W9-AFU-502

OTHER A TO Z GUIDES FROM
THE SCARECROW PRESS, INC.

1. *The A to Z of Buddhism* by Charles S. Prebish, 2001.
2. *The A to Z of Catholicism* by William J. Collinge, 2001.
3. *The A to Z of Hinduism* by Bruce M. Sullivan, 2001.
4. *The A to Z of Islam* by Ludwig W. Adamec, 2002.
5. *The A to Z of Slavery & Abolition* by Martin A. Klein, 2002.
6. *Terrorism: Assassins to Zealots* by Sean Kendall Anderson and Stephen Sloan, 2003.
7. *The A to Z of the Korean War* by Paul M. Edwards, 2005.
8. *The A to Z of the Cold War* by Joseph Smith and Simon Davis, 2005.
9. *The A to Z of the Vietnam War* by Edwin E. Moise, 2005.
10. *The A to Z of Science Fiction Literature* by Brian Stableford, 2005.
11. *The A to Z of the Holocaust* by Jack R. Fischel, 2005.
12. *The A to Z of Washington, D.C.* by Robert Benedetto, Jane Donovan, and Kathleen DuVall, 2005.
13. *The A to Z of Taoism* by Julian F. Pas, 2006.
14. *The A to Z of the Renaissance* by Charles G. Nauert, 2006.
15. *The A to Z of Shinto* by Stuart D. B. Picken, 2006.
16. *The A to Z of Byzantium* by John H. Rosser, 2006.
17. *The A to Z of the Civil War* by Terry L. Jones, 2006.
18. *The A to Z of the Friends (Quakers)* by Margery Post Abbott, Mary Ellen Chijioke, Pink Dandelion, and John William Oliver Jr., 2006
19. *The A to Z of Feminism* by Janet K. Boles and Diane Long Hoeveler, 2006.
20. *The A to Z of New Religious Movements* by George D. Chryssides, 2006.
21. *The A to Z of Multinational Peacekeeping* by Terry M. Mays, 2006.
22. *The A to Z of Lutheranism* by Günther Gassmann with Duane H. Larson and Mark W. Oldenburg, 2007.
23. *The A to Z of the French Revolution* by Paul R. Hanson, 2007.
24. *The A to Z of the Persian Gulf War 1990–1991* by Clayton R. Newell, 2007.
25. *The A to Z of Revolutionary America* by Terry M. Mays, 2007.
26. *The A to Z of the Olympic Movement* by Bill Mallon with Ian Buchanan, 2007.

The A to Z
of Witchcraft

Michael D. Bailey

The A to Z Guide Series, No. 77

The Scarecrow Press, Inc.
Lanham • Toronto • Plymouth, UK
2009

Published by Scarecrow Press, Inc.
A wholly owned subsidary of
The Rowman & Littlefield Publishing Group, Inc.
4501 Forbes Boulevard, Suite 200, Lanham, Maryland 20706
http://www.scarecrowpress.com

Estover Road, Plymouth PL6 7PY, United Kingdom

British Library Cataloguing in Publication Information Available

Library of Congress Cataloging-in-Publication Data

The hardback version of this book was cataloged by the Library of Congress as
follows:

Bailey, Michael David, 1971–
   Historical dictionary of witchcraft / by Michael D. Bailey.— 1st ed.
     p. cm. — (Historical dictionaries of religions, philosophies, and movements ;
   no. 47)
   Includes bibliographical references.
   1. Witchcraft—History—Dictionaries. I. Title. II. Series.
   BF1566 .B25 2003
   133.4'3'03—dc21   2003011520

ISBN 978-0-8108-6864-9 (pbk. : alk. paper)
ISBN 978-0-8108-7027-7 (ebook)

∞™ The paper used in this publication meets the minimum requirements of
American National Standard for Information Sciences—Permanence of Paper
for Printed Library Materials, ANSI/NISO Z39.48-1992.

Printed in the United States of America

To my father

Contents

Editor's Foreword

A book on witchcraft at the dawn of the new century? Most definitely so. Without a good knowledge of the subject, one cannot understand earlier periods in Europe and European overseas colonies when there was widespread concern with witches, so intense that it culminated in witch-hunts and burnings. Nor can one understand the situation in many other ancient or "primitive" cultures well beyond Europe, indeed, almost worldwide, where a belief in creatures resembling witches was—and sometimes still is—very strong. Nor can one even understand the present (and doubtless future) with the emergence of modern witchcraft, also known as *Wicca*. This book, fortunately, takes a broader view, looking back, looking beyond Western civilization, and looking into the present (bordering on the future).

Obviously, most of *The A to Z of Witchcraft* concentrates on witchcraft in the older, more traditional sense. It therefore includes entries on persons who strongly influenced the mood of the times, who wrote about witches and how to find them, who brought them to trial and sometimes had them burned, or who defended them and gradually convinced broader society that perhaps those punished were not actually witches, maybe there was no such thing. This amidst other entries on how to ascertain if someone was a witch, how to extract a confession from such a person, what the punishment could be, and also why so many witches were women. But the most intriguing entries are often about the appearance of similar phenomena in other cultures and especially the return of witchcraft in the West, long after it seemed to be disappearing, and in surprising new forms. The trajectory is easier to follow (thanks to a brief chronology), easier to understand (thanks to a general introduction), and easier to read (thanks to a substantial bibliography).

This book was written by an academic, and not a practicing witch, as is increasingly the custom. So he views the subject of witchcraft from without and not within, which is a better vantage point for most of us and helps us grasp the many twists and turns of an endlessly intriguing subject. Michael D. Bailey has been interested in European witchcraft ever since he was a student at Northwestern University, writing his dissertation and later his first book on the rise of witchcraft in late-medieval Europe and on one of the preeminent early authorities to write about witchcraft, the German Dominican Johannes Nider. He also studied medieval history in countries where the witch-hunts were most virulent, Germany and Switzerland. Since then, Dr. Bailey has taught at Bethany College, the University of Cincinnati, Saint Louis University, and currently at Iowa State University, where he continues to write on various aspects of the medieval period, sorcery, and witchcraft. For this historical dictionary, he has expanded his horizons substantially to bring in the wider world and the current period, which make the whole matter considerably more interesting and in some ways more comprehensible, or less, depending on one's intellectual position.

Jon Woronoff
Series Editor

Acknowledgments

I would like to thank, first of all, Richard Kieckhefer, who has taught me much about the history of European witchcraft, both directly and through his writings, and who initially recommended to Scarecrow Press that I should author this dictionary. Thanks go also to Jon Woronoff, who invited me to undertake the project and has seen me through it. I began this project while at the Department of History at the University of Cincinnati, wrote most of the entries during a year I spent as a Visiting Scholar at the Medieval Institute of the University of Notre Dame, and completed the book while I was a member of the Department of History at Saint Louis University. I am grateful to each of these institutions for their support. Both in my academic life and beyond, Christine Caldwell has helped me in ways too extensive to recount. My thanks to her here is only a small indication of what I owe her.

Chronology

Ca. 1750 B.C.E. The Code of Hammurabi, one of the first written law codes, contains sections dealing with magic and legal charges of sorcery and witchcraft.

Ca. 400 B.C.E. By this time, magicians (*magoi*) come to have a very negative reputation in ancient Greece. They are condemned by Plato, among others.

Ca. 150–400 C.E. Early Christian writers such as Tertullian, Origen, and John Chrysostom condemn magic by associating it with demonic forces, while defending Christian miracles as non-magical.

375 The Council of Laodicaea forbids Christian clergy from practicing any form of magic.

425 Augustine completes *The City of God,* sections of which become foundational for later Christian demonology and the theory of demonic pacts associated with magic and witchcraft.

438 The imperial law code of Theodosius II prescribes severe penalties for those convicted of practicing magic or divination.

529 The code of Justinian reiterates earlier severe penalties for magic and divination.

789 Charlemagne issues legislation against sorcerers and magicians for his entire kingdom.

Ca. 906 An early version of the canon *Episcopi,* describing groups of women who believe that they fly through the night with the goddess Diana, appears in a collection of legal canons made by Regino of Prüm.

1022 The first known burning of heretics in medieval Europe occurs at Orléans.

Ca. 1140 Gratian's *Decretum,* one of the first standard texts of medieval canon law, includes several sections dealing with magic, sorcery, and superstition, including a version of the canon *Episcopi.*

1184 Pope Lucius III issues the decree *Ad abolendam,* which orders bishops and other ecclesiastical officials to rigorously investigate cases of heresy.

1215 The Fourth Lateran Council of the church regularizes procedures to be used against heretics.

1231 Pope Gregory IX commissions the first papally appointed inquisitors to hear cases involving heresy.

1233 Pope Gregory IX issues the decree *Vox in Rama,* in which he describes heretics gathering to worship a demon in the form of a toad or a pallid man, and then engaging in sexual orgies, similar to later notions of witches' sabbaths.

Ca. 1250–1275 Thomas Aquinas establishes much of the basic scholastic understanding of magic and demonology in his many theological works, including his *Summa contra gentiles* (Summa Against the Gentiles) and *Summa theologiae* (Summa of Theology).

1258 Pope Alexander IV orders papal inquisitors not to inquire into matters of sorcery unless the sorcery also involves "manifest heresy," primarily meaning the worship of demons.

1307–1314 Arrest and trial of the Knights Templar in France. Although charges of sorcery do not figure significantly in these events, the trial exhibits many of the features—diabolism, conspiracy theories, and forced confessions—that later characterize witch trials.

1324–1325 Trial of Lady Alice Kytler in Kilkenny, Ireland, for practicing sorcery with the aid of a demon.

Ca. 1324 The inquisitor Bernard Gui writes his handbook *Practica inquisitionis heretice pravitatis* (The Practice of Inquisition into Heretical Depravity), which includes sections on sorcery and demonic magic.

1326 Pope John XXII issues the Decretal *Super illius specula*, in which he declares a blanket excommunication on anyone who summons demons or enters into pacts with them for the purpose of performing sorcery.

1376 The inquisitor Nicolau Eymeric writes his highly influential inquisitorial manual *Directorium inquisitorum* (Directory of Inquisitors), in which he proves the necessarily heretical nature of all magic involving the invocation of demons, and hence the legal jurisdiction of ecclesiastical inquisitors over most types of sorcery.

1398 The theological faculty of the University of Paris condemns various forms of superstition and the practice of sorcery in 28 articles.

Ca. 1400 One of the earliest known witch-hunts in European history (although in reality the trials probably dealt only with simply sorcery and *maleficium*) takes place in the Simme valley in the western Alps.

Ca. 1425–1500 The beginnings of the major European witch-hunts can be traced to this period. The number of trials in which harmful sorcery, or *maleficium*, is linked to diabolism rises significantly, and many early treatises on witchcraft are written.

1426 The Franciscan preacher and moral reformer Bernardino of Siena witnesses an early trial for witchcraft in Rome.

Ca. 1428 The Lucerne chronicler Hans Fründ describes witchcraft in the diocese of Sion in the western Alps.

Ca. 1436 Claude Tholosan, a secular judge in the French region of Dauphiné, writes a treatise *Ut magorum et maleficiorum errores manifesti ignorantibus fiant* (That the Errors of Magicians and Witches May be Made Clear to the Ignorant), detailing the practices of witchcraft based on trials he had conducted in Dauphiné and arguing that secular courts should have jurisdiction over this crime. Also around this time, an anonymous clerical author writes *Errores Gazariorum* (Errors of the Gazarii), a brief but extremely lurid description of witchcraft and the witches' sabbath.

1436–1438 The Dominican theologian Johannes Nider writes his *Formicarius* (The Anthill), a long moralizing treatise containing some of the most extensive early accounts of witchcraft to appear in Europe.

1440–1442 The French cleric Martin Le Franc writes the long poem *Le Champion des Dames* (The Defender of Ladies), which includes a section on witchcraft.

1458 The French inquisitor Nicholas Jacquier writes the influential treatise *Flagellum haereticorum fascinariorum* (Scourge of Heretical Witches), one of the first major treatises devoted exclusively to witchcraft and witch-hunting.

1474 Heinrich Kramer (Institoris) is made inquisitor in southern Germany, where he presides over numerous witch trials.

1478 The Spanish Inquisition is established.

1484 Pope Innocent VIII issues the bull *Summis desiderantes affectibus*, ordering that inquisitors in German lands should not be hindered or prevented from exercising their authority in matters of sorcery and witchcraft. The bull is later included in the *Malleus maleficarum*.

1486 *Malleus maleficarum* (Hammer of Witches) is written by the Dominican inquisitor Heinrich Kramer.

1487 *Malleus maleficarum* is published in the first of many printed editions.

Ca. 1500–1575 The steady rise in the number of witch trials, evident since the early 15th century, levels off in this period, and in some areas the number of witch trials even declines.

1532 The *Carolina* legal code is enacted for all the lands of the German Empire. It deals, in part, with matters of witchcraft.

1542 The Roman Inquisition is established by Pope Paul III.

1563 A statute ordering the death penalty for witches is passed in England. Stringent witchcraft laws are also passed in Scotland. Johann Weyer publishes *De praestigiis daemonum* (On the Deceptions of Demons), a treatise that is skeptical of various aspects of witchcraft.

1566 The first major witch-hunt in England takes place at Chelmsford, Essex.

Ca. 1575–1675 Witch-hunting reaches its height in most regions of Europe.

1580 The French political philosopher Jean Bodin publishes his very influential treatise on demonology and witchcraft, *De la démonomanie des sorciers* (On the Demonomania of Witches).

1582–1594 A series of witch-trials take place in the archbishopric and electoral principality of Trier in the German Empire.

1584 The skeptical English thinker Reginald Scot publishes his *Discoverie of Witchcraft*.

1589 Dietrich Flade, vice-governor of Trier and the highest ranking victim of any witch-hunt in Europe, is executed. Peter Binsfeld, suffragan bishop of Trier, writes a *Tractatus de confessionibus maleficorum et sagarum* (On the Confessions of Witches), defending the necessity of witch trials and the procedures used in them.

1590–1591 A group of supposed witches from North Berwick, Scotland, are put on trial; the Scottish king James VI takes part in the proceedings.

1593 The skeptical theologian Cornelius Loos, who had criticized a recent wave of witch-hunting in Trier, is forced to recant publicly. He is then exiled from Trier to Brussels.

1595 The French magistrate and important demonologist Nicholas Rémy publishes his *Daemonolatreiae* (Demonolatry).

1597 King James VI of Scotland (from 1603 also James I of England) publishes his *Daemonologie* (Demonology).

1599 The first edition of the Jesuit Martin Del Rio's *Disquisitiones magicarum* (Disquisitions on Magic) is published.

1604 A new witchcraft act is passed in England, establishing much harsher penalties for the crime.

1608 The Italian friar Francesco Maria Guazzo publishes his *Compendium maleficarum* (Handbook of Witches), which becomes the most important and influential such manual used in Italy. In England, William Perkin's *Discourse on the Damned Art of Witchcraft* is published posthumously.

1609–1614 A major outbreak of witch-hunting occurs in the Basque lands in southwestern France and northern Spain.

1623–1633 Severe witch-hunts take place in Bamberg, Germany, under the so-called *Hexenbischof* (Witch-Bishop) Johann Georg II.

1631 The German Jesuit Friedrich Spee publishes (anonymously) the *Cautio criminalis* (Warning for Prosecutors), a harsh critique of the procedures by which most witch trials are conducted.

1633–1634 A famous case of mass possession occurs among nuns in a convent at Loudun, France.

1645–1646 The infamous witch-hunter Matthew Hopkins directs the most intense witch-hunt in English history, primarily in the counties of Essex and Suffolk, leading to the execution of more than 200 victims.

1661–1662 During the "great Scottish witch-hunt," hundreds of trials and executions occur throughout the country.

1669 Severe witch-hunts occur in Mora in central Sweden. These in turn help trigger hunts in other areas of the country.

Ca. 1675–1750 In this period, most regions in Europe see a steady reduction and end of witch-hunting.

1682 King Louis XIV reclassifies the crime of witchcraft in France as mere "superstition," no longer warranting capital punishment, effectively ending legally sanctioned witch-hunting in that country.

1689 Cotton Mather preaches about the dangers of witchcraft in Boston, Massachusetts.

1692 The famous witch trials of Salem, Massachusetts, take place.

1736 The Witchcraft Act of 1604 is repealed in Great Britain, effectively decriminalizing witchcraft in that country.

1782 A woman named Anna Göldi is executed for witchcraft in the Swiss Canton of Glarus. This is the last execution for witchcraft in Europe carried out under full and unequivocal legal sanction.

1793 Two women are executed for witchcraft in Posnan, Poland, which is at that time just passing under Prussian authority. Local courts sanction the execution, but it seems clear that if higher authorities, either Polish or Prussian, had been able to act, the sentence would not have been carried out.

1828 The German scholar Karl-Ernst Jarcke advances the argument that historical witchcraft was actually a pre-Christian, pagan religion.

1888 The Hermetic Order of the Golden Dawn, an elite secret society devoted to ritual magic, is founded in England.

1899 The amateur folklorist Charles Leland publishes *Aradia, or the Gospel of the Witches,* an account of the history and beliefs of the supposedly ancient religion of witchcraft in Italy.

1921 The British academic Margaret Murray publishes *The Witch-Cult in Western Europe,* the first of three studies in which she argues that historical witchcraft was actually a form of an ancient pagan fertility religion.

1937 British anthropologist E. E. Evans-Pritchard publishes *Witchcraft, Oracles and Magic among the Azande,* a very influential study of African systems of magic and witchcraft.

1954 Gerald Gardner publishes *Witchcraft Today,* laying the foundations for modern witchcraft, or Wicca.

1966 Anton Le Vey founds the Church of Satan in San Francisco, the most important group within modern Satanism. This movement is not, however, associated in any direct way with modern Wicca.

1972 In a decision by the Internal Revenue Service, the Church of Wicca becomes the first Wiccan organization to achieve official federal recognition as a religion in the United States.

1979 The Wiccan author Starhawk publishes *The Spiral Dance.* Margot Alder publishes *Drawing Down the Moon.* Both become foundational books for modern Wicca in the United States and elsewhere.

1989 Aidan Kelly, a student of Wicca, publishes *Crafting the Art of Magic,* a thorough study of Gerald Gardner's papers relating to his development of modern witchcraft. The British academic Tanya Luhrmann publishes *Persuasions of the Witch's Craft,* the first major study of modern witchcraft done outside the movement.

1999 Ronald Hutton publishes *The Triumph of the Moon,* the first major academic historical study of modern witchcraft and neo-paganism.

Introduction

Witchcraft is an important and difficult historical subject. Throughout human history, most cultures and societies have conceived of certain categories of malevolent people who are supposedly able to access or exhibit powers of great supernatural evil. In Europe during the Middle Ages and the early-modern period, such people were believed to be in league with the devil and bent on the destruction of Christian society on earth. For over 300 years, from the 15th to the 18th centuries, social fear and legal paranoia led to the prosecution, and ultimately the execution, of tens of thousands of people for the supposed crime of witchcraft. The period is often described as being the era of "the great witch-hunts," or, by more sensationalistic authors, simply as the "burning times." Accurate figures are difficult to establish, but it seems that the number of trials for witchcraft exceeded 100,000 during this period, and the number of people executed as witches exceeded 50,000. Such figures are low in comparison to some overly credulous accounts (one occasionally still encounters claims that the victims of the witch-hunts numbered in the hundreds of thousands or even millions), and they certainly pale when compared to the scale of deadly repression exercised by some governments in the modern world. Nevertheless, especially in regions of particular intensity, the witch-hunts were a major preoccupation of early-modern religious and state authorities. Moreover, the number of trials alone surely does not indicate all those whose lives were affected in some way, and certainly almost never for the good, by suspicions of witchcraft during this time.

The primary focus of this dictionary will fall on the historical phenomenon of witchcraft as defined and constructed in Europe during the era of the great witch-hunts. Other varieties of magic and conceptions of harmful sorcery in other periods of history and in other world cultures will, however, also be treated to some extent. Because the concept of witchcraft in medieval and early-modern Europe was informed by ideas, beliefs, and practices from the earlier Christian era, as well as from classical antiquity, some attention must also be given to those periods. Outside of the major Western civilizations, ideas of harmful magic and witchcraft have manifested in many ways. In particular, African varieties of witchcraft have been studied and often used as a basis for comparison with historical witchcraft in Europe. Such anthropologically informed scholarship has done much to increase understanding of how belief in witchcraft can function at a social level. Other magical beliefs and practices around the world have themselves been influenced by aspects of European witchcraft. For example, conceptions of harmful sorcery and those who practice it associated with the religion of Voodoo in Haiti and elsewhere in the Caribbean seem heavily influenced by Christian notions of witches. In addition, some treatment will be given to the modern world because not all of the beliefs that characterized historical witchcraft in Europe vanished with the end of the witch-hunts, and some have persisted even to the present day. Moreover, there now exists a substantial movement (or movements) of modern witchcraft, commonly termed *Wicca*. Although there is no credible evidence of any direct connection between the modern and historical variants of witchcraft in the Western world, some individuals and groups within modern witchcraft maintain that such connections do exist, and certainly some groups outside of modern witchcraft persist in associating modern witches with historical stereotypes.

DEFINITIONS

Anyone trying to understand witchcraft in a broad yet accurate historical sense must confront a number of problems, of which perhaps none is more basic than the difficult question of how to define exactly what elements constitute witchcraft. Seen in one way, witchcraft appears as a virtually universal and seemingly perennial aspect of almost all human cultures. Regarded in another way, the concept of witchcraft is highly contingent on historical time and place. Certainly, the crime for which tens of thousands of people went to their deaths in Europe and colonial America in the 15th, 16th, and 17th centuries—the period of the great European witch-hunts—could only have existed, and can only be understood, within the specific Christian culture that prevailed at that time. By those who fear its reality, witchcraft has always been defined as a set of actions, practices, and behaviors that certain people actually perform to supposedly terrible effect, and witches are believed to cause great evil in the world through the harmful sorcery that they work, generally in close alliance with dark, supernatural forces. If one accepts this belief, then such a crime is certainly worthy of the harshest penalties any society can impose. To those skeptical of the reality of witchcraft, on the other hand, it exists only, or at least predominantly, as a construct in the minds of those who would use it as an excuse to persecute, and those accused of witchcraft are innocent victims caught in a deadly web of false beliefs and pious convictions.

These problems of definition are not just modern ones. Even during the period of the great European witch-hunts, when belief in the real existence and effectiveness of witchcraft was far more widespread than it is today, there were always those who doubted elements of the witch-stereotype. Given the level of general belief in magic and supernatural power in pre-modern European society, at least some of the people brought into court on charges of witchcraft probably were actually trying to perform some form of harmful sorcery that they thought would be effective against others in their communities. This does not mean, however, that these people necessarily thought that they had sold their souls to the devil or that they, in fact, gathered with others at secret conventicles in order to worship demons, as they were typically accused of doing (although certain individuals might actually have engaged in such activities in some way). Likewise, even some authorities, convinced of the power of the devil in the world and certain that some people were indeed entering his service in order to gain supernatural powers, were nonetheless skeptical about the existence of a vast, diabolically organized, conspiratorial cult of witches, and feared that a large number of false confessions were being obtained by the courts through the excessive use of torture and by other means. Authorities in the late-medieval and early-modern periods also had to explain the apparent newness of the threat posed by large numbers of witches—nothing like it had ever been described in earlier sources—while still maintaining the supposedly perennial nature of demonic power and diabolic evil.

Taken in the broadest sense, witchcraft can be defined as the performance of various harmful acts through sorcery. The belief that certain people can and do work such harmful sorcery appears to have existed in almost every human culture throughout history. Witchcraft is also generally regarded as a low or common form of magic, as opposed to high or learned magic, which requires much arcane knowledge and training and is limited to certain elite groups within society. Acts of witchcraft typically involve only simple gestures, spells, or rituals, and witches are usually uneducated people of low social status, more frequently women than men. In many cases, the power of witchcraft is often regarded as somehow inherent in the witch herself, as opposed to lying in the ritual actions or spells that she performs. This special status that marks the witch herself as being intrinsically evil, as opposed to just performing evil acts, might be inherited from other family members or derived from some personal association with dark, supernatural forces.

All of these definitions of witchcraft might be applied to aspects of magic (itself a word that is extremely difficult to define precisely for all situations in which it is used) in many different human cultures and historical contexts. Yet the actual word "witchcraft," as well as its cognates in other European languages such as the German *Hexerei* or even to some extent the earlier French *sorcellerie,* developed to describe a particular phenomenon that existed, or at least was widely believed to exist, in Europe at the end of the Middle Ages (traditionally defined as the period up to about 1500) and the subsequent early-modern era (the 16th through the 18th centuries). In this particular context, all the conditions described above pertained, to a greater or lesser degree, but witchcraft actually had a far more specific definition. Witches were generally, although not necessarily, simple and uneducated people, mostly women. And witches were certainly thought to perform harmful sorcery, most commonly termed *maleficium* by secular and ecclesiastical authorities writing in Latin. But the real crime of witchcraft lay in the intense diabolical elements that authorities were convinced underlay these other aspects of the phenomenon.

Witches were believed to perform their harmful sorcery through the agency of demons whom they were able to command, often with only a few simple words, signs, or gestures. In order to attain this power over demons, authorities were convinced, witches offered worship to demons, in violation of the most basic tenets of the Christian faith. Beyond even this, witches were thought to have forsaken their faith entirely and to have surrendered themselves to the service of Satan. They were believed to be members of widespread, satanic cults that met secretly at night, in the presence of the devil or some other presiding demon, to worship, celebrate, and perform a wide variety of horrible acts. This was the image of the witches' sabbath that first appeared in Europe in the early 15th century and persisted for the rest of the period of the witch-hunts. The more credulous and extreme among the authorities on witchcraft often wrote of hundreds if not thousands of witches infesting a given region, attending sabbaths, and acting in concert as members of an organized sect. Thus, the evil that witches represented was not simple human malice. Rather, they were seen as battalions in the demonic legions of Satan operating in secret to subvert and bring about the destruction of the Christian world. This concept of witches as comprising a widespread, conspiratorial, and entirely malevolent force in the world supported, indeed necessitated, the major efforts at witch-hunting that were undertaken primarily in the 15th, 16th, and 17th centuries.

PRECEDENTS: MAGIC AND RELIGION
IN THE ANCIENT AND MEDIEVAL WORLDS

The figure of the witch, defined not only as someone who performed secretive and harmful sorcery, but also as someone who worked this sorcery through the agency of demons and who, forsaking the true faith, worshiped demons and the devil, only developed toward the end of the Middle Ages, appearing for the first time in the early 15th century. Although such a conception of witchcraft was only possible in a Christian society, still, in the most general terms, the two essential elements of witchcraft as conceived during the period of the witch-hunts—that it involved the performance of maleficent sorcery that caused real harm in the world, and that it also entailed serious violations of religious beliefs and practices—can be seen in the very earliest conceptions of magic to appear in ancient Western civilizations. Like witchcraft itself, magic is a difficult concept to define precisely, and distinctions between magical and religious rituals are notoriously difficult to draw. Yet almost all human cultures, it would seem, have posited certain boundaries, and indeed a certain opposition, between these two concepts.

In European history, at least by the fifth century B.C.E., as the city-states of Greece were entering into their golden age, religion, that is, the public and communal cults of the city-states, was being defined to some extent in opposition to magic, that is, other systems for accessing supernatural power that were either private, secretive, or anti-social. Although priests engaged with the gods and other supernatural entities for the greater civic good, and functioned to maintain stability and social order, magicians in ancient Greece were private individuals, either seeking their own gain or hiring themselves out as professionals to whom other people would turn seeking individual magical services. The distinction was amplified by the fact that foreign religious systems were often categorized as magic. In fact, the Greek word *mageia* derived from the name for the Persian priestly cast, called *magoi* in Greek. In other words, while the rituals and practices of the Greek civic cults were "religion," the foreign rites and practices of the Persians were "magic." In addition, the Greek word *goeteia* was often used to describe the lower forms of magic, even further removed from religious ritual, and this concept is perhaps as close as the Greeks ever came to something like later European witchcraft.

The boundaries between all of these concepts and practices, however, were extremely tenuous. They certainly appear so to modern historians, and probably were for the ancients as well. For example, the two most famous images of sorceresses to appear in Greek literature are Circe and Medea. While both would later be considered witches and would contribute to the development of the idea of witchcraft in medieval, Christian Europe, in ancient legend both were also religious figures. Circe was a demigoddess, and Medea was either a demigoddess or a priestess of a foreign cult.

In the ancient Hebrew tradition, too, magic was often defined in terms of being harmful and anti-social but was also seen as a religious error, and the priests of foreign religions were deemed to be magicians. In the Book of Exodus in the Bible, listed among other regulations placed upon the Israelites, is the command not to permit a sorcerer or seer (Hebrew *kashaph*) to live, rendered famously in the 17th century King James' translation: "Thou shalt not suffer a witch to live" (Exodus 22:18). Such people were considered criminals due to the harmful magic that they employed. In 1 Samuel 28:3, just prior to the famous story of the Witch of Endor, King Saul is described as having driven out all the sorcerers and diviners from his kingdom because such people constituted an anti-social threat to the stability of his realm. The contrast between magic and religion is more clearly developed in other passages, such as Exodus 7:8–12. Here Moses and Aaron confront Pharaoh during the Israelites' captivity in Egypt, and, in order to demonstrate the power of the Hebrews' god, Aaron casts down his staff and it becomes a serpent. The priests of Pharaoh's court are able to replicate this feat with their own staffs by resorting to their "secret arts." Aaron's serpent devours theirs, however, thus proving the superiority of divine power. In 1 Kings 18:20–40, the prophet Elijah confronts the pagan priests of Baal, who have been corrupting the people of Israel. He has them build an altar and place sacrifices on it, and then pray to their god to send fire from heaven to consume the sacrifices. Though they try for many hours, no fire comes. Then Elijah builds an altar, and for good measure douses his sacrifice with water. Still, at his prayer, a great fire descends from heaven and consumes the sacrifice.

As Judaism developed into a fully monotheistic religion, that is, a system of belief maintaining not just that Israel had only one god, while other peoples might have many, but that the one god of Israel was in fact the single supreme deity of the entire universe, the idea of magic as a deviation from proper religious practice became further developed. This process culminated, however, only in the early Christian era. Although Judaism was monotheistic, it never had a clearly defined concept of the devil, that is, the principal opponent of the one god responsible for all evil in the universe, such as developed in Christianity. For early Christian authorities the power of Satan and the legions of lesser devils he commanded was set very directly against the power of God and the church in the world, and much magical practice became fully demonized. While holy men and women might perform miracles by calling on divine power, all other such wonders were actually the work of demons. The strict dichotomy was expressed in the New Testament account of Christ's chief apostle, Simon Peter, and the magician Simon Magus of Samaria (Acts 8:9–24). Seeing that the wonders that the apostles could perform were greater than those he could achieve, Simon Magus offered Peter money in exchange for some of his power. Later apocryphal accounts developed the rivalry between the miracle-working apostle and the demonic magician even further. In one story, Simon Magus tried to fly up to heaven, borne aloft by demons. At a word from Peter, however, the power of the demons failed and Simon Magus crashed to earth.

Because, in Christian cosmology, all demons were evil spirits in the service of the one great evil, Satan, who was the enemy of both God and humankind, all magic, insofar as it entailed involvement with demonic forces, was inherently evil. The anti-social and religiously deviant aspects of magical practice were fully merged. It was the great church father Augustine of Hippo, who lived from 354 to 430 C.E., who gave this new Christian conception of magic its full form. In his most important work, *The City of God,* Augustine described the entire world in terms of the struggle between divine and demonic forces. All evil arose from demons, and all evil sorcery derived from demonic power. Moreover, Augustine fully articulated the concept of the pact made between the demon and the human magician who called upon it. Implacably hostile to humanity, demons would only offer their services in exchange for worship. Thus for Christian authorities the real crime of demonic magic, as ultimately for witchcraft, lay not in the harm that magic was supposedly able to cause, but in the religious violation of demon-worship that such magic was believed to entail.

With the full demonization of magic by Christian authorities achieved at least by the fifth century C.E., one might think that the concept of diabolic witchcraft would have appeared in late antiquity. This, however, was not the case. Rather, the initial general effect of the Christian conception of demonic magic seems to have been actually to reduce the culpability of human magicians. That is, Christian religious authorities recognized their real enemies as being the devil and his demons, who lay behind any harmful sorcery that a human magician might work. The magician was guilty only of having succumbed to temptation and the deceits of these demons. The punishments that religious authorities, mainly bishops, prescribed in cases involving sorcery were in fact generally more lenient than those laid out by secular Roman authorities in the harsh late-imperial legal code.

On into the early Middle Ages, for many centuries, clerical authorities remained relatively lenient in their treatment of sorcery. There are several possible reasons for this. First, in the wake of the influx of pagan Germanic tribes into the territories of the Western Roman Empire, and the expansion of Roman Christianity into lands that had never lain within the boundaries of the empire, clerical authorities probably focused more of their energies on spreading the religion, converting pagans, and stamping out or subsuming within Christian belief the elements of paganism that persisted among the great majority of people in the emerging medieval kingdoms of Europe. Also, in the wake of the collapse of the Roman imperial system, for many centuries the church's own institutions and systems for exerting power and control were relatively weak and certainly not highly centralized. Above all, perhaps, clerical authorities did not, in general, seem to perceive demonic power, and hence demonic sorcery, as a serious threat during this period. The famous 10th century canon *Episcopi* (a document of church law named after its first word in Latin, "Bishops") warned bishops and their officials to take all steps necessary to eradicate the magical practices of *sortilegium* and *maleficium* from the regions under their control. The canon then went on to describe the widespread belief that there existed groups of women who would ride through the night sky with the pagan goddess Diana. Centuries later, this belief would contribute directly to the idea of the night flight of witches to a sabbath. In the 10th century, however, the canon declared that such ideas were merely delusions and deceptions of the devil, and that they had no basis in reality. Other documents show that many clerical authorities felt only penance and correction were needed to combat such beliefs, and that harsher punishments were not in order.

This is not to say that clerical authorities in the early Middle Ages did not accept the reality of demonic sorcery. But they were either unable or unwilling (most likely both) to respond to such beliefs and practices with widespread and highly organized campaigns of persecution. Insofar as harmful sorcery, *maleficium,* remained a crime to be prosecuted and punished in the early Middle Ages, it was mainly secular authorities who exercised jurisdiction over such cases. In Germanic legal codes, as in the law codes of the ancient world, *maleficium* was defined as a crime not primarily for its implications of religious deviance, but for the real harm that such sorcery was believed to be able to achieve. Such prosecutions, however, could not generate the necessary levels of fear and panic to spark a real witch-hunt, as would occur in later centuries. Although secular authorities in the early Middle Ages were certainly not unaware of the church's position that most, if not all, sorcery involved trafficking with demons, they do not seem to have stressed the point, and so the idea of sorcerers being in league with the devil and part of a larger conspiratorial assault on the entire Christian world never developed to the extent it later would. Also, sorcerers were not typically accused of membership in satanic cults, and no concept like the later witches' sabbath ever developed in the early medieval period. Rather, individual accusations of sorcery tended to be settled without generating other accusations or anything like a widespread hunt.

An important aspect underlying the lack of any truly rampant persecution of sorcerers in the early Middle Ages was the use of accusatorial procedure in most European courts. This was a legal method whereby an accuser, a private person who felt himself to be afflicted or aggrieved in some way, not only brought the initial charge of a crime, but also bore the responsibility of prosecuting the case and demonstrating the guilt of the person accused. For a crime like sorcery, secretive by its very nature, hard evidence was usually difficult if not impossible to find, and witnesses were similarly scarce. In such cases, accusatorial procedure relied on the judicial ordeal (or for certain elite groups trial by combat) to determine guilt or innocence. Typically, the accused would be made to grasp a heated iron. If, several days later, the wound was judged to have healed sufficiently, the person was deemed innocent. Another common ordeal was for the accused to be immersed in a pool of water. If they did not immediately float to the surface (a sign that the pure water had not rejected them as being evil), they were judged innocent. In theory, such methods left the determination of guilt or innocence in the hands of God. In practice, they were uncertain at best. Since the accuser was responsible for proving his case, and was subject to legal penalties if the person accused was judged innocent, entirely frivolous cases were rare, and the sort of wild accusations that later typified the witch-hunts were almost unthinkable.

Around the 12th century, important developments began to take place that would lay the foundations for the emergence of witchcraft and witch-hunting centuries later. Perhaps most directly, Roman law was rediscovered across Europe, and the new legal method of inquisitorial procedure began to be used, first by ecclesiastical courts but then by secular courts as well, instead of the older accusatorial procedure. Under inquisitorial procedure, a private person could still bring a charge of some crime, but now judges could also initiate inquests themselves. In either case, after the initial accusation, the responsibility for prosecuting the case lay with the judges or magistrates. Rather than relying on practices like the ordeal, judges employed more rational methods, such as examination of witnesses and interrogation of the accused, as well as collection of any evidence that might be available. In cases of sorcery or witchcraft, however, where secrecy still prevailed, evidence and witnesses were rare. Thus, the confession of the accused was virtually the only way to achieve a conviction. Since it was assumed that guilty people would lie to protect themselves, judges could employ torture. Under normal circumstances, use of torture should have remained limited and strictly regulated. In cases of witchcraft, however, where the crime was believed to be so severe, panic usually ran high, and the devil was often thought to exert his power to prevent guilty witches from confessing, the use of torture was often uncontrolled and excessive. In such cases, authorities could extract a lurid confession from virtually anyone accused.

Although the development of inquisitorial methods and use of torture provided a legal procedure that made rampant witch-hunting possible, legal changes alone were not enough to lead to the concept of witchcraft as developed in the late-medieval and early-modern periods. Authorities also had to be prepared to see a vast demonic conspiracy behind accusations of simple *maleficium*. Here, too, important changes began to occur around the 12th century. As part of the so-called "Renaissance of the 12th Century," the general revitalization of intellectual life in Europe, classical Greek and Roman, Hebrew, and Arabic texts were rediscovered and began to circulate more widely among educated, mainly clerical, elites. Among these texts were learned treatises on magical arts, including astrology and alchemy, and also works discussing forms of magic and divination performed through the invocation of spirits or demons. These authoritative sources took the reality and power of demonic magic seriously, and so clerical writers in Europe followed suit. By the middle of the 13th century, the great scholastic authority Thomas Aquinas was devoting significant sections of his major theological works to exploring and explaining the powers of demons. Aquinas' writings were arguably the most important treatment of demonology in the Western Christian tradition since Augustine in the fifth century. By the early 1300s, the older, less intensely focused clerical attitude toward demonic sorcery had given way to profound concern at the very highest levels of the church. Pope John XXII, who reigned from 1316 until 1334, was deeply worried about the threat posed by practitioners of demonic sorcery. He ordered papal inquisitors to take actions against this crime, and he passed an automatic sentence of excommunication against anyone who engaged in such activities. By the later 14th century, the theologian and inquisitor Nicolau Eymeric crafted a definitive theological and legal argument that all demonic sorcery was heretical and necessarily involved the worship of demons. The stage for the emergence of diabolical witchcraft was set.

THE EMERGENCE OF WITCHCRAFT AND THE AGE OF THE EUROPEAN WITCH-HUNTS

In the early 15th century, the fully developed idea of European witchcraft—of witches as demonic sorcerers who worshiped the devil and formed a vast, conspiratorial, diabolic cult dedicated to the destruction of the Christian world—began to emerge. Especially in lands in and around the western Alps, where some of the first true witch-hunts took place, the number of trials involving charges of harmful and maleficent sorcery increased significantly. In addition, even when the initial accusations might still focus only on traditional aspects of *maleficium,* judicial authorities increasingly began interjecting their own notions of diabolism and demonic conspiracy into the trials. The decade of the 1430s seems to have been a critical turning point. Within only a few years, a number of treatises and other learned accounts describing witchcraft were written. While these accounts all differed from one another in various ways, they all described witchcraft not just in terms of demonic *maleficium,* but also as an organized sect and diabolical conspiracy. Several of the authors of these treatises were associated in one way or another with the great church Council of Basel, which met from 1431 until 1449. This council seems to have served as an important center for the development and diffusion of the emerging stereotype of witchcraft. Clerics from across Europe came to Basel to attend the council, and might well have taken notions of witchcraft back with them when they left.

The last three quarters of the 15th century, from approximately 1425 until 1500, mark the beginnings of the witch craze in Europe. The first real witch trials occurred in this period and, although initially they were fairly localized to the lands around the western Alps, they spread and increased steadily in number. The century also saw the publication of the first major treatises on witchcraft, beginning with the group of writings clustered around the 1430s, and culminating in the publication of the most famous medieval witch-hunting manual, *Malleus maleficarum,* or

Hammer of Witches, written by the Dominican inquisitor Heinrich Kramer (Institoris in Latin) and first printed in 1487. Although the *Malleus* never served as the sole or definitive source on all aspects of witchcraft and demonology, it was very popular, circulated widely, and was reprinted many times. Certainly by the end of the century, the stereotype of witches as demon-worshipers and servants of Satan, as laid out in the *Malleus* and other similar works, was widely established across Europe. Individual witch trials and even some small-scale hunts (compared to what was to come) were occurring with increasing frequency in many lands. The rise of the great European witch-hunts was not a smooth trajectory, however, and shortly after 1500 there occurred a long lull in the escalation of witch-hunting.

Beginning around the turn of the century, and for at least the first half of the 1500s, the number of witch trials in many regions of Europe leveled off, and in some areas even declined. In an apparent corollary development, the production of new treatises on witchcraft dried up and older treatises fell somewhat out of favor. For example, no new edition of the *Malleus maleficarum* was printed from 1521 until 1576. Scholars are uncertain why this lull should have occurred. Some cite the influence of Renaissance humanism. In this period, humanist ideas spread from Italy to the rest of Europe. Humanist thinkers were often skeptical of witchcraft, or at least of the existence of large cults of witches. In addition, insofar as the conception of diabolical witchcraft rested on principals of medieval scholastic demonology, fear of witches may have been reduced by the humanists' many critiques of scholasticism in general. It must be noted, however, that while humanism differed from scholasticism as an intellectual method and in its approach to older, authoritative texts, nothing in Renaissance humanist thought challenged the basic Christian notion of the devil or the real existence of demons. Thus nothing in Renaissance humanism was inherently opposed to belief in witchcraft.

Historians have also argued that the first phase of the Protestant Reformation in the 16th century may have contributed to the lull in witch trials. The relationship between the Reformation and the continued development of the witch craze in Europe is complex. On the one hand, Protestant theologians naturally tended to disregard many aspects of earlier Catholic theology and were not inclined to regard medieval clerical authors, such as those who wrote the earliest treatises on witchcraft, as being in any way authoritative. However, Protestant theologians certainly did not deny the existence or real power of demons or the devil, and ultimately Protestant theories of witchcraft were virtually identical to Catholic ones. If anything, Protestantism was even more concerned about the power of the devil in this world than medieval Catholicism had been. In the short term, however, it seems as if the initial shock of Martin Luther's successful break with the Catholic Church and the other subsequent breakaways that he helped to inspire, as well as the Catholic response, occupied so much of the attention of religious and secular authorities across Europe that little energy was left to expend on concern over witches at least for a time.

In the long run, though, the Reformation may have contributed significantly to the severity of later witch-hunts by helping to promote the jurisdiction of secular courts over this crime. Witchcraft had always been a crime under both church law, as a form of idolatry and demon-worship, and secular law, since *maleficium* was believed to cause real harm, injury, or death. In fact, secular courts were often more severe in their handling of cases of witchcraft than were many ecclesiastical courts. In Protestant lands after the Reformation, ecclesiastical courts were done away with, and secular authorities became responsible for the enforcement of moral and religious codes. A similar process was already underway in many Catholic lands, but the Reformation doubtless accelerated this development. When witch-hunting began to rise again after the mid-1500s, secular courts were responsible for the vast majority of witch-trials across Europe. The only major exceptions were in Spain and Italy, where the Spanish Inquisition and Roman Inquisition respectively oversaw many cases. It is worth noting that witch-hunting was much less severe in these regions, with fewer overall trials per capita and significantly fewer executions than in many northern lands.

In addition to possibly contributing to some of the legal developments that underlay the witch-hunts, the Reformation and Catholic Counter-Reformation certainly caused matters of religious belief and personal morality to be brought to the fore of the European consciousness for most of the 16th and early 17th centuries. While confessional conflict does not appear to have been directly responsible for many accusations of witchcraft, the heightened and sustained religious tensions that pervaded much of European society in these years probably did contribute to concerns about religious deviance and moral corruption, and ultimately to the fear of witches within many communities. The religious wars sparked by confessional conflict that engulfed Europe in the 16th and 17th centuries also certainly contributed to harsh economic conditions and social strife that then produced accusations of witchcraft. The period from 1550 to 1650 is sometimes known as "Europe's iron century." War, agrarian failures, popular revolts, inflation, and economic and social dislocations on a wide scale wracked the continent. It is certainly no coincidence that the idea of witchcraft and the fear of witches that emerged first in the 15th century found new life in the late 16th and early 17th centuries, and that this was the period of the most intense witch-hunting in many regions of Europe.

After the lull in the early 1500s, around in the middle of that century the number of witch trials across the continent began to rise again, and the period from approximately 1575 to 1675 marked the height of the European witch-hunts. Not only did the number of trials rise to the highest levels ever in most regions of the continent, but almost all of the worst panics and largest hunts occurred during this period. In addition, the production of treatises on witchcraft and witch-hunting resumed. The *Malleus maleficarum* was reprinted again in 1576 and several times thereafter, and even more popular and influential new treatises appeared by Jean Bodin in 1580, Nicholas Rémy in 1595, Martin Del Rio in 1599, and Francesco Maria Guazzo in 1608. By the middle of the 17th century, however, witch-hunting was again declining across much of Europe. Scotland and Scandinavia experienced their most severe outbreaks of witch-hunting in the 1660s and early 1670s respectively, and the persecution of witches in the British colonies in New England crested with the trials at Salem, Massachusetts, in 1692. Elsewhere in Western and Central Europe, however, the number of witch trials fell off rapidly, and many states began to officially end witch-hunting. In France, for example, King Louis XIV effectively ended witch trials in 1682, and in England Parliament repealed the witchcraft act in 1736. In Eastern Europe, concern over witchcraft and witch-hunting developed late, and in regions of Poland, Hungary, and Russia, the worst trials occurred in the 18th century. This regional anomaly aside, however, the period from 1675 until 1750 can generally be seen as one of steady decline in witch-hunting. By the end of the 18th century, the legal persecution of supposed witches had ended across Europe.

GENERAL NATURE OF THE WITCH-HUNTS

During the main period of witch-hunting in the 16th and 17th centuries, fear of witches manifested itself in many forms. Nevertheless, certain generalizations about the pattern of witch-hunting can be made. A trial would most often begin with an accusation of *maleficium*. Such charges usually arose as a result of some sort of otherwise unexplainable misfortune—the sudden death of a child, cows no longer giving milk, a crop failure, or other similar events. As for the direction the charges took, that is, who was accused of being a witch, this usually reflected long-standing interpersonal animosities of the sort that could be quite common in small, tightly knit communities. People in pre-modern Europe were accustomed to sudden and unexplained calamities and did not automatically assume that witchcraft lay behind all such events. However, when established animosity existed, often having developed over years, then people might indeed become ready to explain their misfortune as being the result of malevolent witchcraft directed against them by certain of their neighbors or often enough even by family members. *Maleficium* might be a particularly attractive explanation for a misfortune that occurred soon after some quarrel or other conflict, especially if, in the course of the argument, the other party had uttered a curse or made some sort of general threat.

In theory, almost anyone could be a witch. In practice, however, those most likely to be accused of witchcraft were people who lived on the margins of their communities. The poor, especially those who begged from the rest of the community and thereby continually strained the social bonds between themselves and the community, the elderly, especially elderly women who had neither husbands nor children to care for them, or anyone who acted strangely or in an anti-social manner were all typical targets of witchcraft accusations. For a variety of social and cultural reasons, women in general were especially vulnerable to charges of witchcraft, and across Europe an average of 75 percent of those executed for this crime were female. In some regions, as high as 90 percent of the victims of witch trials were women, although in some other regions, men were in the majority. As many scholars have noted, witchcraft was a gender-related crime but by no means a gender-specific one.

Although most everyone in medieval and early-modern Europe was familiar with religious teachings about the power of demons and the association of witches with the devil, the majority of witch trials began with charges only of *maleficium,* and elements of diabolism did not usually figure prominently in the initial accusations. Most people, it would seem, were concerned about the potential harm witches could do to them and not about any larger, diabolical conspiracy existing in their midst. Once accusations were brought into the courts, however, authorities would be sure to inject charges of diabolism into cases in which these were not already present, and clearly the general populace was not averse to this occurrence and fully accepted that witches were indeed in league with Satan.

Once a trial began, it could proceed in several ways. The simplest possibility, and probably what happened in a large number of cases, was that an acquittal or conviction would be attained and the process would end there, with just the single, isolated trial. Also likely, however, was that a single trial might lead to a larger hunt. Other people might begin coming forward with accusations of witchcraft, the magistrates conducting the trial might broaden the scope on their own, or the accused witch might name accomplices, either voluntarily or under torture. Thus, even a single accusation could lead to numerous trials. In most cases, after several trials, and in all likelihood several convictions and executions, this sort of medium-level hunt would end of its own accord. Judges would become satisfied that they had found all the witches present in a community and no further accusations would be made. In some cases, however, a hunt could spiral out of control if, for whatever reason, the initial few trials created a high enough level of panic in the community, or concern among the prosecuting officials was raised to a sufficient level. In these cases, accusations would not dry up, and zealous magistrates might press their investigations, convinced that more witches would be uncovered. Often, the use of torture became more intense, and thus confessions came more quickly and became more extreme. A fair sign that a hunt was getting out of control was that the typical stereotype of the witch began to break down and accusations came to fall increasingly on men and on wealthier and more socially prominent people.

Not many hunts became widely out of control, but when they did, they could claim scores or even hundreds of victims and threaten to destroy entire communities. Because the uncontrolled use of torture could virtually guarantee confession and conviction in almost all cases, and because even a single witch might accuse dozens more, there was no natural break to the process. Such large-scale hunts typically ended only when the authorities involved reached a crisis of confidence. That is, they had to become convinced that they were extracting mostly false confessions and therefore were attaining mostly false convictions. Only then would they either stop the trials or at least become more cautious in their acceptance of evidence and use of torture. In the face of more acquittals than convictions, the level of panic that could grip a community usually then subsided, and the hunt came to an end.

REGIONAL VARIATIONS

Any discussion of the general pattern of witch-hunts for all of Europe is complicated by the degree of regional variance in levels of concern and responses to this crime in the 16th and 17th centuries. Although the basic idea of witchcraft was accepted in almost all European lands, including colonial possessions overseas, nevertheless there were important differences in the acceptance of certain aspects of the witch-stereotype, and certainly in the patterns of prosecution that fear of witches created. Central Europe was without a doubt the heartland of the witch-hunts. The lands of the German Empire and the Swiss Confederation experienced the greatest overall numbers of witch trials and also the most severe panics and largest hunts. Yet even within this region, because of the political fragmentation of the Empire and the independence of the numerous Swiss cantons, significant geographical variations in the level of witch-hunting were evident. In general, Switzerland and the southern and western regions of the German Empire, where political fragmentation was highest and there existed numerous small and essentially autonomous states and legal jurisdictions, saw the most severe hunts. In the northern and eastern parts of the German Empire, including the large southeastern region of Bavaria, where political entities were larger, witch-hunting was significantly less severe.

Similarly in France, at the time the largest unified state in Europe in terms of population, many thousands of witch trials were conducted in the 16th and 17th centuries, but accusations and especially executions for the crime of witchcraft, measured per capita, were far lower than in the smaller states within the German Empire. In France, too, there were major variations in the intensity of witch trials from region to region. Overall, far more witch-hunting took place on the fringes of the country than in the central regions, or more accurately, than in those regions that were more firmly and fully under the centralized control of the royal government in Paris. Across Europe, this pattern would hold. In those regions that had large, centralized legal bureaucracies, witch trials were less frequent and large-scale hunts, involving dozens or even hundreds of trials, were extremely rare. Larger-scale bureaucracies tended to be more careful in their conduct of trials and to focus more on matters of legal procedure, such as proper application of the restrictions on the use of torture. This in turn significantly reduced, although by no means eliminated, convictions for witchcraft and worked to prevent individual accusations from sparking major hunts. In regions of greater local legal autonomy, on the other hand, magistrates were often more careless in their adherence to proper legal procedures and were more likely to be swept along by the level of panic that could be generated in a community when one or more serious accusations of witchcraft were made.

In the British Isles, England had some episodes of severe persecution of witches, but overall the level of witch-hunting was lower than on the continent. For various reasons, continental notions of diabolism—the idea of a conspiratorial cult of witches gathering at nocturnal sabbaths and worshiping the devil—never gained as much acceptance in England as elsewhere in Western and Central Europe, and many witch trials focused only on the practice of *maleficium*. In addition, England had never fully adopted inquisitorial procedure, and most especially torture was extremely limited under English law. These factors worked to keep the intensity of fear over witchcraft and the level of witch-hunting down. Scotland, by comparison, where notions of diabolism gained a wider credence and where the central government was less able to enforce restrictions on the use of torture, experienced more major witch-hunts, although the overall intensity was still not as severe as in Central European lands. Also the British colonies in New England experienced more severe witch-hunting (again per capita) than in the mother country. Here, concern over witchcraft was deeply enmeshed with broader Puritan concerns over morality, temptation, and the power of the devil.

In Northern and Southern Europe—Scandinavia and Mediterranean lands—the persecution of witches was relatively light, although some large-scale hunts certainly did occur. In Spain and Italy, perhaps somewhat ironically, this reduced intensity was primarily a result of the existence of the Spanish and Roman Inquisitions in those lands. Although ecclesiastical inquisitors had been among the first to develop the notion of diabolical witchcraft, in the 16th and 17th centuries the Spanish and Roman Inquisitions were large, centralized, bureaucratic organizations. As such, they exerted the same restraint on witch trials as other centralized legal bureaucracies elsewhere. In the lands of Eastern Europe, witch-hunting came late and also endured later than in western lands, with the most severe hunts in many regions only coming in the early 18th century. Here, too, however, there were significant regional differences. The only eastern state to experience major hunts on the scale of some of those in German lands was Poland. Hungary had fewer witch trials, although still a significant number. Further east, in Russian lands, witch-hunting was very late and very limited. Among other factors, the Eastern Orthodox Church never operated under the same model of intense diabolism as was present in both Catholic and Protestant lands to the west.

DECLINE OF WITCH-HUNTING AND SURVIVAL OF WITCH-BELIEFS

As early as the mid-17th century in some lands, and certainly by the 18th century across much of Europe (excluding the east), large-scale witch-hunting was in decline. This did not mean, however, that belief in the reality of witchcraft or the potential threat posed by witches was declining. Rather, the decline of witch-hunting preceded any lessening in actual belief in witchcraft and was caused primarily, it would seem, by a more limited sort of purely legal skepticism. In a sense, the witch-hunts undermined themselves by their own severity, and more and more authorities became concerned with the abuses of legal procedure, primarily the rampant use of torture, that took place in many courts, and the obviously large number of false convictions that were being extracted. While not denying the power of the devil or the possible existence of real witches, authorities increasingly became convinced that witchcraft did not exist as a widespread threat. With the application of more careful legal procedures, more people accused of witchcraft were shown to be innocent, and the level of fear and panic that had fueled the largest hunts was dissipated. Gradually, this legal skepticism was supplemented by a level of real skepticism about the very possibility of witchcraft. Nevertheless, belief in the real existence of at least some witches remained widespread among most of the European population, if not among the ruling elites, well into the 19th century.

Although belief in the reality of witchcraft remained widespread at many levels of European society, the legal prosecution of witches and conduct of witch trials required cooperation between populations and ruling elites, and in the course of the 1700s government after government put an end to witch trials. The last legal executions for witchcraft took place toward the end of this century. The end of officially sanctioned witch-hunting certainly had an effect on the nature of commonly held witch-beliefs and popular reaction to suspected cases of witchcraft. Greater historical shifts would be needed, however, to end the widespread belief in harmful sorcery and the existence of witches.

Belief in witchcraft in the most general sense—that of harmful sorcery or *maleficium*—seems almost a universal aspect of pre-modern human societies and functions to meet a variety of social needs. In almost all cultures in which it appears, the concept of witchcraft, however specifically defined, serves mainly as an explanation for unexpected misfortune or natural calamities, and as an outlet to express social conflict within tightly knit communities existing in a largely agrarian context. Such cultures support the belief in harmful sorcery and witchcraft in many ways, and ultimately it is the very nature of these cultures that must change in order to undermine these ideas. In Europe, the widespread belief in the existence of witches does not appear to have declined significantly until the profound demographic, economic, political, legal, and social changes brought about as a result of the industrial revolution permeated most regions of the continent and most levels of European society, and this process was not complete until the 19th and in some areas even well into the 20th century.

Even as this process was underway, however, ideas of magic and occultism were taking new forms. Already in the 18th century, European elites began to form numerous secret societies, the most well known of which were the Masonic orders. Certain elements within these elite groups, such as the Rosicrucians or Illuminati, were drawn to magic and occult practices. By the end of the 19th century, in 1888, the Hermetic Order of the Golden Dawn was founded in England as a socially elite, secret society explicitly devoted to the study and practice of magic and occultism. At the same time, spiritualism was becoming extremely popular with the urban middle classes of Europe, and all manner of seers and mediums, such as the famous and outrageous Madame Blavatsky, were capturing the public imagination with their claims of supernatural powers and ability to commune with the dead and foretell the future. Even today, the continued prominence of astrology, tarot reading, and other forms of divination—to say nothing of the actual practice of ritual magic by some groups—speaks to the continued willingness of many people in modern, industrialized, and technologically sophisticated society to believe in the existence of magical or occult forces.

WITCHCRAFT IN OTHER WORLD CULTURES

In Europe, witchcraft developed along a particular historical trajectory, deeply influenced by Christian concepts of evil, the devil, and demonology, but shaped also by unique European social and legal developments. For these reasons, the great witch-hunts that occurred in Europe from the 15th to the 18th centuries have never been matched elsewhere in the world. Nevertheless, witchcraft in a more general sense, understood to mean simply the practice of harmful forms of sorcery by malevolent individuals, can be said to have existed in virtually every human culture throughout history. As these figures have almost universally inspired fear and anxiety, so attempts at suppression of witchcraft and the eradication of witches have also occurred throughout human history, although never on the scale of the witch-hunts of Europe.

Witchcraft has been a concern, it seems, from the very dawn of humankind. In ancient Mesopotamia, people believed that the world was full of hostile supernatural forces and demons bent on the destruction of human civilization. Both magical and religious rituals were widely employed to combat these hostile forces, which appear to have threatened to undermine human society in much the way that witchcraft was later conceived in Christian Europe. Authorities were concerned to expose and punish any witches—individuals who aided or directed these demonic or hostile forces—and to devise means of protection from this threat. The Babylonian magical ritual *maqlu*, for example, meaning "burning" and referring to the incineration of certain magical effigies, was designed to counter witchcraft. The ancient Greek and Roman responses to such supernatural threats have already been described briefly above, and they provided at least one basis for later European conceptions of and reactions to witchcraft.

Throughout the ancient Near-East and into South- and East-Asia, belief in harmful magic and malevolent, witch-like figures is known to have existed. As late as the 18th century, a major panic over the supposed threat of harmful sorcery and the perceived existence of a conspiracy of evil sorcerers occurred in China. Beliefs akin to witchcraft have also been widespread in Africa and civilizations in the Americas. Since, especially in Africa, these beliefs have persisted openly into the modern era, they have been much studied by European anthropologists and in turn by historians seeking to make comparisons to historical witchcraft and witch-beliefs in Europe. Many similarities are evident. In most African societies, for example, women are far more commonly associated with witchcraft than are men. In addition, witches are often perceived to be not merely individual practitioners of harmful magic, but somehow organized and threatening to all of human society. In attempting to distinguish "witchcraft" from mere "sorcery," anthropologists have often categorized as sorcery those beliefs that involve humans learning to manipulate supernatural forcers in certain ways. Witchcraft, by contrast, is defined as operating (or being believed to operate) through some innate power found in the witch herself. Following this distinction, any person might learn to perform acts of sorcery, but only those born with innate power can be witches, and this power marks them as being inherently evil beings. This distinction is useful for many African and other world cultures, but would not seem to apply to Europe, where, historically, witches were believed to acquire their evil powers from the devil or from demons, not from any internal ability that they naturally possessed. European witches were, however, certainly often seen as inherently evil beings, because they had supposedly abandoned the true Christian faith and surrendered their souls to the devil.

Many traditional African magical beliefs were brought to the Americas during the period of the slave trade. In the Caribbean and elsewhere, these beliefs merged with the Christian beliefs of the slaves' colonial masters, and this resulted in the emergence of new, syncretistic systems. Voodoo (or, as more of its practitioners prefer, Vodoun) and Santería are the most commonly known examples of new systems of belief created out of the merger of traditional African and European concepts of magic and religion. Both Vodoun and Santería are properly identified as religions practiced by many people in the Caribbean, in Latin America, and to some extent in major centers of Hispanic population in North America. Both include certain practices that could be seen as more magical than religious, however, particularly those practices focusing on providing protection from harmful sorcery, and both include beliefs in malevolent figures similar in many ways to witches. Clearly, notions of witchcraft have not been limited to European societies, and they are not confined solely to the pre-modern period of world history.

HISTORICAL STUDY AND MODERN WITCHCRAFT

In the course of the 19th century, European scholars first began to address the question of historical witchcraft and the witch-hunts of the late-medieval and early-modern periods in a serious way (although many of their conclusions were based more on their own ideological convictions than on the historical evidence). As early as 1828, the German scholar Karl-Ernst Jarcke advanced the theory that those persecuted for witchcraft had in fact been practicing an ancient, pagan religion. His purpose was in some way to justify, or at least to rationalize, the witch-hunts as a serious effort on the part of ecclesiastical and secular authorities to enforce a real Christianization on the populace. In 1862, the French historian Jules Michelet published his study, *La sorcière,* making a similar argument, but to opposite effect. Michelet presented the supposed religion of witchcraft as a means of positive popular resistance against the oppressive authority of the church in the Middle Ages. The witch-hunts were for him not a rational and necessary step in the progress of European history, but an instance of terrible persecution and repression by zealous and unenlightened religious authorities.

Also in the 19th century, the Romantic Movement had spurred a major interest in folk-culture among European elites. Professional and amateur folklorists began cataloging and studying popular or traditional beliefs and practices, which of course at this time still included a belief in *maleficium* and other elements of witchcraft. While not typically credulous of these beliefs themselves, many 19th-century folklorists were clearly fascinated by and drawn to such subject matter. Academic anthropologists as well began delving into the structures, and possible realities, of ancient myths. In his *Teutonic Mythology,* published in 1844, Jacob Grimm argued that the historical stereotype of witchcraft included many elements drawn from traditional Germanic folk culture and the remnants of pre-Christian religious beliefs. In 1890, the first edition of James Frazier's *The Golden Bough* appeared, in which he explored the apparent unities between the mythologies of many ancient cultures, centered on the supposed existence of a single ancient fertility goddess and her consort who enacted a ritual of life, death, and rebirth that gave form to the seasonal cycle of the year. By the early 20th century, Frazier's ideas, and a focus on mythology rather than actual ancient cultures, were falling out of favor with many professional anthropologists, but were becoming highly popularized, and *The Golden Bough* sold extremely well to a general readership.

Frazier's notions of a single basic fertility myth underlying the core mythologies of many ancient cultures was profoundly influential on the emergence of modern witchcraft in the 20th century through the person of Margaret Murray. Murray was a British Egyptologist and amateur anthropologist who became interested in the historical phenomenon of witchcraft in medieval and early-modern Europe. In looking through the sources on witchcraft, she came to believe that she saw the vestiges of just the sort of ancient religion that Frazier had postulated. Clerical authors had, in her view, twisted the actual practices of this religion into diabolical rituals, but in the supposed orgies and depraved feasting of a witches' sabbath, Murray saw pagan fertility rituals. These festivals were presided over by an ancient, horned fertility god, such as the Greco-Roman Pan or Celtic Cernunnos, whom clerical authors had transformed into the Christian devil. In 1921, Murray published her first book on witchcraft, *The Witch-Cult in Western Europe,* in which she advanced her basic argument that historical witchcraft had in fact been a remnant of an ancient fertility religion. In *The God of the Witches*, published in 1933, she presented her theories about the nature of the witches' sabbath and the corruption of the pagan horned god into the Christian devil by clerical authorities. By the time of 1954's *The Divine King of England,* Murray was maintaining that every English king from the time of William the Conqueror in the 11th century to James I in the 17th had been members of the secret religion of witchcraft, which survived as a powerful but clandestine force throughout this period.

From the start, many scholars were as skeptical of Murray's theories as they were intrigued. As her claims became more outlandish, skepticism increased. Since the 1950s, all of her theories and arguments have been largely disproved. Although it now seems clear that certain elements of the stereotype of witchcraft, especially night flight and the transformation of witches into animals, were indeed rooted to some extent in the remnants of ancient beliefs and folk-practices that were widespread across Europe, there is no evidence that historical witchcraft was in any way directly connected to pre-Christian pagan religions. Instead, historical European witchcraft was a thoroughly Christian construct, derived primarily from biblical, patristic, and medieval scholastic notions of magic and demonology. Certainly, the widespread witch-hunts of the 16th and 17th centuries were in no way an attempt by Christian authorities to destroy a surviving archaic pagan religion that continued to exist in their midst.

Nevertheless, Murray's notions provided a basis for the initial development of modern witchcraft, often termed *Wicca*, in Europe in the second half of the 20th century. The man most responsible for this development was Gerald Gardner, an English civil servant and amateur student of world religions who spent much of his life in the Far East before retiring to England. Once back in his native country, he claimed to have discovered and been inducted into a coven of traditional, hereditary witches who practiced an ancient religion and who could trace their lineage back to the Middle Ages. In 1954, he published *Witchcraft Today,* in which he claimed to be introducing the genuinely ancient beliefs and practices of this coven to the world. In fact, the book was largely a mixture of the theories of Margaret Murray (with whom Gardner had collaborated as a member of the British Folklore Society in the late 1930s and who wrote an approving preface to *Witchcraft Today*), aspects of world religions, and ritual magic and occultism (Gardner had been made an honorary member of the *Ordo Templi Orientis*, an elite magical society, by the famed occultist Aleister Crowley, who in turn had years earlier been a member of the Hermetic Order of the Golden Dawn). Nevertheless, Gardner's book served as the primary genesis of the modern movement of witchcraft, and his followers and those inspired by him were convinced that they were merely continuing the practice of an ancient, pre-Christian form of religion.

In many ways a reaction to the apparent bankruptcy many people saw in the traditional Western religions in the wake of the horrors of the first half of the 20th century, Wicca, along with other varieties of neo-paganism, flourished in the counter-culture atmosphere of the 1960s and 1970s. The movement originated by Gardner was never strongly unified or cohesive, and many different traditions of modern witchcraft quickly emerged. By 1979, the movement as a whole came of age with the publication of two important works, both by American authors. Starhawk, a witch and political activist, wrote *The Spiral Dance,* which unified essentially Gardnerian forms of Wiccan belief and practice with a lyrical internal spirituality that embraced personal liberty, environmentalism and respect for nature, and especially feminism and female spiritual empowerment. The book largely superseded Gardner's *Witchcraft Today* to become the essential expression of modern witchcraft. In the same year, the journalist and practicing witch Margot Adler wrote *Drawing Down the Moon,* the first serious study of the origins and development of the Wiccan movement. Adler recognized that, especially in light of near-universal scholarly dismissal of the theories of Margaret Murray and serious suspicions about Gerald Gardner's reliability, the claim that modern Wicca was a direct continuation of an actual ancient religion that had survived underground for over a millennium could not be seriously maintained. However, the supposed pseudo-history of the Wiccan faith could be viewed as a foundation myth without in any way undermining the value of current Wiccan beliefs and practices.

Most modern witches now fully accept that, rather than continuing an ancient form of pre-Christian religion, they are practitioners of a new religion creatively based on ancient forms and principals. An aspect of this religion continues to be the working of spells and ritual magic, which modern Wiccans believe have real power. In this sense, they are, in fact, continuing in the true historical tradition of witchcraft, which has always placed this phenomenon, in various ways, at the juncture where religious belief meets magical practice.

The Dictionary

– A –

ABSALON, ANNA PEDERSDOTTER (?–1590). The victim of perhaps the single most famous **witchcraft** accusation made in **Scandinavia**, Anna was the wife of the Lutheran minister and famous scholar Absalon Pedersen Beyer. The charges against her arose mainly out of popular opposition to the attempts by Absalon and other Protestant clergy to remove holy images from the churches of Bergen, Sweden, in accordance with Lutheran teachings. Because the clergymen themselves were too highly placed for their efforts to be resisted directly, opposition focused on Anna. She was first acquitted of charges in 1575, but more accusations arose years later. She was tried again and executed in 1590. Her trial later became the basis for a play and then the film by Carl Theodore Dreyer, *Day of Wrath*.

ACCUSATORIAL PROCEDURE. This refers to the basic system of criminal procedure that was used in most courts of law, mainly secular but also to some degree ecclesiastical, in medieval Europe prior to the 13th century. It was then gradually replaced in most lands, first in ecclesiastical courts but eventually in secular courts as well, by **inquisitorial procedure.** Although the earlier accusatorial procedure by no means precluded prosecutions for crimes of magic or **sorcery**, it was difficult to ensure a conviction for such crimes under this system. By contrast, inquisitorial procedure made prosecuting such crimes significantly easier, and so provided a necessary condition for the emergence of **witchcraft** and **witch-hunting** in the late-medieval and early-modern periods.

Under accusatorial procedure, all legal actions had to be initiated by accusations coming from private persons who felt themselves afflicted or injured in some way. Accusers, however, did more than just initiate trials. They also acted as prosecutors and were responsible for proving the guilt of the person or persons whom they had accused. If the accused did not admit their guilt, and if no positive proof could be provided, the matter was placed in the hands of God. Most often, the accused would be made to undergo an ordeal. They might be dunked in water, or made to put their hand in boiling water, or forced to hold hot irons. If they were able to stay immersed in the water for a sufficient period of time in the first case, or if their wounds healed reasonably well in the second or third, they were judged to be innocent. Nobles, instead of undergoing an ordeal, might have access to trial by combat, in which, in theory, God would ensure that the innocent won and the guilty lost. Importantly, if by whatever mechanism the accused would be judged innocent, the accuser then fell under the penalty of law for bringing a false accusation.

For crimes such as sorcery or, later, witchcraft, secretive by their very nature, positive proof was very difficult to obtain. Thus almost all cases would have been decided by ordeal. Since the accuser could be severely punished in cases of wrongful accusation, fear of divine judgment would have prevented many specious accusations. Moreover, even when accusers honestly suspected that sorcery was being used against them, given the extremely secretive and indirect nature of the crime, complete certainty was probably rare. Thus the threat of legal repercussions for false accusations kept the number of trials for sorcery low. The inquisitorial system, on the other hand, although in many ways more rational, facilitated trials for sorcery and later witchcraft by making prosecution the responsibility of the court, not the individual accusers.

ADLER, MARGOT (1946–). An American journalist, author, and practicing pagan, Adler wrote the first important study of the emergence of **neo-paganism** and modern **witchcraft**, or **Wicca**, in America. Her book *Drawing Down the Moon,* published in 1979, the same year as **Starhawk**'s *The Spiral Dance,* became an important text for modern witchcraft. From a historical perspective, in particular, it recognized that much, if not all, of modern witchcraft's connection to the historical witchcraft of the medieval and early-modern periods was fictitious.

Raised in New York City in a non-religious household, Adler studied at the University of California at Berkeley and at Columbia University's School of Journalism. She began a career in broadcast journalism and was also active in political, environmental, and feminist causes. She was first introduced to modern neo-paganism in the early 1970s while in England investigating the history of the druids. Returning to New York, she entered a coven and began practicing modern witchcraft as established by **Gerald Gardner**. Approached to write a book about modern witchcraft, she began researching the origins and development of the movement.

Adler soon realized that many of the claims made by Gardner, that modern witchcraft was directly linked to the witches of the medieval and early-modern period, and that witchcraft represented a genuine preservation of an even more ancient, pre-Christian religion, were false. Nevertheless, she recognized that most religious beliefs ultimately rested on pseudo-history in which real historical fact and myth were merged to meet the needs of belief. Modern Wiccan and neo-pagan groups could recognize the largely mythical nature of this pseudo-history, she argued, and still retain the force and value of their beliefs. These ideas, among others, were set out in *Drawing Down the Moon*.

AFRICAN WITCHCRAFT. Historically, the belief in various forms of harmful magic or **sorcery**, often termed **witchcraft** by Western observers, has been widespread across sub-Saharan Africa. Moreover, these beliefs have remained prevalent and socially respectable in many African societies, while in Europe they have declined significantly since the period of the major **witch-hunts** ending in the 18th century. Thus in the 20th century, as anthropologists began to study these African beliefs, scholars of European witchcraft sought to apply the information gathered from African case studies for comparative purposes to their own work on historical witchcraft in medieval and early-modern Europe. Such comparisons have limitations, the most obvious being that European witchcraft was grounded so completely in specific aspects of Christian theology and **demonology**, and especially the Christian concept of the **devil**, while African witchcraft operates in an entirely different religious and cultural context. Nevertheless, some interesting parallels emerged.

Generalizations about African witchcraft are made difficult because beliefs and practices vary between different African societies. Perhaps the most famous study was made in the early 20th century by the British anthropologist E. E. Evans-Pritchard. Focusing on the Azande of southern Sudan, he discovered three distinct categories of magic among these people. Good magic was used by **witch doctors**, diviners, and oracles to predict the future and to protect against harmful magic. Evil sorcery was used to harm other people. This form of magic often involved using material objects in the performance of spells and typically targeted individuals. A third category, which Evans-Pritchard labeled witchcraft, entailed an internal, hereditary power passed down from fathers to sons and, more often, from mothers to daughters. It manifested, supposedly, in the witch's stomach as a small black swelling. Witches were to some extent organized and gathered at secret meetings to practice their magic. They could attack individual people, but were also responsible for all manner of hardships and afflictions suffered by the entire community, including crop failures, lack of game, infertility, and even poor government. Other African societies make similar distinctions. For example, the Bechuana of Botswana distinguish between "day sorcerers" and "night witches." Day sorcerers might work magic either to help or harm people, but usually do so on an individual basis and for specific reasons, often for pay. Night witches are more inherently malevolent. They are typically pictured as old women who seek to harm the entire community.

The widespread belief in Africa of the existence of certain categories of people who seek to harm society as a whole is reminiscent of the historical European concept of witchcraft as a diabolical conspiracy directed against the entire Christian world. Across Africa, these people are frequently seen as female, they gather at secret assemblies to plan and work their evil magic, and they are often described as flying at night to these gatherings. All of these factors present more parallels between European and African witchcraft. The conclusion drawn by many scholars is that there are certain fears and concerns common to almost all pre-modern, largely agrarian societies, and particularly to societies composed of small, tightly knit communities. Ideas of witchcraft, in a very general sense, seem to be a common response to and explanation for certain kinds of hardship and misfortune in such societies. The notions of secret, nocturnal gatherings and **night flight** seem to indicate that basic notions of **shamanism** and encounters with spiritual forces, good or bad, are a common feature of many human societies and a basis for many systems of religious and magical beliefs. While no true witch-hunts ever developed in any region of Africa on the scale that was seen in Europe during the early-modern period, witchcraft has been, and to some extent continues to be, greatly feared in many African societies, and a variety of steps can be taken to protect a community from witchcraft or to punish suspected witches. Many types of counter-magic have developed, and in some areas such as Zambia groups of professional witch-finders emerged. These were people, usually men, who were employed to discover the presence of witches in a community and to eliminate them. In addition, popular lynching of witches could occur, and is still known to occur occasionally in the present day. The fear of witchcraft and violence directed toward suspected witches could become severe enough that authorities, especially European colonial authorities, felt the need to intervene. For example, in 1914, a witchcraft ordinance was issued in Zambia that prescribed punishment for making accusations of witchcraft or using certain forms of magic to discover supposed witches. Ironically, in many areas European colonial rule in Africa seems to have exacerbated the very economic and social tensions that often underlie accusations of witchcraft.

African beliefs and systems of magic have also influenced some modern religions that incorporate a significant amount of what could be labeled magical rituals. In particular, African slaves brought to the Americas and forced to convert at least nominally to Christianity retained many of their traditional beliefs. African deities and other supernatural entities were merged with Christian saints and a number of syncretistic beliefs emerged. The modern religions of **Santería** and **Voodoo** are prominent examples of such syncretism. These religions are practiced mainly in the Caribbean and elsewhere in Latin America, as well as in large Hispanic communities in North America.

AGE, CORRELATION WITH WITCH ACCUSATIONS. By far the most common image of a witch is that of an old hag. From surviving evidence, it seems clear that the majority of people accused of **witchcraft** throughout the historical period of the European **witch-hunts**

were in fact old **women**. There is also an opposite stereotype of the witch as a young seductress, but this seems to have been more common in literary representations of witchcraft (the models being classical figures like **Circe** or **Medea**) than in actual accusations. Moreover, an elderly witch could also be seen as sexually driven, since during the medieval and early-modern periods old women were often regarded as being sexually voracious. The actual factors producing such a high number of elderly people among the accused were several. Suspicion of witchcraft often developed slowly in a community, and many years of strange or threatening behavior might be needed before an initial accusation came to be leveled at an individual. Also, the elderly, and especially elderly women, could easily become marginalized socially, thereby making them easier targets for accusations. Widows, in particular, might be seen as a burden by their families, or as an obstacle to property inheritance. Also, the elderly could easily suffer from some form of senility, producing odd behavior and making them vulnerable to accusations.

AGRIPPA (HEINRICH CORNELIUS AGRIPPA VON NETTE-SHEIM) (1486–1535). More important for the history of magic than the history of **witchcraft** per se, Agrippa was one of the most famous magicians and occult philosophers of the early-modern period. He completed his major work, *De occulta philosophia* (On Occult Philosophy) in 1510, when he was only 24 years old, but he did not publish this work until 1533. It became one of the most important compendiums of magical and occult knowledge of the period.

Agrippa was born in Cologne and educated at the university there. He was drawn to the study of the Kabbalah, the Jewish system of mysticism and occult knowledge, and to neo-platonic and **Hermetic magic** and occult systems. He led a peripatetic life, holding many positions throughout **France** and the **German Empire**. His involvement with magic often raised concerns on the part of local authorities and frequently prompted his relocation. Many stories began to circulate about Agrippa's life. He was widely considered to be a magician involved in the blackest arts, such as demonic invocation, and was at times suspected of witchcraft. He supposedly had a demonic **familiar**, which took the form of a large black dog, and he was rumored to be able to reanimate corpses with his magic.

Rumors aside, the only direct involvement he seems to have had with witchcraft was as a defender of accused witches. On one occasion, while living in Metz, he became involved in a witch trial. A woman was being accused of witchcraft, primarily on the grounds that her mother had been convicted and executed for this crime. Agrippa successfully defended the woman, arguing that the crime of witchcraft, involving a deliberate **pact** with the **devil**, had to be entered into voluntarily. A witch's power could not simply be inherited from another person.

ALBERTUS MAGNUS (ca. 1190–1280). Born in the German region of Swabia, Albertus Magnus (Albert the Great) was a Dominican friar and an important medieval philosopher and theologian. He taught theology at the university in Paris, where his most famous student was **Thomas Aquinas**, and later he went to the Dominican *studium* at Cologne. Albertus viewed some magic as a form of natural science, distinct from demonic **sorcery**. In the area of **demonology**, however, he helped to develop notions of explicit and tacit **pacts** that humans might enter into with **demons**. His student Aquinas would develop this position more fully, and such ideas formed an important basis for later notions of **witchcraft**. Like many famous medieval scholars, Albertus himself developed a popular reputation as an **alchemist**, astronomer, and **sorcerer**. While he certainly did engage in the study of certain occult sciences, which he viewed as legitimate, he thoroughly condemned demonic sorcery.

ALCHEMY. An occult science that developed in antiquity and was rediscovered in Europe, along with other forms of learned magic and occult practices, in the 12th century, alchemy involved the manipulation of the secret properties of chemicals and other natural materials. Above all, alchemists sought to discover the so-called philosopher's stone, which would allow them to transmute lead or other common materials into silver and gold. As a clearly learned form of magical practice, like **astrology**, alchemy had little direct connection to **witchcraft**. Alchemists might, however, as a result of the secretive nature of their work, become suspect of practicing more sinister forms of magic.

ALEXANDER IV, POPE (?–1261). By the 1250s, papal inquisitors, whose purpose was to investigate cases of **heresy**, were increasingly dealing with matters of **sorcery**, and questions were being raised as to whether such matters properly fell under their jurisdiction. In 1258, Alexander IV (pope from 1254 to 1261) ruled that sorcery was not a matter of concern for papal inquisitors, unless the sorcery involved acts that "manifestly savored of heresy" (*manifeste saperent haeresim*). Since any case of sorcery that involved the invocation or worship of **demons** met this condition, Alexander's ruling provided an important basis for later inquisitorial action against sorcerers and witches. *See also* INQUISITORIAL PROCEDURE.

ALEXANDER V, POPE (ca. 1340–1410). Reigning for only a short time from 1409 to 1410, Alexander V, in his first year as pope, sent a letter to the Franciscan inquisitor Pontus Fougeyron in which he announced his concern over the existence of many people, both Christians and **Jews**, who performed demonic **sorcery** and worshiped **demons**. In particular, he stated that such people were forming "new sects" (*novas sectas*). The use of this phrase was not original to Alexander, but serves to illustrate how, in the early 15th century, **witchcraft** was clearly perceived as a new and serious threat to the church and Christian society in Europe.

APOSTASY. Referring to a complete renunciation of the basic principles of faith, apostasy was considered to be one of the chief crimes entailed in **witchcraft**, along with **idolatry**, during the medieval and early-modern periods. Upon entering a heretical cult of witches, usually at a witches' **sabbath**, new witches were generally believed to be required to renounce the Christian faith entirely and pledge themselves to the service of the **devil**. Unlike normal **heresy**, which involved errors of belief or practice that could be corrected, apostasy was often seen as an unforgivable crime, a kind of treason against God that required the most severe form of punishment possible.

AQUINAS, THOMAS (ca. 1225–1274). A Dominican friar and one of the most important theologians of the Middle Ages, Aquinas was born in Italy and studied in Paris and Cologne under the direction of the Dominican scholar **Albertus Magnus** (Albert the Great). Aquinas later became a professor of theology at Paris and in Italy. In numerous works, most notably his *Summa contra gentiles* (Summa Against the Gentiles) and *Summa theologiae* (Summa of Theology), he systematized medieval theology according to scholastic logic. Although his works were at first controversial, they later became widely accepted as authoritative, especially by other Dominican authors. Many early clerical authorities who wrote on **witchcraft** cited Aquinas heavily, including the Dominicans **Johannes Nider**, **Jean Vineti**, and **Heinrich Kramer**, the author of the *Malleus maleficarum*.

Aquinas did not write about witchcraft himself—he lived centuries before the idea of diabolic witchcraft fully developed in Europe—but he did discuss the operations of **sorcery** and the power of **demons** in several of his works. He worked out a logical system to explain how demons, as spiritual beings, could affect the physical world, including how demons operating as **incubi** could impregnate women, and how they might influence human actions. He also discussed the evil nature of demons and demonic sorcery. Such sorcery, he argued, always entailed at least a tacit **pact** between the human sorcerer and the demon that the sorcerer invoked. Demons submitted to carry out the wishes of sorcerers in order to ensnare and corrupt them. Such basic notions of **demonology** and the nature of demonic sorcery became foundational for later ideas of witchcraft.

ASTROLOGY. Throughout ancient, medieval, and early-modern Europe, most people believed that the stars and planets exerted influence on many aspects of the terrestrial world, including human beings, and that stellar bodies could be used to predict the future. Astrology, the study of the stars and their effects, was practiced as a real, if often occult, science by educated elites, but many forms of astrology were also practiced at a popular level. Perhaps the most common use of astrology was the practice of making horoscopes to predict the future and divine the destiny of individual people. Astrology also entered into many other forms of magical and occult operations, since the power of the stars was thought, for example, to affect **alchemy** and even demonic invocations. Astral magic, which claimed to draw down and manipulate the power of heavenly bodies, was obviously intimately connected to astrology. There was, however, little direct connection between astrology and **witchcraft**.

AUGUSTINE OF HIPPO, SAINT (354–430). The most important of the so-called Latin Fathers of the Christian church, and probably the most important intellectual figure in the history of Western Christianity, Augustine's writings on **demonology** and the nature of magic provided a basis for all further consideration of these subjects throughout the Middle Ages and the early-modern period in Europe. Above all, his ideas about demonic involvement in most forms of magic and the necessity of **pacts** between the human magician and the **demon** were essential to later conceptions of **sorcery** and **witchcraft**.

Born in North Africa, Augustine studied in Carthage and later in Italy. Although his mother was a Christian, he did not convert to Christianity until 385. He then returned to North Africa, where he became a priest and later bishop of the city of Hippo. For the rest of his life, Augustine devoted himself to demonstrating the superiority of Christianity to **pagan** religions. Of particular importance to the history of magic and later witchcraft were his arguments that pagan deities were in fact Christian demons and that pagan religious practices were empty superstitions. He distinguished sharply between magic performed with the aid of demons and legitimate Christian miracles performed by divine power. He discussed the nature of demons in many works, especially in his treatise *De divinatione daemonum* (On the Divination of Demons), written in 406, and in sections of his greatest work, *The City of God,* written from 413 to 425. Because demons were inherently evil, he reasoned, they would not serve humans who invoked them unless those human sorcerers entered into pacts with the demons and worshiped them.

– B –

BABA YAGA. A famous witch in Russian folklore, Baba Yaga was pictured as an old woman who lured people to her home where she cooked and devoured them. She especially liked to practice such **cannibalism** on young **children**. Much more a demonic monster than a human figure, she lived in a hut beyond a river of fire. The hut was surrounded by stakes set with human heads and was built on chicken legs, so that it could move at her command. She often flew through the air in an iron cauldron. She is clearly related to other night-flying, child-devouring monsters that later became associated with **witchcraft** in the traditions of Western lands, such as the Roman **strix**.

BACCHANALIA. A religious celebration in honor of the Roman god of wine, Bacchus, the rites, real or supposed, of the Bacchanalia became an important basis for the idea of the witches' **sabbath** in later medieval Europe. In ancient Greece, worshipers of the god of wine and fertility, Dionysos (who later became the Roman Bacchus), gathered at night, often in secluded wilderness areas. Their celebrations usually involved a number of women led by male priests, and entailed rites involving the consumption of wine, ecstatic dancing, and animal sacrifice. The god, Dionysos, was represented by a horned **goat**, a traditional symbol of fertility. The celebrations were often associated with sexual frenzies. In Roman times, the Bacchanalia became so associated with uncontrolled revelry, sexual activity, and immorality, that it was outlawed by the Roman Senate in 186 B.C.E. The description of a Bacchanalia by the Roman historian Livy became an important literary model for the later idea of the sabbath.

BACON, ROGER (ca. 1213–1291). An English Franciscan philosopher and scholar, Bacon was one of the most important natural scientists of the Middle Ages. In particular, he studied **alchemy, astrology**, mathematics, and optics. He developed a popular reputation as a sorcerer because of his unconventional scientific experiments and his pursuit of occult learning. There is no evidence, however, that Bacon was ever significantly interested in matters of demonic **sorcery** (as some medieval scholars were), and he certainly was never associated with **witchcraft** in any way.

BAMBERG WITCH TRIALS. The scene of some of the most severe **witch-hunts** in the **German Empire**, the persecution of witches in and around the city of Bamberg was particularly intense during the reign of Bishop Johann Georg Fuchs von Dornheim, the so-called *Hexenbischof* or "witch-bishop," from 1623 to 1633. Bishop Johann established a large staff to carry out the hunt for and prosecution of witches, and he had a special prison constructed, the *Hexenhaus* or "witchhouse," containing cells and interrogation chambers to hold suspected witches. The hunts in Bamberg began to spiral out of control, and many prominent citizens were accused. Eventually, the situation became so bad that an appeal was made to the emperor Ferdinand II. Finally, in 1630 and 1631, he issued mandates that proper legal procedures should be more carefully adhered to in all cases of suspected **witchcraft** in accordance with the **Carolina law code** that supposedly governed the entire empire. From this point, and especially with the death of Bishop Johann and other important persecutors, the number of trials in Bamberg gradually decreased.

BAPHOMET. An image of the **devil** or a **demon** as a horned, half-**goat** creature, Baphomet is of medieval origins. The word may be a corruption of the name of the Islamic prophet Muhammad (often incorrectly rendered as Mahomet in medieval Christian sources), conceived by Christian authorities as a demon or idol. In the early 14th century, the **Knights Templar** were accused of possessing an idol shaped like the head of Baphomet, which they supposedly worshiped. In the 19th century, the image of Baphomet was revived among occultists and enthusiasts of ritual magic. Perhaps the most famous image of the horned goat-devil was drawn by the French occultist Eliphas Lévi, and the well-known British occultist **Aleister Crowley** took the name Baphomet at one point in his career. In the 20th century, a version of the image of Baphomet—a goat's head inscribed in an upside-down **pentagram**—was adopted by the **Church of Satan** as its official symbol. The image has also often been associated with **witchcraft**, but no practitioners of **Wicca** or other forms of modern **neo-paganism** use the image in any way, although practitioners of modern **Satanism** continue to do so.

BASEL, COUNCIL OF (1431–1449). This great church council, held in the city of Basel in the first half of the 15th century, was an important center for the early diffusion of the idea of **witchcraft** across Western Europe. Several of the most important early theorists of witchcraft were present at the council or associated with it in some way, and clearly many clerics first learned of witchcraft while at Basel.

In the early 15th century, full-fledged demonic witchcraft, that is, witchcraft that involved not just the practice of harmful **sorcery** (*maleficium*) against others, but also involved the worship of **demons** or the **devil**, **apostasy** from the faith, gatherings at a **sab-**

bath, and all the attendant horrors that implied, was a fairly new and localized phenomenon. Some of the earliest true witch trials were only just beginning to take place, mainly in lands in and around the western Alps—the dioceses of Lausanne and Sion, and the territories of Dauphiné and Savoy. The Council of Basel brought churchmen from across Europe together just to the north of these regions.

Several of the first learned authorities to write on witchcraft were present at the Council of Basel. Perhaps most important among these men was the Dominican theologian **Johannes Nider**. In his major work on witchcraft, the *Formicarius* (Anthill), he included several accounts of witches in the Simme valley in the Bernese *Oberland,* that is, the alpine territory of the city of Bern, and elsewhere in the diocese of Lausanne. He also wrote about the supposed witchcraft of **Joan of Arc**, about whom he learned while at the council from clerics who had come from Paris. The French cleric and poet **Martin Le Franc** was also at Basel, and there composed his poem *Le Champion des Dames* (The Defender of Ladies), in which he included a long section about witchcraft. Moreover, there is strong evidence to suggest that the anonymous clerical author of the ***Errores Gazariorum*** (Errors of the Gazarii), another important early description of witchcraft, was associated with the council in some way.

In addition, many ecclesiastical authorities involved in the prosecution of witches were present at the Council of Basel, for example George de Saluces, who was later bishop of Lausanne from 1440 until 1461, and under whose direction several **witch-hunts** were conducted. Also the inquisitor Ulric de Torrenté, who conducted some of the earliest witch trials in the diocese of Lausanne, might have been at the council for some time. Most famously, **Nicholas Jacquier**, who later conducted numerous witch trials as an inquisitor in northern **France**, attended the council in 1432 and 1433. He also wrote the important treatise on witchcraft *Flagellum hereticorum fascinariorum* (The Scourge of Heretical Witches) in 1458.

BASQUE LANDS, WITCHCRAFT IN. The Basque lands comprise a small region in southwestern **France** and northern Spain, lying on either side of the Pyrenees. They were the scene of some of the most intense **witch-hunting** in both countries. The major Basque witch-hunt began in 1609. In France, the judge **Pierre de Lancre** was appointed to the Pays de Labourd and began to investigate cases of **witchcraft**. He quickly became convinced that the entire region was infested with witches. He wrote of thousands of witches gathering at great **sabbaths**, and he is often credited with executing up to 600 supposed witches, although in all likelihood the figure should be under 100. In Spain, cases of witchcraft fell under the jurisdiction of the Spanish **Inquisition**, and in 1609 the inquisitor **Alonso de Salazar Frias** was appointed to the regional tribunal at Logroño. Unlike Lancre, he was skeptical of many of the charges being made in the courts. In 1611 and 1612, he conducted a thorough investigation of the procedures being employed in witch trials in the region. He found many lapses in procedure and became convinced that many of the convictions being obtained were false. Based on his report, the central council of the Spanish Inquisition in Madrid, the *Suprema,* established much stricter oversight and guidelines for witch trials. By 1614, the severe outbreak of witch-hunting on both sides of the Pyrenees was over and the region was returning to normal.

BAYLE, PIERRE (1647–1706). An important philosopher, born in **France** and later a professor at the university in Rotterdam, Bayle was a strong advocate of liberalism and religious toleration. He treated the subject of **witchcraft** at length in his *Réponse aux questions d'un provincial* (Responses to the Questions of a Provincial), written in 1703. He did not deny the potential reality of **sorcery** or witchcraft, or the power of the **devil**. Instead he advocated a more moderate form of **skepticism**, arguing that many acts attributed to witchcraft could also arise from natural causes, and that human authorities could rarely, if ever, be certain in assigning blame to witches. He also felt that the excessive use of **torture** led to many false convictions in cases of witchcraft, that many convicted witches were in fact deranged or confused, and that authorities should not place so much credence in popular beliefs and concerns.

BEKKER, BALTHASAR (1634–1698). One of the most important and perhaps the most thorough opponent of **witch-hunting** in the 17th century, Bekker was a Dutch clergyman. In 1690, he published the first volumes of his *De Betoverde Weereld* (The Enchanted World), which was soon translated into German, English, and French.

A rationalist thinker following the model of the French philosopher René Descartes, in this work, he exhibited a complete **skepticism** about the very existence of **witchcraft**, unlike many other opponents of the witch-hunts who chose to criticize only the faulty procedures of witch trials, which they felt were producing numerous false convictions, while still maintaining the potential reality of witchcraft in the world. Drawing on a new, mechanistic understanding of the universe, Bekker did not deny the reality of **demons**, but he did deny that they could exert any influence or power over the natural world or human affairs. Rather than attribute certain occurrences to witchcraft, he maintained, authorities should look for natural explanations for these events, whatever they were. Because demons lacked any real power in the world, there was no basis for the supposed **pact** between witches and the **devil**. For his beliefs, Bekker was labeled an atheist and ultimately was expelled from the Dutch Reformed church.

BENANDANTI. The apparent remnants of an ancient fertility cult practicing a form of archaic **shamanism**, the *benandanti* were people in the northern Italian region of Friuli who believed that they traveled at night in spirit form to battle witches. The name *benandanti* translates as "those who go well" or "well-doers." They consisted of men and women who had been born with the caul, the inner fetal membrane, still intact and covering their bodies. Such births are frequently taken as a sign of supernatural power in many cultures. Upon reaching maturity, the *benandanti* were initiated into their cult. On certain days they were summoned, while they slept, to travel in spirit form to battle witches, also in spirit form. The *benandanti* were armed with fennel stalks and the witches with sorghum stalks. If the *benandanti* were victorious, the fertility of the land and abundant crops in the coming season were assured. When awake and in their physical forms, the *benandanti* were also thought to have certain supernatural powers, especially the power to perform magical **healing**.

In 1575, the *benandanti* first came to the attention of ecclesiastical inquisitors. These authorities immediately suspected that the *benandanti* were themselves witches, a claim that the *benandanti* vigorously denied. An **inquisition** was instituted, and inquests and trials lasted until well into the 1640s. Over this period, inquisitors did succeed, to some extent, in convincing the local populace and even some of the *benandanti* themselves that they were in fact involved in **witchcraft** and attending witches' **sabbaths**. As was typical for **Southern Europe**, however, the trials were well-controlled, **torture** was rarely employed, and no major **witch-hunt** developed.

Scholars now agree that the *benandanti* are among the best examples of the surviving remnants of ancient pagan fertility cults in medieval and early-modern European society. The roots of the beliefs surrounding the *benandanti* are clearly ancient. By the 16th century, however, they had become thoroughly Christianized. The *benandanti* often maintained that they were summoned by angels to battle witches and that they were agents of God in this struggle against evil. They thus reveal how surviving fragments of ancient beliefs and practices could combine with Christian belief and notions of witchcraft.

BERKELEY, WITCH OF. The story of the witch of Berkeley supposedly took place around the time of the Norman conquest of England in 1066. The chronicler **William of Malmesbury** included it in his history of the kings of England, the *Gesta regum,* and the story continued to circulate throughout the medieval and early-modern periods. A powerful sorceress lived at Berkeley. She performed demonic magic and had clearly entered into some sort of **pact** with the **devil**. Upon receiving a premonition of her own death, she asked her children, since they could not save her soul, at least to try to protect her body after death by sewing it into the skin of a stag and placing it in a stone coffin fastened by three chains inside a church. On the first two nights after her death, **demons** assailed the church in which she lay and broke two of the chains. On the third night the devil himself appeared and commanded the woman's corpse to come with him. The body replied from inside the coffin that it could not, at which point the devil broke the third chain and carried off the corpse on an enormous black horse. Although horrific in its depiction of the connection between **sorcery** and ensnarement of a human soul by demons, the story of the witch of Berkeley does not contain any overt descriptions of the worship of demons or other elements of **diabolism** that would later come to comprise the stereotype of **witchcraft**.

BERNARDINO OF SIENA (1380–1444). One of the most popular preachers in the early 15th century, Bernardino was a Franciscan friar who was active across northern Italy. He was particularly concerned with matters of immorality that he felt threatened to corrupt the entire community in which they were found, especially **sorcery** and **witchcraft**, sodomy, and toleration of **Jews**. In fiery sermons, he called for the extirpation of these supposed sins. He witnessed an early witch trial in Rome, probably in 1426 (some sources give 1424 or other years). He later tried to instigate trials for witchcraft in his native Siena in 1427, and was associated with a witch trial in Todi in 1428. Through his sermons, Bernardino can be seen as helping to begin the spread of concern over sorcery and witchcraft that would soon escalate into the earliest **witch-hunts** in Europe.

BIBLE, WITCHCRAFT IN. The most famous reference to **witchcraft** in the Bible is the passage from Exodus 22:18, given in the 17th century King James' Version as "Thou shalt not suffer a witch to live." Throughout the period of the European **witch-hunts**, this passage served as the biblical justification for the execution of witches. In fact, the original text referred to soothsayers or diviners, but throughout the medieval and early-modern periods, the passage was understood as referring to sorcerers and witches. Other biblical passages of significance for the later history of witchcraft include the story of the **Witch of Endor** (again originally described only as a pythoness or diviner) to whom King Saul went to consult with the spirit of the dead prophet Samuel. Later Christian authorities regularly assumed that the "witch" must in fact have summoned a **demon** who took the form of the prophet. Other important episodes include the encounter between Moses and Aaron and the magicians of the Egyptian pharaoh in Exodus 7:8–13, and the story in 1 Kings 18 in which the prophet Elijah defeated the priests of Baal in a magical contest. Later authorities held that priests of **pagan** religions depicted in the Bible actually worked their magic by summoning demons. The victory of God's prophets in both of these contests was used to show the superiority of divine miracle to demonic **sorcery** or witchcraft.

The most significant magical figure from the New Testament was **Simon Magus** of Samaria. He was a magician who confronted the apostles of Christ in Acts 8:9–24. Seeing that their power was superior to his, he offered the apostle Peter money to be granted similar power. Peter, of course, refused. In later apocryphal literature, the rivalry between Simon Magus and Peter (also called Simon Peter) was elaborated, and Simon Magus became the archetype for practitioners of demonic sorcery throughout the Middle Ages. He was, however, never described as a witch.

BINSFELD, PETER (ca. 1540–1603). A theologian and suffragan bishop of **Trier**, Binsfeld was a major German authority on **witchcraft**. He played a key role in the severe outbreak of **witch-hunting** that took place at Trier in the late 1580s and early 1590s, and he wrote a *Tractatus de confessionibus maleficiorum et sagarum* (Treatise on the Confessions of Witches), first published in 1589. His purpose was to justify the witch trials at Trier, and in particular to defend the value of the confessions made by accused witches as evidence against other witches. He drew on all the previous major Catholic works on witchcraft, such as the *Malleus maleficarum* and the treatises by **Alfonso de Spina** and **Jean Bodin**, and he criticized more **skeptical** authorities such as **Johann Weyer**. He was also instrumental in opposing the skeptical authority **Cornelius Loos**, who had written a treatise in response to the severe witch-hunts he had witnessed in Trier.

BLACK MASS. Generally conceived as an elaborate perversion of the Catholic Mass, involving the inversion of liturgical ritual and often nude rites and sexual **orgies** dedicated to Satan, the Black Mass actually has no historical reality, and certainly no association with **witchcraft**, either historical or modern. Although the witches' **sabbath**, as conceived in the late-medieval and early-modern periods, involved mocking Christian rites, worshiping the **devil**, and engaging in sexual orgies, no historical account describes any rituals directly perverting the Catholic Mass. There is evidence from the 17th century that certain nobles at the court of French king Louis XIV hired priests to perform unorthodox Masses containing sacrilegious and erotic elements, but this seems to have been done more for titillation than out of any serious worship of the devil. Only in the 18th century did the concept of a Black Mass develop and was then projected back into earlier periods. Some secret and possibly occultist organizations of the 18th century, such as the infamous Hellfire Club in England, were rumored to perform Black Masses, but most likely they simply engaged in irreverent and libertine revels that gained a darker tint in rumor and gossip. Practitioners of modern witchcraft, or **Wicca**, do not engage in any rituals resembling a Black Mass, nor do most practitioners of modern **Satanism**. The largest Satanist group, the **Church of Satan**, founded by Anton LaVey, explicitly rejects the Black Mass. Nevertheless, the stereotype of witches and other **neopagans** performing Black Masses persists.

BODIN, JEAN (1529/30–1596). One of the greatest political thinkers of the 16th century, Bodin is most famous for his *Six livres de la République* (Six Books of the Republic), published in 1576. Here, he presented one of the first modern arguments about the nature of political sovereignty, maintaining that ultimate sovereignty lay with the people who comprised a state. This work established Bodin as one of the most progressive political thinkers of his time. In terms of the history of **witchcraft**, however, he is most well known for his work *De la démonomanie des sorciers* (The Demonomania of Witches). First published in 1580, this book went through 10 editions before 1604, and for the remainder of the period of the **witchhunts** stood as one of the preeminent authoritative sources on witchcraft. Nowhere near as liberal on this subject as he was in other areas of political theory, Bodin argued forcefully for the real danger posed by witchcraft and the need for authorities to uncover and destroy this crime.

Born in Angers, **France**, Bodin became a Carmelite monk, but left the monastery to pursue a university education at Toulouse, where he excelled in classics, philosophy, economics, and above all law. Eventually, he became a professor of law. In 1561, he went to Paris in the service of the king, until the publication of the *Six livres* lost him royal favor and he became a provincial prosecutor in Laon. His *Démonomanie* was in part based on his own experience with witch trials. Bodin was convinced of the reality and threat of witches, arguing at length against such **skeptics** as **Johann Weyer**. His theories on witchcraft may be linked to his larger political thought in that he saw in political authority a reflection of divine order on earth. Thus, he was convinced that secular magistrates had to take all measures necessary to protect this order from the diabolical threat of witchcraft.

BOGUET, HENRI (ca. 1550–1619). An eminent lawyer and author of one of the most important legal treatises on **witchcraft** in early-modern Europe, Bouget based his writings on his own experience with witch trials and his personal examinations of many witches. In his *Discours des sorciers* (Discourse on Witches), he not only described witchcraft but collected existing legal statutes and codified the procedures legal authorities should take against witches. As a practical handbook for dealing with witchcraft, the *Discours* was at least as important as other major works on witchcraft and **demonology** such as those by **Jean Bodin**, **Nicholas Rémy**, and **Pierre de Lancre**.

BONAE MULIERES. Literally meaning "good women," *bonae mulieres* was a common term by which authorities writing in Latin described various women or female creatures found in many European folk legends who flew or otherwise traveled at night and often needed to be placated with offerings of food or drink. Aspects of the *bonae mulieres* are reflected in the women who were thought to ride with the pagan goddess **Diana**, as described in the **canon** *Episcopi* and other sources, as well as older beliefs in malevolent, female, nighttime demons such as the **strix** or **lamia**, or the Germanic concept of the **Wild Hunt**. All of these notions came to inform the developing stereotype of **witchcraft** in various ways, contributing most especially to the notion of the **night flight** of witches to a **sabbath**.

BONIFACE VIII, POPE (ca. 1235–1303). As pope from 1294 to 1303, Boniface came into conflict with many powerful European rulers, such as the English king Edward I and especially the French monarch Philip IV. After Boniface was dead, his political enemies continued to struggle against his successors in the papacy. As part of this conflict, servants of the French crown posthumously accused Boniface of **heresy**, murder, and sodomy, of performing ritual magic, and of being in league with **demons**. Although the magic the pope was accused of performing was more akin to learned **necromancy** than **witchcraft**, and although the charges against him were clearly politically motivated, the case, along with the similar trial of the **Knights Templar** at about the same time, served to some degree as a harbinger of later developments, culminating ultimately in the earliest **witch-hunts**.

BOOK OF SHADOWS. In modern **witchcraft**, or **Wicca**, collections of magical rituals, prayers, spells, beliefs, and teachings are called Books of Shadows. They are the basic texts of the Wiccan religion. The original Book of Shadows was composed by the founder of modern witchcraft, **Gerald Gardner,** and his chief assistant **Doreen Valiente.** Nevertheless, there is no definitive Book of Shadows for the entire Wiccan tradition, which is very fragmented and decentralized. Gardner himself continually rewrote and modified his Book of Shadows, and Valiente, after breaking with Gardner, authored her own rituals as well. Among modern witches, most **covens,** the basic groupings in which the religion functions, have their own Book of Shadows, usually similar to other groups in their tradition but modified to meet the needs and beliefs of that particular coven. Some ceremonies of modern witchcraft can be practiced alone, and some modern witches are entirely solitary, not part of any organized group or coven, so that individual witches can also have their own personalized Books of Shadows.

BRITISH ISLES, WITCHCRAFT IN. All the lands of the British Isles experienced significantly less intense **witch-hunting** than did many areas of the continent. The total number of executions ranged between 1,500 and 2,500, with virtually no executions taking place in Ireland. Particularly in England, the full stereotype of **witchcraft,** linking the practice of harmful **sorcery,** *maleficium,* with intense **diabolism,** attained force only much later than on the continent, and was never accepted, even by authorities, as fully as it was in **France** or the lands of the **German Empire.** For this reason, witchcraft in England, involving only harmful sorcery, was seen as a less serious offense, and in the absence of widespread belief in the diabolical witches' **sabbath,** those accused of witchcraft were rarely required to name additional suspects. Individual cases, therefore, did not explode as easily into widespread hunts. In addition, the judicial use of **torture** was extremely restricted in England. It was permitted only by the specific command of the Privy Council, and only where matters of state were concerned. Thus, it was effectively banned in almost all cases of witchcraft. Not only did restriction of torture reduce the number of convictions in general, but it also contributed to the slow and incomplete English acceptance of the diabolical aspects of witchcraft because evidence of large cults of witches and witches' sabbaths generally rested on confessions obtained through torture. This is not to say that major witch-hunts did not occur in England. For example, the series of trials conducted by the famous witch-hunter **Matthew Hopkins** in 1645 and 1646 claimed over 200 lives. Even this hunt, however, the most severe in English history, was significantly less extensive in scope than the greatest panics on the continent.

Scotland was similar to England in that it experienced only a belated and never fully complete acceptance of continental ideas of diabolism, and similar restrictions were in place regarding the use of torture (although the acceptance of diabolism was higher than in England, and restrictions on torture were not always as effectively enforced). Nevertheless, Scotland experienced significantly more witch-hunting than did England, with some estimates placing the number of executions in Scotland at three times the number in England (during a period when Scotland had only about one fourth of England's population). One reason for this was that the legal system was not as fully centralized in Scotland as in England. Conviction rates in trials heard by unsupervised local magistrates were significantly higher than in those cases heard in Edinburgh or by royal circuit justices. In England, by comparison, almost all cases were heard by royal circuit justices, and conviction rates were generally kept low. In addition, the church in Scotland seems to have been more directly involved in the prosecution of witches than in England. Still, even the largest hunts in Scotland did not approach the scale of the major continental hunts.

In Ireland, virtually no witch-trials are known to have taken place, although the land had a reputation for sorcery, and the belief in harmful magic was certainly widespread. One possible explanation is that the prevalence of belief in fairies allowed the Irish population to explain misfortune without resorting to accusing their neighbors of maleficent magic. Another equally likely explanation is that the Irish often did suspect their neighbors of witchcraft, but refused to bring charges against them in courts, since these operated under English law and were seen as instruments of foreign oppression.

BROOMS. One of the most standard images of the **night flight** of witches was that of witches flying on brooms. The first images of witches on brooms date from the 15th century, most famously associated with the description of **witchcraft** in the poem *Le Champion des Dames* (The Defender of Ladies) by the French poet **Martin Le Franc**. In fact, early sources such as *Le Champion* and also the *Errores Gazariorum* (Errors of the Gazarii) describe witches flying on brooms, staffs, and other common household or farming implements. Other descriptions of flight, such as that found in the famous **canon** *Episcopi*, describe witches riding on animals or **demons** in the form of animals. Nevertheless, the broom became the most common implement for flight supposedly used by witches. Most likely this was because the broom was an extremely standard household item used by all **women**. Generally, witches were thought to have to anoint themselves or their brooms with certain magical potions or **ointments** in order to be able to fly. Often these ointments were supplied to them by the **devil** at a witches' **sabbath**.

BUCKLAND, RAYMOND (1934–). Born in London, Buckland was the person initially most responsible for the introduction of modern **witchcraft**, or **Wicca**, to the United States. While still living in England, Buckland became interested in the study of religions and the occult. He was drawn to the notion of witchcraft as a revived ancient religion by the writings of **Margaret Murray** and **Gerald Gardner**. In 1962, he emigrated to the United States, and a year later, while back in England, met Gardner and was initiated into modern witchcraft. Thereafter, Buckland became Gardner's principal agent in North America. Eventually, Buckland broke with Gardner's variety of witchcraft and founded his own variety, called *Seax-Wicca*, based more closely on ancient Anglo-Saxon traditions. A prolific author, Buckland has written many books and for a long time conducted a correspondence school in witchcraft from his home.

– C –

CAESARIUS OF HEISTERBACH (ca. 1180–1250). A well-known Cistercian abbot of Heisterbach in the Rhineland, Caesarius was a theologian and the author of numerous treatises on religious subjects. His most famous work was the *Dialogus miraculorum* (Dialogue on Miracles), composed in the 1220s and 1230s. In this long, moralizing work he included several stories of **demons** and demonic **sorcery**, particularly **necromancy**. He stands as an example of the increasing concern over such matters on the part of clerical authorities in the late 12th and 13th centuries.

CALVIN, JEAN (1509–1564). After **Martin Luther**, Calvin was the leading figure of the Protestant **Reformation**. Like Luther, while he disagreed with and challenged many aspects of medieval theology, he fully accepted the power of the **devil** and the system of **demonology** on which the idea of **witchcraft** rested, and he fully accepted the reality of the threat posed by witches. He treated these issues in many of his sermons, biblical commentaries, and theological writings, and his doctrines provided a basis for the continuation of **witch-hunting** in Calvinist lands.

CANNIBALISM. One of the more horrible aspects of the witch-stereotype, cannibalism, especially the cannibalizing of babies and young **children**, has a long association with evil **sorcery**, **heresy**, and **witchcraft**. In classical mythology, nocturnal monsters such as the **strix** and **lamia** were believed to kill and often devour children. During the Middle Ages, **Jews** were often suspected of murdering Christian children and eating their flesh, in a dark parody of the Christian Eucharist. Later, the killing and eating of babies was thought to be a standard element of the witches' **sabbath**. Ironically, the association of cannibalism with unorthodox and clandestine religious assemblies probably began with the rise of Christianity itself. In the Roman Empire, when Christianity was seen as a dissident sect, authorities often condemned Christian gatherings as orgiastic festivals, and they sometimes sought to equate the consumption of the Eucharist, which in Christian doctrine is the flesh of Christ, with cannibalism.

CANON *EPISCOPI*. One of the most important legal texts regarding **sorcery**, superstition, and later **witchcraft**, the earliest version of the canon appears in the 10th century in the legal collection of Regino of Prüm. It later was incorporated into other collections of canon law, most importantly the *Decretum* of Gratian in the 12th century. The canon took its name from the first word of its text in Latin, and commanded bishops and their officials to work to eliminate the dangerous practice of sorcery and harmful magic in their diocese. It then went on to describe "certain **women**" who believed that they flew at night in large assemblies with the goddess **Diana**. The canon was careful to state that this did not occur in reality, but that these women were simply deluded by illusions caused by **demons**. The crucial passage reads:

> It is also not to be omitted that some wicked women, turned away after Satan and seduced by the illusions and phantasms of demons, believe and profess that, in the hours of the night, they ride upon certain beasts with Diana, the goddess of the pagans, and an innumerable multitude of women, and in the silence of night traverse great spaces of earth, and obey her commands as of their mistress, and are summoned to her service on certain nights.

The canon then goes on to declare that such flight is only an illusion and deception, and "priests in all their churches should preach with all insistence to the people that they may know this to be in every way false and that such phantasms are imposed on the minds of infidels not by the divine spirit but by a malignant one."

This canon and the popular beliefs that it describes form an important basis for the later concept of the **night flight** of witches to a **sabbath**. Here, however, the women who supposedly engaged in such flight were declared to be deluded. They appear less the willing servants of demons than their victims, and, rather than prosecute such people, the canon enjoins ecclesiastical authorities to work to correct this false and dangerous belief. Centuries later, when many authorities had accepted the existence of witchcraft and become convinced of the very real nature of the witches' night flight and sabbath, the canon proved something of a problem because it stated in authoritative and certain terms that such practices were illusions. The most typical way around this dilemma was to argue that, while the canon stated such practices could be illusory, it did not maintain that they could never be real. Nor did it in any way state that demons were incapable of producing real flight, as well as imaginary flight. Still, many opponents of the **witch-hunts**, or those who were at least **skeptical** about many of the more fantastic elements of the witch-stereotype, such as the idea of the sabbath, continued to make use of the canon in their arguments.

CARIBBEAN WITCHCRAFT. *See* SANTERÍA; VOODOO.

CAROLINA LAW CODE. A criminal law code for all the lands of the **German Empire** was introduced at the Reichstag in Regensburg in 1532, under the authority of the emperor Charles V, thus deriving its name from his (*Carolus* in Latin). The Carolina code, in theory, governed **witchcraft** prosecutions in the German Empire for the remainder of the period of the **witch-hunts**. However, given the political fragmentation of the Empire, local courts could generally apply the law as they saw fit. For example, in the severe witch trials in **Bamberg** in the early 17th century, victims of the trials actually appealed to the emperor that he should enforce the proper application of the Carolina code.

CASTAÑEGA, MARTÍN DE (early 16th century). A Franciscan friar in Spain, Martín witnessed a series of witch trials in Pamplona in 1527. In response, he wrote a *Tratado muy sotil bien fundado de las supersticiones y hechicerías* (Treatise . . . on Superstition and Witchcraft). Published in 1529, this was the first work on **witchcraft** to be printed in the Spanish vernacular. Martín adopted a qualified **skepticism** toward witchcraft. He accepted that some witches really existed, but avoided any discussion of the more extreme elements of the witch-stereotype, such as **night flight** and the witches' **sabbath**. He also argued that many events attributed to witchcraft could be caused by other, natural means, and he was concerned that many people accused of witchcraft were actually mentally ill.

CATS. Cats have long been associated with magic and **witchcraft**. The ancient Egyptians venerated cats and associated them with, among other deities, Isis, the mother-goddess and lunar deity who was also a patron of the magic arts. In Christian Europe, heretics and later witches were often thought to worship cats, or **demons** that had transformed themselves into cats. Most descriptions of the witches' **sabbath** depict the **devil** presiding over these gatherings and receiving worship in the form of a black animal, most often a black cat. Cats were also the most common of the many forms that a demon could take when it became a witch's **familiar**. Cats believed to be familiars were often burned along with the witches they supposedly served, and because of their general association with evil, cats were often killed in large numbers in regions experiencing particular hardship or misfortune, such as famines or epidemics. *See also* GOATS.

CHELMSFORD WITCHES. The first major witch trial in England occurred at Chelmsford, Essex, in 1566. The first statute against **witchcraft** had been passed by Parliament under King Henry VIII in 1542, but was quickly revoked in 1547. A new statute, mandating death for convicted witches, was passed under Elizabeth I in 1563. The Chelmsford case was the first significant trial conducted under this statute. Charges were brought against three **women**—Elizabeth Francis, Agnes Waterhouse, and Agnes' daughter Joan. Elizabeth eventually confessed that she had learned witchcraft from her grandmother, who had given her a **cat** named Sathan as a **familiar**. The cat was in fact the **devil**. She had the cat for 16 years, during which time it aided her in performing various acts of *maleficium*, including aborting one child and later murdering her daughter. Eventually, Elizabeth gave the cat to Agnes, who supposedly turned it into a toad that then continued to assist her in performing *maleficium*, including killing farm animals and causing butter to spoil. Agnes was convicted and hanged. Elizabeth received a lighter sentence, but was eventually hanged after other charges of witchcraft were brought against her years later. Agnes' daughter Joan, however, was aquitted.

The Chelmsford case is typical of English witchcraft in that elements of **diabolism** and a formal **pact** with the devil are not as developed as in trials elsewhere in Europe, and the concept of the witches' **sabbath** is entirely absent. Instead, a demonic familiar figures significantly in the charges. Familiars were a common feature in English witchcraft accusations, while the idea was much less prevalent on the continent. Chelmsford was also the site of several later witch trials, notably one instigated by the self-proclaimed "Witch-Finder General," **Matthew Hopkins**, in 1645.

CHILDREN, WITCHCRAFT AND. Historically, children have figured in **witchcraft** in several ways. On occasion, children could be accused of witchcraft, although this was generally rare. Such accusations usually occurred when one or more of the children's older relatives had already been accused. Also, children could play an important role as accusers themselves. They could bring charges directly, or they could begin a panic among adults by exhibiting symptoms of bewitchment or demonic **possession**. Their adult relatives would then begin making accusations of witchcraft, perhaps directed by the children. The most famous case of a major series of trials being generated by the accusations of children occurred in **Salem**, Massachusetts, in 1692. Most frequently, however, children figured in witchcraft purely as victims. Witches were regularly assumed to use their powers to commit **infanticide**, killing babies and small children, or causing abortions or miscarriages. A standard element of the witches' **sabbath** was the murder and sacrifice of babies to Satan, and the **cannibalism** of babies during the riotous **orgies** that the witches held. This aspect of the witch-stereotype persists to the present day, and some groups continue to allege that practitioners of modern witchcraft, or **Wicca**, and modern **Satanism** ritually abuse and murder children, despite the fact the no credible evidence exists linking such practices to any organized group.

CHURCH OF SATAN. Founded by Anton Szandor LaVey, the Church of Satan is the leading organization for modern **Satanism**. LaVey engaged in a variety of professions, but was always deeply interested in matters of magic and the occult. In 1966, he founded the Church of Satan in San Francisco. His major publications, *The Satanic Bible* (1969) and *The Satanic Rituals* (1972), have been influential far beyond his own church. Most other Satanist groups adhere to LaVey's basic principles, even if they do not accept all aspects of the Church of Satan's particular structure and forms.

Modern Satanism, as conceived by LaVey, has little to do with the traditional Satanism thought to exist in the past (and still believed by many to exist in the modern world). To begin, LaVey's Satanism does not really involve the worship of Satan, at least not in the traditional sense in which Satan is seen as the Christian **devil**, the representation of all evil. The Church of Satan does not (in its own view) advocate immorality or evil. Rather, it adheres to a philosophy of strong individualism and hedonism, so long as the well-being of other people is not adversely affected. The church advocates personal freedom and the pursuit of worldly pleasure, above all physical and especially sexual pleasure, which it maintains have been falsely proclaimed to be evil by Christianity. In this basic philosophy, as well as in his continued interest in occult learning and ritual magic, LaVey can be seen as following in the footsteps of such famous 19th-century figures as **Aleister Crowley**. Thus the Church of Satan does advocate and adhere to its own well defined, if non-Christian, ethical code. In particular, the use of illegal narcotics is strongly disapproved, and the torture or sacrifice of animals is strictly forbidden (in contrast to many popular images of Satanist activity).

Despite the use of magical rituals in the Church of Satan, and the frequent popular association of Satanism with **witchcraft**, the Church of Satan is in no way associated with any aspect of modern witchcraft, or **Wicca**. Modern witches strongly deny any aspect of Satanism in their religion. For their part, members of the Church of Satan and most other Satanist groups reject any association with Wiccan, **neo-pagan**, or other New Age groups. In particular they object to the strong feminist element of much modern witchcraft. It should be noted that the Church of Satan is extremely small, certainly not more than a few thousand members, and other Satanist groups are even smaller.

CHURCH OF WICCA. One of the oldest organizations of modern **witchcraft**, or **Wicca**, in the United States, the Church of Wicca was also the first such organization to receive official recognition as a religion. The church was founded in 1968 by Gavin and Yvonne Frost. The Frosts then set about trying to attain official tax-exempt religious status from the Internal Revenue Service. This came in 1972, and was the first ruling to give Wicca the status of a federally recognized religion. Subsequently, the Church of Wicca became the first Wiccan organization to have its status as an officially recognized religion upheld in court, as a result of a federal appeals court affirmation of a prisoner's rights case in Virginia.

The church follows most of the usual beliefs and rites of Wiccan practice, with one notable exception. The church holds that the nature of the deity is not definable, as opposed to the typical emphasis on the female **Goddess** in most other forms of modern witchcraft. The church also maintains a School of Wicca, the oldest correspondence school for modern witchcraft in the United States.

CIRCE. Along with **Medea**, Circe was one of the great female sorceresses in classical mythology. She was often thought to be the daughter of **Hecate**, goddess of magic, and so was herself a demigoddess. She is most famous for having turned the crew of the adventurer Odysseus into swine when they came to her island. Odysseus forced her to reverse her spell, but became enamored with her and stayed on her island for a year. In the medieval and early-modern periods, Circe became a literary archetype of the witch, especially for the notion of witches as dangerous seducers of men.

COLONIAL AMERICA, WITCHCRAFT IN. Witchcraft was not a significant problem, and **witch-hunts** were extremely rare, throughout almost all of the European colonies in the New World. The major exception occurred in the British colonies in New England, where significant witch-hunting did occur in the 17th century. In all, more than 200 people were put on trial for witchcraft in New England, over half in the single famous outbreak at **Salem**, Massachusetts, and 36 were executed, with 20 of these occurring at Salem alone. This number is significant given that the population of the New England colonies at this time was only around 100,000 people. Thus courts in New England executed something like 50 percent more witches per capita than were sentenced to death in the **British Isles**, even if statistics from Scotland, where witch-hunting was more severe, are included along with figures from England itself.

In many ways, in fact, witchcraft in New England followed more of a continental pattern than the pattern most common in the British Isles. In particular, aspects of **diabolism**—consorting with **demons** or the **devil**, entering into demonic **pacts**, attending **sabbaths**, and cases of **possession**—all figured significantly in cases of witchcraft in New England. In contrast, in England itself, the diabolic aspects of witchcraft were never fully accepted, even by authorities, and most accusations and trials focused instead simply on *maleficium*, the practice of harmful **sorcery**. As a crime, such sorcery was typically regarded as far less serious and threatening to the community as a whole than the demonically inspired conspiracy that underlay the notions of diabolism in witchcraft.

The greater emphasis on diabolism in New England, and the greater concern exhibited by the population as a whole in regard to witchcraft, may be easily explained in terms of religion. Founded as religious havens, these colonial communities were essentially theocratic in nature. Both individually and collectively, the colonists of New England were deeply concerned with matters of moral and spiritual purity, and were wary of any potential signs of demonic assault on their communities. Although witchcraft was regarded as a secular offense and was tried in civil court, members of the clergy played a major role in directing the trials and larger hunts. These men were often readily inclined to view any evidence of sorcery or possession as a sign of a larger satanic conspiracy that needed to be rooted out for the good of the community.

COMO, BERNARD DE (?–1510). A Dominican friar and inquisitor who conducted a number of witch trials at Como in northern Italy, Bernard wrote a brief *Tractatus de strigiis* (Treatise on Witches). The treatise has most often been dated to the early 16th century, but may have been written as early as the mid-1480s. It was later printed in several editions, often with the famous *Malleus maleficarum*.

COVEN. In modern **witchcraft**, or **Wicca**, a coven refers to an organized and set group of witches who practice together. The traditional number of people in a coven is 13, consisting of a leader and 12 members; however, in practice, the number varies widely. As modern witchcraft is a very unstructured religion, covens are self-regulating and determine what rites and ceremonies they will follow. Historically, the term can be traced at least to trials in the mid-17th century in Scotland, and of course the idea that witches met in groups to worship the **devil** and perform harmful **sorcery** was always a basic element of the idea of witchcraft. However, despite the claims of some modern witches to be members of extremely old covens, some up to 800 years, there is no historical connection between the modern ritual coven and the sorts of gatherings and witches' **sabbaths** that were thought to take place in the period of the **witch-hunts**.

CRAFT, THE. An alternate term for the rites and beliefs of modern **witchcraft**, or **Wicca**.

CROWLEY, ALEISTER (1875–1947). One of the most famous occultists and practitioners of ritual magic in modern times, Crowley is idolized by some and vilified by many others. He himself carefully cultivated a dark reputation and seemed to enjoy the approbation of others. His connections to **witchcraft** are tangential at best, but still important.

Born in Warwickshire, England, into an intensely religious family, Crowley came to reject Christianity entirely. He became interested, instead, in many varieties of occultism prevalent in England in the late 19th century. In 1898, he joined the **Hermetic Order of the Golden Dawn**, one of the most important occultist organizations in England, and rose quickly through its ranks. He also came into conflict with the hierarchy of the order, however, and studied many other forms of occultism, esoteric Eastern religions, and so forth. He claimed to have experienced many special revelations and to be the incarnation of several historical occult figures, including an ancient Egyptian priest of the 26th pharaonic dynasty. His *Book of the Law,* written in 1904, claimed that the Christian era was past and espoused a new religion based on esoteric and magical knowledge. His most famous work, *Magick in Theory and Practice* (1929), viewed ritual magic as a means toward union with God (Crowley used the spelling "magick" to distinguish real, mystical magic from illusion or trickery).

Although by no means himself a witch or neo-pagan, Crowley did exert some influence over modern witchcraft, or **Wicca**, and other forms of **neo-paganism**. At the very end of his life, Crowley briefly met **Gerald Gardner**, the founder of modern witchcraft, and many elements of Crowley's magical philosophies and rituals found their way into some of Gardner's early writings on witchcraft. Many of the more explicit elements, however, were later removed by Gardner and especially by his chief disciple **Doreen Valiente**. Nevertheless, Crowley's most basic philosophical principle has proven very influential on modern witchcraft and other varieties of neo-paganism. This principle is known as the "Law of Thelema," and is expressed in *The Book of the Law*: "Do what thou wilt shall be the whole of the law." This is not meant to express complete immorality, but rather profound individuality and respect for human free will. It is echoed in the basic creed common to modern Wicca and most neo-pagan groups: if it harm none, do what you will. The basic "Wiccan Rede" developed by Gerald Gardner ("an' it harm none, do what ye will"), is probably a direct borrowing of Crowley's statement.

CUNNING MEN AND WOMEN. Also called wise men or wise women, witch doctors, or sometimes white witches or wizards, cunning men and women were people who engaged in a variety of activities, such as magical **healing**, fortune telling, and **divination**. Their activities were generally regarded as good or helpful, as opposed to the harmful **sorcery**, or *maleficium*, performed by witches. Cunning men and women were often consulted in cases of perceived bewitchment, either to undo the bewitchment or to identify the witch who had supposedly cast the spell. Cunning men and women claimed to derive their power in various ways. Many maintained that they possessed a hereditary form of power passed down through their family. Others might claim power due to some special occurrence at birth or later in life. Being the seventh son of a seventh son, for example, or being born with the caul were considered signs of supernatural power. Some cunning folk might dabble in more clearly learned forms of magic or divination, such as **astrology**.

Typically activities of cunning men and women included performing magical healing, fertility rituals, or **love magic**. They also acted as fortune-tellers, and performed other forms of divination, such as identifying thieves, locating lost or stolen items, or reporting on the condition of loved ones far away. In short, they performed all the magical services common in pre-modern European society. Although cunning folk were typically not identified as witches by most people, since their magic was beneficial rather than harmful, they could nevertheless fall under suspicion on occasion. Also, during the late-medieval and early-modern periods, when authorities were more concerned with the supposedly demonic nature of almost all magic rather than the particular ends to which magic might be employed, cunning men and women could easily be charged with **witchcraft**.

– D –

DANEAU, LAMBERT (1530–1590). A Calvinist preacher and pastor near the French city of Orléans, Deneau probably became concerned about **witchcraft** due to a number of witch trials that took place in nearby Paris. In 1564, he wrote a treatise *De veneficiis* (On Witches) in the popular form of a dialogue. His purpose was to counter the **skepticism** that still existed regarding many aspects of witchcraft and the full threat that witches supposedly represented to Christian society. Although influenced primarily by the theology of **Jean Calvin**, Daneau was a learned scholar and **humanist**, and he incorporated references to classical Greek and Roman authors, and even medieval canon law, freely into his dialogue. The work proved very popular and was subsequently translated into both English and German.

DEE, JOHN (1527–1608). The most renowned learned magician in Elizabethan **England**, Dee was a brilliant scholar and pursued studies in astronomy, **astrology**, **alchemy**, mathematics, and **Hermetic magic**. He traveled extensively throughout Europe in pursuit of occult learning, was accused of **sorcery** and black magic under Queen Mary of England, and often performed astrological readings for Queen Elizabeth. Despite the charges of sorcery brought against him, which were politically motivated and of which he was acquitted, he had relatively little to do with **witchcraft** during his long life.

Born in London into the family of a minor official in the court of King Henry VIII, Dee entered St. John's College in Cambridge when he was only 15, and devoted the rest of his life to learning. Magic, astrology, and alchemy fascinated him, but he found little serious study of these subjects at Cambridge and so went to the continent. Returning to England, he performed astrological services for Queen Mary and also for her half-sister Elizabeth, whom Mary had imprisoned for political reasons. Dee therefore found himself imprisoned and charged with performing sorcery. These charges were dismissed, however, and when Mary died and Elizabeth ascended to the throne Dee often performed astrological readings for her.

Perhaps most important for the history of witchcraft in England, Dee's contacts with magicians and demonologists across Europe, and the many books he brought back with him to England, facilitated the spread of continental **demonology** to England. Nevertheless, these ideas never gained as firm a hold, even among learned elites, in England as elsewhere in Europe. This was one important reason why concerns over diabolical witchcraft and **witch-hunting** were never as severe in England as in other regions of Europe.

DEL RIO, MARTIN (1551–1608). A famous Jesuit scholar, Del Rio authored the *Disquisitiones magicarum* (Disquisitions on Magic), first published beginning in 1599 and going through numerous editions throughout the next century. This work became probably the most important and most cited treatise on magic and **witchcraft** in the 17th century.

Del Rio was born into a distinguished Spanish family in Antwerp (then part of the Spanish Netherlands). He was an intellectual prodigy and had published an edition and commentary of the tragedies of Seneca by the time he was 19. At 24, he was appointed Attorney General for the region of Brabant. In 1580, however, he chose to enter the Jesuit order, after which he studied and taught at numerous Jesuit centers around Europe. It was in Louvain that he composed his *Disquisitiones*. This wide-ranging work began with a discussion of magic in general before focusing on demonic magic and witchcraft. Del Rio also included a discussion of harmful **sorcery**, or ***maleficium***, and a section of instructions to judges on how they should handle cases of witchcraft, as well as discussing subjects such as prophecy, fortune telling and **divination**, and the role of priestly confessors in dealing with these activities. In many ways the most comprehensive learned treatise on witchcraft in the early-modern period, the *Disquisitiones* was also extremely popular, surpassing such works as the ***Malleus maleficarum*** and **Nicholas Rémy's** *Daemonolatreiae*.

DEMONOLOGY. Referring to the scholarly study of **demons** and the **devil**, demonology has always existed in Christianity as a counterpart to theology, the study of God. As early as the second century C.E., Christian monks in the deserts of Egypt were writing about the nature of demons, which they thought were assailing them constantly. The early church fathers were also demonologists, and the great **Augustine of Hippo** wrote extensively about the nature of demons in some of his major works, including *De divinatione daemonum* (On the Divination of Demons), and sections of *The City of God*. After late antiquity, few major works were written about demons until about the 12th century when the study of demons began to revive as part of the general revitalization of education and intellectual life in Europe known as the "Renaissance of the 12th Century." In the 13th century, the important medieval theologian **Thomas Aquinas** discussed the nature and powers of demons in several of his works.

Throughout the period of major **witch-hunting** in Europe, from the 15th to the 17th centuries, witches were believed to have entered into **pacts** with the devil and to work their harmful **sorcery**, or *maleficium*, through the power of demons. Thus virtually every treatise on **witchcraft** was really a treatise on demonology, or at least contained large sections of demonological material. The knowledge, or supposed knowledge, about the nature, variety, and number of demons was refined as never before. As fallen angels, the demons were thought to retain their rank respective to one another based on the order of angels in heaven (in descending order: seraphim, cherubim, thrones, dominions, principalities, powers, virtues, archangels, and angels). Lucifer, the devil, was the prince of all demons. Chief demons under him included Asmodeus, Astaroth, Baal, Beelzebub, Belial, and Leviathan. These demons were derived principally from the **Bible** and had generally been **pagan** deities worshiped by tribes and nations encountered by the ancient Israelites. Christian authorities considered all such pagan gods to be demons.

Demonologists spent a great deal of effort calculating the number of demons, which was known from the Bible to be "legion." In the 15th century, **Alfonso de Spina** estimated that one third of all the angels in heaven had sided with Lucifer when he fell, and by various calculations he determined this number to be 133,306,668 demons. Other figures were based on the association of the number six with the devil. In the 16th century, one authority determined that there were 66 princes in hell commanding 6,660,000 demons. **Johann Weyer**, who was actually **skeptical** about many aspects of witchcraft, calculated that there were 1,111 legions in hell, each with 6,666 demons, for a total of 7,405,926 demons commanded by 72 princes.

DEMONS. As evil spirits that could be commanded by humans, demons were essential to **witchcraft** as conceived in Christian Europe in the medieval and early-modern periods, since it was through the agency of demons that witches were believed to perform their harmful **sorcery**, or *maleficium*. In exchange for the ability to command demons, witches were thought to have offered worship to the demons or to the **devil** himself. Witches thus became agents of pure evil in their own right, and most Christian authorities, both ecclesiastical and secular, believed they posed a dire threat to society and needed to be eradicated at all costs. The demonic and ultimately diabolical nature of the evil entailed in witchcraft necessitated and justified the extreme measures used in **witch-hunting**.

Most, if not all, pre-modern human cultures have believed in the existence of powerful spirits that could be controlled by human beings for magical purposes. In ancient Greece, such creatures were known as *daimones*. These creatures were not necessarily evil, however, but might have good, evil, or even ambivalent intentions toward human beings. Ancient Judaism also had a complex system of **demonology** that distinguished between good and evil spirits, and this system continued to inform Jewish Kabbalah throughout the medieval and early-modern periods. As Christianity developed, however, demonology developed into a far more rigid system, based largely on the more fully articulated Christian conception of the devil as the one great opponent of God and source of all evil in the world. All demons became associated with the fallen angels who rebelled with Satan and were cast out of heaven. Christian demons, therefore, were entirely evil, and humans who became involved with them in any way were believed to be evil as well.

In the early fifth century, the great church father **Augustine of Hippo** defined the essential nature of the world as being one of conflict between the forces of good, represented by the Christian church, and the forces of evil, led by Satan and his demons. He defined the notion of the demonic **pact** that magicians were believed to make with the demons they sought to control. Seeking to corrupt humans, these demons offered their services only in exchange for worship. Augustine's basic notion of demonic power and the demonic pact underlying much magical activity remained in force for the remainder of the Middle Ages and into the early-modern period.

DEVIL. In Christian cosmology, the devil represents the supreme force of evil in the universe. The concept of the devil actually developed as a composite of several figures from the Hebrew **Bible**, including the serpent that tempted Eve in the Garden of Eden, Lucifer, the rebellious angel who was cast out of heaven, and Satan, who appears in the Book of Job. The Greek *diabolos,* meaning tempter or deceiver, is a translation of the Hebrew Satan. In ancient Judaism, none of these figures represented a supreme force of evil, however. Only in the Christian New Testament does the devil begin to appear as the principal opponent of God and humankind, especially in the Book of Revelation, where the renewed war between God and the devil at the end of time is described. Eventually, Christian authorities became convinced that witches, whom they had long believed performed their harmful **sorcery** through the agency of **demons**, worshiped the devil, who would preside over the witches' **sabbath**. Believing that witches had sold their souls to the devil and become his servants in the world allowed Christian authorities, both ecclesiastical and secular, to justify the extreme measures taken against witches.

Although it is entirely probable that at least some people accused of **witchcraft** during the period of the **witch-hunts** did in fact practice some form of sorcery, and a few of these people may even have worshiped the devil and believed that they gained power from him, there is no evidence that any large cults of devil-worshiping sorcerers ever really existed in Europe. Likewise, some people continue to accuse practitioners of modern witchcraft, or **Wicca**, of worshiping the devil. Modern witches are in fact **neo-pagans** who do not adhere to any elements of Christian belief. Even groups that practice modern **Satanism** do not really worship the devil in the Christian sense.

DEVIL'S MARK. During the period of the **witch-hunts**, many authorities believed that the **devil** marked all witches as a sign of their service to him. This mark could take many forms, and in practice once a person became suspected of **witchcraft** almost any blemish, scar, or bodily mark might serve as evidence. Witches were routinely searched for such marks when they were arrested and brought to trial, through a procedure known as **pricking**. The devil's mark should not be confused with the **witch's mark**, which was believed to be the spot on the flesh where witches would suckle their demonic **familiars**.

DIABOLISM. Witchcraft as conceived in the Christian, European context during most of the medieval and early-modern periods, and certainly during the age of the most intense **witch-hunting** during the 15th, 16th, and 17th centuries, was comprised of two essential elements: the practice of harmful **sorcery**, or *maleficium*, and a range of activities that focused on the supposed worship of the **devil** and supplication of **demons** entailed in the performance of that sorcery.

These latter elements are often referred to collectively in modern scholarship as diabolism.

Essential to the diabolical aspect of witchcraft was the basic belief, firmly held by most Christian authorities at least since the time of the great church father **Augustine** in the fifth century, that most if not all forms of sorcery relied on demonic agency, and that this entailed a heretical **pact** made between the demon and the human sorcerer. The sorcerer would offer or promise to offer the demon certain signs of worship in exchange for which the demon would perform certain acts. Although notions of demonic pacts are rooted in early Christianity, however, the linkage of this concept to the performance of acts of *maleficium* was slow to develop. Even in the late 14th century, the inquisitor **Nicolau Eymeric** had to prove that demonic sorcery necessarily entailed **idolatry** and the worship of demons. Thereafter, however, the full range of diabolism evident in later witchcraft quickly developed, and by the early 15th century the stereotype was already fairly complete.

Witches, in addition to simply entering into pacts with certain demons or offering them worship in exchange for magical power, were believed to have entered into complete **apostasy** from the true faith and to have surrendered their souls to the devil himself. They were members of an organized, conspiratorial, satanic cult, and gathered regularly at secret, nocturnal gatherings known as witches' **sabbaths**, where they would worship the devil, desecrate the cross, Eucharist, and other holy objects, and perform other abominable acts, such as killing and **cannibalizing** babies and small **children**, and engaging in sexual **orgies** with each other, with various demons, and with the devil.

DIANA, GODDESS. A pagan goddess of the moon and the hunt, Diana is the Roman incarnation of the Greek Artemis. As a lunar goddess, she was associated even in ancient times with secret, nocturnal activities. Particularly as part of a trio of lunar goddesses including Selene and **Hecate**, Diana was sometimes associated with dark magic and **witchcraft**.

As Europe became Christian, Diana, as with all **pagan** gods and goddesses, came to be regarded as a **demon**, at least by ecclesiastical authorities. In the early Middle Ages, a belief developed that Diana led large groups of **women** on nocturnal journeys through the night sky. This belief seems based not in any element of traditional mythology surrounding Diana, however, but on the Germanic notion of the **Wild Hunt**, a band of ghosts or spirits who would haunt the countryside at night, destroying and killing as they went. The leader of the hunt was most commonly a female spirit named Berta or **Holda**, but was typically translated as Diana (also sometimes **Herodias**) by ecclesiastical authorities when they wrote in Latin. The most famous image of Diana leading a group of women on a nocturnal flight is contained in the 10th century **canon** *Episcopi*, and such ideas clearly influenced the later development of ideas of **night flight** and the witches' **sabbath**.

In modern witchcraft, or **Wicca**, Diana remains an important figure. Early in the 20th century, **Margaret Murray** used the long association of Diana with witchcraft to claim, without any real evidence, that historical witchcraft was in fact a direct survival of ancient paganism long into the Christian era. Most Wiccans today recognize that Murray's theories are groundless and maintain that Wicca is, at most, a creative revival of certain pre-Christian religious beliefs, and in no way a direct surviving remnant of such religions. However, they still revere Diana as an important pagan goddess. As a lunar deity, she continues to be associated with magic; as a virgin goddess and goddess of the hunt, she is an archetype for the strong feminist and naturalist elements in modern witchcraft.

DIVINATION. Referring to the practice of revealing hidden knowledge or foretelling the future by magical means, divination is one of the most common forms of **sorcery** around the world and throughout human history. The English word sorcery in fact derives from the Latin *sortilegium,* meaning fortune telling or divination, specifically by casting lots. This became the French *sorcellerie*, which meant both sorcery and, eventually, demonic **witchcraft**. In the ancient world, although the practice of divination was widespread, diviners were often viewed with suspicion, either because they were thought to be charlatans, or, if genuine, because they were thought to traffic with evil forces. The marginal status of divination in the ancient world is well illustrated in the **biblical** story of King Saul, who expelled sorcerers and diviners from his kingdom, but then felt compelled to consult the **Witch of Endor** (actually a seer rather than a maleficent witch) before a crucial battle with the Philistines.

For Christian authorities in medieval and early-modern Europe, divination was a crime because, like many other forms of magic, it was thought to involve the invocation of **demons**. In addition, attempting to foretell the future was seen as an affront against the power of God, who alone could know such things. Nevertheless, divination remained common and was widely practiced by professional **cunning men and women** across Europe. Such people were often viewed with suspicion by authorities and could become targets for accusations of witchcraft. However, in most cases the penalties for simple divination were not as severe as for actual harmful sorcery, or *maleficium*. The practice of divination, of course, extends long after the main period of **witch-hunting** ended in Europe, and even today the wide array of horoscopes, tarot readings, and other means of divination attest to the continued practice of what might be the most common and enduring form of magical activity in history.

– E –

EASTERN EUROPE, WITCHCRAFT IN. Widespread persecution of **witchcraft** began significantly later in all the lands of Eastern Europe (primarily Poland, Hungary, and Russia) than in the West. The intensity of **witch-hunting**, however, varied considerably from region to region. In general, those lands in close proximity to the **German Empire** experienced the severest witch-hunts, most closely resembling the Western model. On the other hand, lands that adhered to Eastern Orthodox Christianity, as opposed to Roman Catholicism, experienced significantly less witch-hunting activity.

The Kingdom of Poland experienced by far the most severe witch-hunts in the East. As many as 10,000 executions might ultimately have taken place in Polish lands. However, the hunts began significantly later there than in Western Europe. Large-scale persecution in Poland did not begin until after 1650, and the period of the most intense hunts was between 1675 and 1725, with the largest trials taking place in the 18th century. In general, the hunts in Poland followed the pattern of those in the German Empire. The major factors underlying the large number of trials and executions in Poland were the widespread acceptance of the full stereotype of witchcraft, linking simple harmful **sorcery**, or *maleficium*, with intense **diabolism**, the relative lack of centralized judicial control (which, when present, tended to keep down the number of convictions and the severity of punishment in witch trials), and the widespread use of **torture**.

Given Poland's proximity to and close connections with German-speaking lands, it is not surprising that the Polish hunts followed a German model, or that the hunts were most severe in the western regions of the country nearest to German territories and with a large German-speaking population. The problem comes in explaining why the Polish hunts began so late. From 1655 to 1660, the first northern war between Sweden and Russia ravaged the country, producing severe social and economic disruption and dislocation, which in turn may have led to an increase in concern over witchcraft. In addition, after 1648, the Catholic majority in Poland became increasingly intolerant of Protestantism, and this heightened religious tension may have contributed to a fear of witches. Finally, only in the second half of the 17th century did the secular courts in Poland begin to claim jurisdiction in cases of witchcraft instead of ecclesiastical courts, which generally tended to be less ruthless in their prosecutions.

Hungary, a state almost equal to Poland in population, experienced significantly fewer trials and well under 1,000 executions. As in Poland, the trials only really began in the second half of the 17th century, and were most severe in the early 18th. Witchcraft accusations were often colored by elements of particular Hungarian folklore, particularly the figure of the *táltos*. These were magicians specializing, in particular, in forms of magical **healing**, and who also engaged in a form of **shamanism**, entering trances to encounter and combat forces in the spirit world. Moreover, there is evidence that the decline in trials for witchcraft in the 18th century, imposed from above by the empress Maria Theresa's enlightened legislation, was met by a rise in beliefs about **vampires** and vampirism. Vampires provided an alternate supernatural explanation for misfortune when witchcraft was no longer available.

With perhaps less than 100 known executions, Russia had almost no witch craze to speak of. What hunts there were came late, after the middle of the 17th century, as elsewhere in Eastern Europe. The most obvious reason for this delay in the rise of major witch trials was that only in the middle of the 17th century did the tsar move to make witchcraft a crime for the secular courts, as opposed to ecclesiastical ones. Witchcraft in Russia was marked by an extremely high number of men among the accused. Indeed, only slightly over 30 percent of accused witches in Russia were **women**, in marked contrast to Western lands. Moreover, Orthodox Russia never accepted the intensely diabolical image of the witch prevalent among both Catholic and Protestant authorities in the West. Rather, in Russia, witchcraft remained a crime of simple *maleficium*.

ENDOR, WITCH OF. A famous witch of the **Bible**. In 1 Samuel 28, King Saul, who has exiled all the sorcerers and seers from his kingdom, nevertheless seeks supernatural guidance before a battle against the Philistines. Because God will not answer him, he goes to consult a "witch" (she is actually described as a seer or medium) living in Endor. She summons the spirit of the dead prophet Samuel for the king.

Later Christian theologians in the medieval and early-modern periods generally argued that the Witch of Endor could not really have summoned the spirit of Samuel. Rather she, like other witches and supposed seers, actually summoned a **demon,** who appeared in the form of Samuel. Thus, she became a model for the involvement of witches in demonic magic and in the spreading of demonic deception. Opponents of belief in **witchcraft** also used the story of the Witch of Endor, seeing in it an example of simple human deception. The **skeptical** author **Reginald Scot**, for example, in his *Discoverie of Witchcraft,* argued that the Witch of Endor had no supernatural powers of any sort, divine or demonic, but simply fooled Saul with the aid of a human accomplice.

ENGLAND. *See* BRITISH ISLES, WITCHCRAFT IN.

ERASMUS, DESIDERIUS (1466–1536). Perhaps the greatest scholar of his day, and the most important figure in the history of northern **humanism,** Erasmus was born in the Netherlands, at Rotterdam, and studied at the University of Paris, among other places. A great classical scholar as well as a scholar of the **Bible** and the early church fathers, especially Saint Jerome, he is not nearly so important a figure in the history of **witchcraft** as he is in other areas. Like many other humanists, he was **skeptical** of many cases of witchcraft. He did not deny the existence of **demons** or the **devil**, nor did he deny their real power in the world, but he realized that many witch trials were hopelessly flawed, that the uncontrolled use of **torture** and other improper procedures produced many false confessions, and that many of the people accused of witchcraft were simple peasants with little chance of defending themselves. As a textual scholar of the Bible, he also realized that there was no biblical basis for witchcraft as it was conceived in his day.

ERICTHO. A famous witch in classical literature, Erictho appears in the Roman poet Lucan's epic poem *Pharsalia* about the war between Julius Caesar and Pompey. Unlike some other major sorceresses in Greco-Roman mythology and literature, such as **Circe** or **Medea**, both of whom are depicted as beautiful, if dangerously powerful, **women**, Erictho is a hideous, almost semi-demonic figure. She lives in Thessaly, a land long associated with **sorcery** in ancient times. On the eve of the decisive battle, the son of Pompey comes to consult with Erictho, asking her to **divine** the future by summoning the spirits of the dead. Lucan describes in great detail how she uses body parts stolen from graves in her magic. In the later Middle Ages and early-modern period, the figure of Erictho became a model for the image of the witch as a hideous old hag.

ERRORES GAZARIORUM. The "Errors of the Gazarii" is a brief but extremely lurid tract describing the actions of a heretical sect of witches (*gazarius* was a common term for **heretics** at this time). Written by an anonymous cleric, most likely an inquisitor, probably in Savoy around the middle of the 1430s, it is among the first writings to describe witches as being members of a secret, conspiratorial, satanic cult. Gathering at a **sabbath** (here termed a "synagogue"), the witches renounced the Christian faith, worshiped the **devil**, who usually appeared in the form of a black **cat** or other animal, killed and devoured babies and small **children**, and engaged in sexual **orgies** with each other and with **demons**. They also performed a variety of acts of harmful **sorcery**, or *maleficium*, including producing **poison**, killing and causing infertility, and raising destructive **storms**.

Surviving in only two manuscript copies, the *Errores* exists in two distinct versions—an earlier and shorter version and a slightly later and significantly expanded version. The longer version of the tract describes witches flying on staves, making it one of the earliest sources to accept as a reality what was to become the stereotypical image of the **night flight** of witches. In most other respects, **witchcraft** as depicted in the *Errores* is similar to what is found in other early writings on the subject by **Johannes Nider, Claude Tholosan, Hans Fründ**, and **Martin Le Franc**. The tract seems to have been associated in some way with the **Council of Basel**, and the later version was probably influenced by early witch trials conducted in the diocese of Lausanne.

EUGENIUS IV, POPE (1383–1447). Eugenius reigned as pope from 1431 until 1447, during a period when the full stereotype of **witchcraft** was just beginning to emerge as a clearly defined concept, when some of the first real **witch-hunts** were taking place in lands in and around the western Alps, and when many of the first treatises and authoritative accounts describing witchcraft were written. He himself was at least to some extent directly concerned with matters of demonic **sorcery** and witchcraft. In 1434, he issued a letter in which he briefly discussed magicians performing demonic magic, and in 1437, he issued a letter to all papal inquisitors in which he declared that there were many people practicing demonic sorcery throughout Christendom. Throughout his reign, Eugenius was involved in nearly constant strife with the **Council of Basel**, to the extent that the council eventually declared Eugenius deposed and appointed the duke of Savoy, Amadeus VIII, as anti-pope Felix V in his stead. Refusing, obviously, to recognize this deposition, in 1440 Eugenius issued a statement to the council in which he declared that the lands of Savoy were well known to be full of witches, who were called *stregule* or *stregonos* in the vulgar tongue. Eugenius was clearly motivated by his opposition to the council and Amadeus/Felix, but regardless of this fact, the lands of Savoy were the location of many early witch trials, and the pope's statements might have reflected widely held opinion about the perceived prevalence of witchcraft in this region.

EVIL EYE. Also known as fascination, the evil eye refers to the power of witches to effect harm simply through their gaze or the glance of their eyes. This is surely one of the most widespread of all forms of folk-magic, and the evil power of glances or stares is known in many world cultures. For example, in Europe alone it exists in France as the *mauvais oeil*, in Germany as the *böse Blick*, and perhaps most famously in Italy as the *mal occhio*. The term itself arises from the **Bible**, Mark 7:21–22, where Christ states, "from within, out of the heart of men, proceed evil thoughts, adulteries, fornications, murders, thefts, covetousness, wickedness, deceit, lasciviousness, an evil eye, blasphemy, pride, foolishness" (this from the King James' Version; the term is *oculus malus* in the medieval Latin Vulgate).

Drawing on pre-modern scientific thought that the eye saw by emitting rays rather than receiving them, theories of natural magic held that the evil eye might work by transmitting harmful intentions along these rays, thereby affecting the person held in the gaze. **Demonological** theories maintained that witches simply signaled to **demons** by the glance of their eyes the victims whom they sought to afflict. Fairly common among folk beliefs was the idea that the evil eye might be either intentional or unintentional. That is, some witches might deliberately seek to harm through the glance of their eyes, but others might be unaware that their gaze contained such power, or at least be unable to control or deliberately employ such power. Many forms of amulets and charms were devised for protection from the evil eye.

EXORCISM. Referring to the casting out of demonic spirits and curing cases of demonic **possession**, the practice of exorcism in the Christian tradition is based on such **biblical** passages as Luke 9:1 ("Then Jesus called the twelve together and gave them power and authority over all demons"). Very early in the history of Christianity, the office of exorcist became one of the minor orders of the church. Thus an exorcism could refer to the formal religious ceremony of casting out a **demon** performed by a cleric, and remains to this day an official (although little-used and somewhat disreputable) rite of the Roman Catholic Church (Protestant denominations long ago abandoned the official rite of exorcism). In addition, however, the word *exorcism* could be used more generally to describe the act of commanding a demon, just as other words such as *adjuration* and *conjuration*, and in texts on **witchcraft** and **demonology** written throughout the medieval and early-modern periods the Latin verb *exorcizare* was often used almost interchangeably with the verbs *adjurare* and *conjurare*. Taken in this second sense, a legitimate exorcism could be performed by any faithful Christian as a defense against witchcraft or remedy for bewitchment. Because witches performed all of their harmful **sorcery** through the power of demons, afflicted people could invoke the power of Christ to ward off or overcome the demonic assault. Exorcisms in this sense, as well as the official ecclesiastical ceremony, were extremely important during the entire period of the **witch-hunts**. The official rite of exorcism was often sought as a cure for demonic possession, which could be brought about by witchcraft or taken as a sign of bewitchment. Non-clerical witch doctors, folk magicians, and **cunning men and women**, however, often also claimed to wield a religious or at least quasi-religious authority over demons. Although recognizing the ability of all the faithful, clerical or not, to call on the name and power of Christ to expel demons, religious authorities were often suspicious of lay witch doctors. In many regions, particularly where witch-hunting was especially severe and panic ran high, such people were often accused of being witches themselves.

EYMERIC, NICOLAU (1320–1399). A Dominican friar and inquisitor in the Kingdom of Aragon, Eymeric wrote his most important work, the influential inquisitorial manual *Directorium inquisitorum* (Directory of Inquisitors), in 1376 while in exile at the papal court in Avignon. Like the *Practica inquisitionis haeretice pravitatis* (Practice of Inquisition into Heretical Depravity) of the inquisitor **Bernard Gui** half a century earlier, Eymeric's treatise was a general handbook of procedures to be used in conducting an **inquisition**. As such, it included sections on **sorcery** and demonic invocation. In terms of the development of learned, clerical thought about magic, however, Eymeric's handbook is even more important than Gui's, for Eymeric established the basic argument that demonic invocation necessarily entailed the worship of **demons**. Thus, all demonic magic was de facto heretical and subject to the jurisdiction of ecclesiastical courts and papal inquisitors.

As an inquisitor, Eymeric seems to have been particularly interested in sorcery and demonic magic. Several years prior to writing his more general *Directorium,* he wrote a *Tractatus contra daemonum invocatores* (Treatise Against Invokers of Demons), which served as a basis for the sections on sorcery and demonic magic in his later manual. Eymeric presented long, theological arguments to demonstrate that demons could not be summoned or commanded for magical purposes without some form of worship being offered to them. Ultimately, he argued that simply to invoke a demon for supernatural aid, when a true Christian should turn in prayer to God, was to show the demon a form of adoration (*latria*) due only to God. This amounted to **idolatry** (*idolatria*), and meant that all demonic magic could be considered a form of **heresy**. Eymeric's arguments formed the basis of the church's position against demonic sorcery for the rest of the Middle Ages and into the early-modern period. Eymeric never discussed **witchcraft** in his writings, and clearly was concerned primarily with learned demonic magic, or **necromancy**. His argument that all demonic magic involved the worship of demons, however, obviously had important consequences for the development of the concept of witchcraft and the persecution of witches in later years.

– F –

FAMILIARS. Various typically lesser **demons** who were thought to attend witches in some assumed animal form were generally known as familiar spirits, or more simply as familiars. This aspect of the witch stereotype is somewhat unique in being more developed in English, Irish, and Scottish sources than in continental ones. A demonic familiar might appear in almost any animal form. Toads, owls, rats, mice, and dogs were all common, but **cats** were especially associated with familiar spirits. A witch might be given a familiar by the **devil**, or might inherit a familiar from another witch. The demon then attended the witch and performed magical services for her. The witch, in turn, cared for her familiar much as one would care for a household pet, which is of course what many supposed familiars in fact were. In particular, witches were thought to feed their familiars with their own blood, which the familiar might suck from a small protuberance somewhere on the body, the so-called **witch's mark**. One of the earliest examples of a demon resembling a familiar appears in the case of **Alice Kyteler**. Accused of **witchcraft** in Ireland in 1324, Alice was supposedly attended regularly by a demon known as Robert or Robin Artisson, who could appear as cat, a shaggy dog, or an Ethiopian. Unlike witches with later familiars, Alice would have sexual relations with Robert and would sacrifice animals to him, especially roosters. Such accusations seem to lie somewhere between the later concept of the familiar and the worship of demons and sexual **orgies** that typified the witches' **sabbath**, where demons or Satan himself would typically preside in the form of a black cat or other animal. *See also* GOATS.

FASCINATION. *See* EVIL EYE.

FAUST. Perhaps the most famous story of a human entering into a **pact** with Satan is that of Faust. Faust was not a witch but rather the archetypical learned magician of the Renaissance period. The legend appears to have been based on the life of Georg (or, later, Johannes — it is possible that there were two different men) Faustus, a traveling magician who seems to have been widely known in southern Germany in the early 16th century. Stories began to circulate that he had sold his soul to the **devil** in exchange for magical knowledge and power. He was supposedly served by a **demon** named Mephistopheles, who sometimes accompanied him as a **familiar** in the form of a large black dog with fiery red eyes. Aided by Mephistopheles, Faust pursued worldly pleasure and arcane knowledge. At the end of Faust's life, the devil came to claim his soul, killing him in a terrible manner. The Faust legend circulated widely in various forms. The first printed "Faustbook" appeared in 1587 in Germany. In England, Christopher Marlowe's play *Dr. Faustus* was published between 1589 and 1592. Perhaps the most famous version of the legend appeared in the early 19th century in Goethe's play *Faust*.

FLADE, DIETRICH (?–1589). Probably the highest-ranking victim of any **witch-hunt** in European history, Flade was a prominent citizen of **Trier**, an archbishopric and also at that time an independent electoral principality of the **German Empire**. He was selected by the prince-archbishop to oppose the spread of Protestantism in the region and he became head of the secular courts. In 1580, he also became vice-governor of Trier, and in 1586, he was appointed as rector of the university there even though he was a layman and not a cleric. In the 1580s, the number of witch trials in Trier began to escalate, apparently because of a period of bad weather, agrarian failures, and economic difficulties. At first, the secular courts, under Flade's direction, were hesitant and cautious in cases of **witchcraft**. This, however, roused the opposition of more zealous witch-hunting authorities, notably the suffragan bishop of Trier, **Peter Binsfeld**. Eventually, Flade himself was accused of witchcraft. He fled from Trier in 1588 but was captured and returned to the city. Put on trial in August of 1589, he confessed a month later and was executed.

FLYING. *See* NIGHT FLIGHT.

FRANCE, WITCHCRAFT IN. France was the largest state in Europe, in terms of population, during the period of the **witch-hunts**. In all, perhaps 4,000 people were executed for **witchcraft** across this large kingdom. This figure is less than one fifth the number of executions in the **German Empire**, however, whose various lands together had approximately the same sized population. Within France, the most intense witch-hunting took place in those regions located on the peripheries of the kingdom and which, more importantly, were resistant to the increasing power of the centralized royal government in Paris; for example, the **Basque lands** in the extreme southwestern portion of the country. Thus, the history of witchcraft in France fits a basic pattern found across Europe that the most severe witchcraft panics and the most intense and destructive hunts generally took place in regions of great local legal autonomy. Regional courts and justices were more easily caught up in the local social, economic, or communal tensions that produced accusations, and often shared in the local panic of a community that began to feel itself under assault by witches. More centralized courts, or at least centrally controlled or supervised courts, on the other hand, could often remain more impartial to local conditions and were generally more concerned with the proper execution of judicial procedures, the rational collection and evaluation of evidence, and so forth, all of which tended to dampen the flames of an incipient witch-hunt.

Cases from local French courts could typically be appealed to the regional *parlements*. In some cases, these bodies proved willing to accept almost all accusations of witchcraft and thus did little to slow the development of witch-hunting. In many cases, however, the *parlements* overturned local rulings, both stopping the progress of that particular case and sending a message back to the local courts that rampant witch-hunting should not be allowed. In particular, the *parlement* of Paris, which heard appeals from most of northern France, proved very **skeptical** and cautious in matters of witchcraft as in matters of **heresy** and crimes of religious belief in general. To the extent that this central *parlement* set standards for others across the nation, it played a significant role in holding down trials for witchcraft in France.

In the later 17th century, the right to try cases of witchcraft without outside oversight or interference was one of the many specific issues on which various regional authorities resisted the ever-growing power of King Louis XIV and his centralized government. It is perhaps not surprising that in 1682, Louis, seeking to undermine an area of local resistance to the authority of the crown, issued an edict that reclassified the practice of magic and **sorcery** as a mere superstition and not a capital offence, thereby effectively bringing legal witch-hunting to an end in France.

FRÜND, HANS (ca. 1400–1468). A civic chronicler from Lucerne, Hans Fründ was the author of a brief report on **witchcraft** supposedly taking place in the Alpine region of Valais in the diocese of Sion. The activities he described were set in the year 1428, and so his is one of the earliest reports of full-fledged witchcraft in European history. His account may in fact be closer to actual witch-beliefs and perhaps even activity than those of other early authorities, most of whom were clerics and whose understanding of witchcraft was colored by learned **diabolism**. Fründ was a layman, although obviously educated. His account of witchcraft contained less diabolism and more of a focus on simple *maleficium*, that is, harmful **sorcery**. Nevertheless, he did describe a sect of witches and something like a witches' **sabbath**, including **cannibalism**, sexual **orgies**, and the worship of **demons**. His report is in many ways notably similar to other early accounts of witchcraft from the early 15th century, such as those by **Johannes Nider** and **Claude Tholosan**, and that contained in the anonymous *Errores Gazariorum* (Errors of the Gazarii), thus indicating, perhaps, how quickly a basic understanding of witchcraft became widespread among various authorities in the course of the 1420s and 1430s.

– G –

GARDNER, GERALD (1884–1964). The founder of modern **witchcraft**, or **Wicca**, Gardner claimed that he had been initiated into a **coven** of hereditary witches in England, a group that supposedly followed practices that had been passed down from the time of historical witchcraft during the period of the great **witch-hunts** and even before. In fact, Gardner claimed that witchcraft actually represented an ancient, pre-Christian fertility religion. In a deliberate attempt to revive this religion, he published *Witchcraft Today* in 1954, and thus launched the movement that would evolve into modern Wicca.

Gardner was born into a well-off family near Liverpool, England. He later moved to East Asia, where he worked for many years in Ceylon (now Sri Lanka), Borneo, and Malaysia. He became deeply involved in the study of eastern religions and occultism. In 1936, he retired from his position as a colonial civil servant for the British government and returned to England, where he continued to pursue his interest in esoteric religions and the occult. He became an amateur archeologist, both in Britain and in the Middle East, and joined the Folklore Society, where he collaborated with **Margaret Murray** on a paper on historical witchcraft. In 1938, while living in Hampshire, he joined the Fellowship of Crotona, a mystical, quasi-Masonic group. Within this group, supposedly, was a secret inner circle whose members styled themselves as hereditary witches. Gardner claimed that he was initiated into this group in 1939. An 18th-century statute made it a crime in England to claim to be a witch, and this law was only repealed in 1951. At that point, Gardner began to go public with his supposed discovery of an ancient religion. His first book, *Witchcraft Today,* aroused tremendous interest and immediately made him a celebrity. Over the next few years, he and his most important disciple, **Doreen Valiente**, wrote several works on the nature and rituals of modern witchcraft. These writings became the basis for what became known as the Gardnerian tradition of witchcraft. The principal text of the rituals of witchcraft is the so-called **Book of Shadows**, of which Gardner produced several versions.

Although Gardner's writings (some of the most important of which were collaborations with Valiente) provided the basis for modern witchcraft, other traditions soon began to emerge. Valiente herself formed a second **coven**, and by 1957 this group had broken with Gardner, upset over the level of publicity and media attention that he continually sought. Other groups followed. In the 1960s and 1970s, the practice of witchcraft had grown significantly, and many different, independent Wiccan groups came into existence in both Europe and North America. Gardner's notion, based on the theories of Margaret Murray, that modern witchcraft was a direct survival of an ancient fertility religion, has been thoroughly disproved and is no longer accepted by many Wiccans today. The development of Wicca has been influenced by other factors, above all feminist ideologies, and other texts, such as **Starhawk**'s *The Spiral Dance,* have become as important, if not more so, than Gardner's original *Witchcraft Today.* Nevertheless, all branches of modern witchcraft owe something to Gerald Gardner.

GEILER VON KAISERSBERG, JOHANN (1445–1510). A theologian who had studied at both Freiburg and Basel, Johann Geiler von Kaisersberg served as a preacher in the cathedral at Strasbourg beginning in 1478. His *Die Emeis* (The Ants) is a collection of Lenten sermons delivered in 1508. Twenty-six of these sermons deal with **witchcraft**, and another treats the subject of lycanthropy, the transformation of people into **werewolves**. Intended for a wide audience, *De emeis* was one of the first major works on witchcraft to appear in the German vernacular.

GEOGRAPHY OF WITCH-HUNTING. *See* AFRICAN WITCHCRAFT; BRITISH ISLES, WITCHCRAFT IN; COLONIAL AMERICA, WITCHCRAFT IN; EASTERN EUROPE, WITCHCRAFT IN; FRANCE, WITCHCRAFT IN; GERMAN EMPIRE, WITCHCRAFT IN; SCANDINAVIA, WITCHCRAFT IN; SOUTHERN EUROPE, WITCHCRAFT IN; SWITZERLAND, WITCHCRAFT IN.

GERMAN EMPIRE, WITCHCRAFT IN. During the years of the great **witch-hunts** in Europe, the lands of the German Empire were without doubt the heartland of the witch craze. At the beginning of the period of the major witch trials in the 15th and 16th centuries, the Empire was comprised not only of the German states of central Europe, but also the Netherlands, Lorraine, Franche Comté, the Swiss Confederation, Austria, Bohemia, Silesia, and even parts of northern

Italy. In the course of the period of the witch-hunts, the Empire lost its Swiss territories, as well as the northern Netherlands, and these changing boundaries mean that statistics can vary. The inclusion of **Switzerland**, in particular, would add considerably to the number of trials and executions. Limited just to those lands that remained within the Empire for this entire period, however, the best estimates place the number of executions for **witchcraft** near 30,000, or still roughly half of all the executions that took place throughout Europe.

Perhaps the most significant factor behind the extremely high number of executions that took place in German lands was the fact that the German Empire as a whole was politically very weak and disunited. In fact, the Empire was a loose confederation of numerous kingdoms, principalities, duchies, and other smaller territories, each with its own jurisdiction and legal authority. In theory, the entire Empire was governed by the **Carolina law code**, introduced in 1532, but in practice, local authorities exercised nearly total autonomy. This is significant for the prosecution of witchcraft because it has been shown that witch-hunting was generally more severe in regions of limited centralized bureaucracy and legal control. Local authorities, if allowed to have jurisdiction, were far more likely to be concerned about witchcraft and to allow a few accusations to turn into a major hunt. Centralized bureaucracies, on the other hand, were more removed from the immediate situation, and thus the immediate fear and tension out of which accusations arose, and also tended to be more concerned with matters of proper procedure, above all the limitation of **torture**, thereby making unambiguous convictions more difficult to achieve.

The contrast between smaller regions and legal jurisdictions and larger states with centralized and highly bureaucratized legal systems is born out by the distribution of witch-hunting within German lands. In general, the most severe hunts took place in the states of the southern and western parts of the Empire, where political fragmentation was highest. In the north and east, where the German states tended to be larger and to have more centralized bureaucracies and legal structures, as well as in the large southeastern state of Bavaria, a proportionally smaller number of witches (relative to the larger populations of these sizeable lands) was tried, and fewer of those tried were executed. The same pattern is also evident for the large territories of Austria and Bohemia, both part of the Empire but ruled directly by the Habsburg dynasty and thus subject to centralized imperial control unlike the other German territories. Only about 1,000 witches were executed in each of these two large states, which combined had a population of around 4,000,000 people, during the entire period of the witch-hunts.

GERSON, JEAN (1363–1429). A prominent late-medieval theologian and chancellor of the university at Paris, Gerson wrote several works condemning **sorcery** and superstition, including treatises *De probatione spirituum* (On Testing Spirits) and *De erroribus circa artem magicam* (On Errors in the Magic Art). He was only one of several theologians in the late 14th and early 15th centuries to address such issues with greater concern than clerical authorities had typically exhibited earlier. Although he wrote before the concept of diabolic **witchcraft** had fully developed, his concerns indicate one possible basis for this subsequent development.

GIFFORD, GEORGE (?–1620). A preacher at Maldon in Essex, where some of the most intense **witch-hunts** of the **British Isles** took place in the late 16th century, Gifford wrote two important treatises on **witchcraft**, *Discourse of the Subtle Practices of Devils by Witches and Sorcerers* (1587) and *A Dialogue Concerning Witches and Witchcrafts* (1593). In these works, he adopted a position of moderate **skepticism** toward witchcraft. That is, Gifford felt that the **devil** was the true enemy of Christian society, and that the devil was powerful enough to work his evil in the world without the cooperation of human witches. Focusing too much on human witches, he felt, distracted authorities' attention from the real source of evil in the world. Nevertheless, Gifford did support the execution of witches for trafficking with **demons** and the devil.

GILLES DE RAIS (1404–1440). A French nobleman and eventually Marshal of France, Gilles de Rais rose to prominence for his military accomplishments during the course of the Hundred Years War. A companion of **Joan of Arc**, he was later tried and executed on charges of **heresy** and murder. Like Joan, he is often regarded as having been executed for **witchcraft**, although in reality he was never accused of this crime, and even the charges of demonic magic made against him were somewhat tangential to his ultimate conviction. Having become extremely powerful in the course of the war, Gilles made many political enemies. He also incurred significant debts in the course of the 1430s, and was forced to begin selling off his land. His enemies seem to have conspired against him largely because if he were convicted of heresy, they could confiscate rather than purchase his lands. Gilles was brought up on a number of particularly terrible and graphic charges. Before an ecclesiastical court, he stood accused of performing **alchemy** and demonic magic, of summoning and worshiping **demons**, making **pacts** with them, and sacrificing **children** to them. He was also tried before a secular judge for the sexual murder of over 100 children.

By the time of his trials, Gilles had clearly developed a dark reputation, which his enemies were able to exploit. Although most of the charges against him were clearly fabricated by his political opponents, he may well have been a murderous pedophile, and it is certainly possible that he turned to alchemy or even darker magics in an attempt to alleviate his financial problems. Ultimately, he confessed to practicing alchemy and murdering children. His case, however, was hardly one of typical witchcraft.

GLANVILL, JOSEPH (1636–1680). The chaplain of King Charles II of England, Glanvill attempted to prove the existence of **witchcraft** and other supernatural and occult phenomenan in his *Saducismus triumphatus* (Saducism Overcome). He felt that those who were **skeptical** of such phenomena were merely trying to disguise their own atheism, since to deny witchcraft one had to deny the reality of the **devil's** power, and ultimately, for Glanvill, this meant denying the power of God as well. His work became popular not so much for its learned reasoning as for its collection of colorful stories and examples of witchcraft.

GOATS. After **cats**, goats were the animals most typically associated with **witchcraft** in medieval and early-modern Europe. Demonic **familiars** might take the form of a goat in order to serve a witch, but the most common association of goats with witchcraft occurred in images of the witches' **sabbath**. Here, a **demon** or the **devil** himself was typically thought to preside over the assembly of witches, often in the form of a goat. Witches had to kneel before this animal, worship it, and often give the *osculum infame,* the **obscene kiss,** to the creature's hindquarters. This image derived from medieval stereotypes of **heresy** and of heretics, who were often thought to worship demons in the form of goats, and ultimately from **pagan** worship of certain horned, semi-animalistic deities, such as a Greco-Roman Pan or Celtic Cernunnos. Both were fertility gods, and the goat has long been a symbol of fertility and especially masculine virility. This notion is preserved in modern witchcraft, or **Wicca,** in which a **Horned God** is worshiped as the male counterpart and consort of the **Goddess.** The goat, and especially the goat-headed image of the devil known as **Baphomet,** also remains a prominent symbol among practitioners of modern **Satanism.**

GODDESS, THE. In modern **witchcraft,** or **Wicca,** the Goddess is the primary deity. She is the companion of, and is generally seen as superior to, the God or **Horned God,** who represents the male aspect of divinity. Although a supreme deity, the Goddess is above all a nature and fertility deity. She is regarded as being the Earth itself and embodies all creative and productive forces, particularly magic. She is in some ways a conglomeration of all early **pagan** female mother-deities.

The worship of powerful fertility goddesses is ancient and seems to have existed in almost all human cultures. Modern witches identify the Goddess with such ancient female fertility deities and mother-goddesses as the Sumerian Inanna, Babylonian Ishtar, Egyptian Isis, Phoenician Astarte, and Greco-Roman Demeter. Also particularly associated with the Goddess are the Greco-Roman triad of moon-goddesses **Diana** (Artemis), Selene, and **Hecate,** all of whom, especially Hecate, were associated with magic in classical times. Innana, Ishtar, Isis, and Asarte were also all lunar deities, associated with magic and frequently the underworld.

GREGORY IX, POPE (ca. 1170–1241). Reigning as pope from 1227 to 1241, in 1233 Gregory issued the decretal letter *Vox in Rama* (A Voice in Rama) to the archbishop of Mainz and bishop of Hildesheim, discussing certain supposed practices attributed to **heretics** in the

Rhineland. In particular, Gregory described a heretical gathering presided over by a **demon** in the shape of a giant toad. New members of this heretical sect had to kiss this creature, and also a pallid man whose kiss was as cold as ice. The heretics then feasted until a large **cat** appeared, which the heretics also had to kiss on its hindquarters, and then they engaged in a sexual **orgy**. Although there is no mention of **sorcery** in the letter, this description clearly served as a basis for later accounts of the witches' **sabbath**.

GRILLANDUS, PAULUS (late 15th–16th century). A papal judge who presided over several witch trials around Rome in the early 16th century, Grillandus wrote a *Tractatus de haereticis et sortilegiis* (Treatise on Heretics and Witches) around 1525. It was frequently printed, and, after the *Malleus maleficarum*, was one of the most important and influential treatises on **witchcraft** written prior to the major rise of **witch-hunting** in the later 16th century.

GUAZZO, FRANCESCO MARIA (?–early 17th century). An Italian friar of the order of Saint Ambrose, Guazzo was a known expert on **witchcraft** and **possession**. In 1605, he was summoned to the Rhineland by the duke of Cleves to assist in a case of witchcraft. This, however, seems to have been Guazzo's only practical experience with **witch-hunting**. Returning to Italy, he wrote what became one of the standard treatises on witchcraft, *Compendium maleficarum* (Handbook of Witches), at the request of the archbishop of Milan. The work was completed in 1608. The *Compendium* was an encyclopedic account that drew to some extent on Guazzo's personal experience, but was based mainly on earlier Catholic literature on witchcraft, including the treatises by **Johannes Nider** and **Heinrich Kramer**, as well as on the work of such recent authorities as **Nicholas Rémy** and **Martin Del Rio**. Guazzo's treatise became popular more because of its completeness than its originality. In Italy, it became the standard source on witchcraft for the remainder of the period of the witch-hunts.

GUI, BERNARD (1261–1331). A Dominican friar and papal inquisitor in the southern French region of Languedoc, Gui is most well known as the author of one of the first major inquisitorial manuals, *Practica* *inquisitionis haereticae pravitatis* (Practice of Inquisition into Heretical Depravity), completed by 1324. In this work, Gui included some sections on **sorcery** and **divination**, as well as on clearly learned demonic magic, or **necromancy**. He never described diabolic **witchcraft** per se, but his writings were an important basis for later inquisitorial thought in this area.

Born in Limousin, Gui entered the Dominican order in 1279. He studied theology at Montpellier and then served as prior of several Dominican convents in Languedoc until 1307, when he was appointed a papal inquisitor and began operating from Toulouse. He remained in this office until 1324, when he became bishop of Lodève. Throughout his tenure as an inquisitor, Gui seems never to have conducted an **inquisition** into a case of sorcery personally. Nevertheless, sorcery was becoming a concern for religious authorities in southern France at this time. In 1320, **Pope John XXII** ordered the inquisitors of Toulouse and Carcassonne to take action against those who invoked or worshiped **demons** as a part of magical ceremonies. In his *Practica,* Gui included several sections of procedures to be used specifically against clerics who engaged in demonic invocation, including a long description of complex, necromantic ritual magic. He also included a section on sorcery and divination generally. While Gui clearly assumed all such magic was demonic in nature, he actually described acts quite different from the overtly demonic practices of learned magic. Instead, he discussed what seems to be a much more common sort of magic, aimed at **healing**, discovering thefts, locating lost objects, or inspiring love, and performed via everyday objects and simple rituals. Gui's association of such common magic with demonic invocation was fundamental for the later prosecution of sorcery and eventually witchcraft in inquisitorial courts.

– H –

HALE, MATTHEW (1609–1676). An English judge, and later Chief Justice of the King's Bench, Hale is most well known for conducting the trial of two witches in Bury Saint Edmunds in 1662. In this notorious case, which began when several **children** exhibited signs of bewitchment and accused two old **women**, he allowed hearsay and unsupported

spectral evidence, and even refused to give credence to clear evidence of fraud and perjury on the part of some of the children, all in his zeal to attain convictions. Later, as Chief Justice, he was able to help set the tone for the conduct of witch trials across **England**. When accusations of **witchcraft** arose in **Salem**, Massachusetts, in 1692, again from the testimony of children, the noted Boston minister **Cotton Mather** used Hale's conduct of the Bury Saint Edmunds trial as a model.

HALLOWEEN. The period around the present date of Halloween has long carried supernatural significance and has often been associated with death and the spirits of the dead. The Celtic tribes of Europe celebrated the feast of Samhain, their new year and hence a festival associated with death and rebirth, on November 1. On the night before this festival, the boundaries separating the living and the dead were believed to be particularly weak. The Romans, who by 43 C.E. had conquered most Celtic territory in Western Europe, combined two of their own holidays with the Celtic Samhain: the feast of Feralia, which commemorated the dead, and the feast of Pomona, goddess of apples and other fruits, which celebrated fertility and rebirth. In the seventh century, Pope Boniface IV, seeking to Christianize these pagan holidays and incorporate them into the church's liturgical calendar, declared November 1 to be All Saints' Day, to honor Christian saints and martyrs. Later, around the year 1000, the church declared November 2 to be All Souls' Day, commemorating all the Christian dead. All Saints' Day was also known as All Hallows, and so the night before became Hallows Eve and eventually Halloween.

Such modern Halloween traditions as trick-or-treating probably have their roots in the medieval celebration of All Souls' Day, when people would give pastries and other food to the poor, and eventually to children, in exchange for their promise to pray for the souls of the gift-givers' dead relatives. Even older was the tradition of leaving offerings of food and wine for the spirits of the dead thought to roam free on this night. The custom of dressing up in costumes also extends far into the past, when people sought to disguise themselves from wandering spirits. However, Halloween was not particularly associated with witches during the medieval or early-modern periods. Rather, if any one night was thought to be a time of particular celebration and revelry for witches, it was **Walpurgisnacht** (April 30).

In modern times, and especially in the United States, certain religious groups have tired to associate Halloween with **witchcraft** and **Satanism**. This might find its historical roots in colonial times, when the Puritan settlers of New England opposed the celebration of Halloween on moral grounds (the holiday was more widely celebrated in the southern colonies). In the later 20th century, Halloween has finally become a real witches' holiday, as practitioners of modern witchcraft, or **Wicca**, as well as practitioners of other forms of **neopaganism** have revived the celebration of the Celtic Samhain.

HAND OF GLORY. In medieval and early-modern sources, witches were often described as taking the limbs of corpses, and especially their hands, for magical purposes. The Hand of Glory was one particular use to which such a limb could be put. The hand of a hanged murderer was removed from the corpse, often while it still hung on the gallows, then pickled and dried. It was then used to hold candles or the fingers themselves could be lighted. Supposedly, the hand had the power to immobilize or incapacitate anyone within a house, and was often employed by thieves.

HARTLIEB, JOHANN (ca. 1410–1468). Court physician to Duke Albrecht II of Bavaria, Hartlieb was one of the first authorities to write on **witchcraft** in a vernacular language. Around 1456, he published his *Buch aller verbotenen Kunst* (Book of All Forbidden Art). He was very credulous, and accepted, for example, the full reality of **night flight** and the witches' **sabbath**, opposing the tradition derived from the **canon** *Episcopi* that these were only demonically inspired illusions.

HEALING, MAGICAL. Curing diseases and healing injuries have historically always been among the principal functions of common magic. Across Europe in the Middle Ages and early-modern period, a wide variety of healers and **cunning men and women** practiced such magic. In common culture, for the most part, such people were easily distinguished from witches, who performed harmful magic, or *maleficium*, and who were typically believed to cause disease rather than cure it. Authorities, however, especially clerical authorities, often did not recognize such distinctions. They placed less importance than most average people on the effects of magic and were more concerned with the means by which magic supposedly operated. Because they believed that most magical operations depended on invoking demonic power, such acts were still evil even if (occasionally) used to achieve beneficial ends. Many authorities believed, for example, that witches might cause a disease or injury only to cure it later. They supposedly did this not out of compassion for their neighbors, but in order to corrupt their souls by involving them in operations of demonic power.

In practical terms, because most witch trials began with accusations of *maleficium*, magical healers, who were not commonly seen to perform such harmful **sorcery**, were generally safe. If a **witch-hunt** developed, however, and accusations increasingly came to be directed by authorities rather than arising naturally, magical healers and cunning folk were certainly at risk. Authorities, who at best regarded them as frauds and charlatans, could become convinced that they were witches, and as the level of panic generated by a hunt increased within a community, common people, too, could begin to become suspicious of the nature of magical healers' supposed power.

HECATE. A classical goddess of night, death, and malevolent magic, Hecate was also a lunar deity and was often associated with **Diana** and Selene. Even in the ancient world Hecate was regarded as a dangerous and often evil entity. She was imagined as a three-faced spirit that haunted crossroads and roamed about at night, visible only to dogs (a dog's howl was taken as a sign that Hecate was near). She caused nightmares and insanity and was particularly associated with dark magic and **witchcraft** in the ancient world. The mythical sorceresses **Circe** and **Medea** were sometimes believed to be daughters of Hecate. In the Christian Middle Ages, when all **pagan** deities were transformed into **demons**, many of Hecate's terrifying attributes and her strong association with witchcraft were transferred to the more general figure of Diana.

HERESY. Any belief contrary to a formally established doctrine of the church is considered a heresy. In the Middle Ages, the practice of demonic **sorcery** was deemed to be heretical because clerical authorities decided that such acts must entail the worship of **demons** and thus were considered a form of **idolatry**, a violation of the first commandment. The most influential figure in establishing an argument for the heretical nature of demonic sorcery was the 14th-century theologian and inquisitor **Nicolau Eymeric**. Because witches were thought to perform sorcery by demonic means, they were also considered heretics. Many aspects of **witchcraft**, and especially many elements of the witches' **sabbath**, derived from earlier medieval stereotypes about heretics and heretical assemblies. Heretics were commonly described as worshiping demons, often in the form of some animal such as a **cat** or **goat**, murdering **children**, desecrating the sacraments, and engaging in sexual **orgies** with one another. All of these stereotypes were later transferred onto witches. During the period of the **witch-hunts**, many authorities argued that denying the reality of witchcraft or the existence of witches was also heretical, because the church had declared such things to be real.

HERMETIC MAGIC. A major source of magical and occult knowledge in European history was the body of writings traditionally attributed to Hermes Trismegistus (the Thrice-Great Hermes) and referred to collectively as the *Corpus Hermeticum*. Thrice-Great Hermes was a mythical figure—a blend of the Greek god Hermes and the Egyptian god of wisdom, Thoth. He stood as a personification of arcane, magical knowledge, and supposedly wrote over 20,000 books containing his wisdom. In fact, the *Corpus Hermeticum* was composed by various authors over several centuries. Much of it was lost in ancient times, but some writings remained known throughout the Middle Ages, and more were rediscovered in the Renaissance of the 14th and 15th centuries. Hermetic writings became a basis for much learned or high magic in the Renaissance and continued to be a basis for systems of learned magic and occult science in Europe thereafter. For example, when occultists in 19th century England organized into a group, they designated themselves the **Hermetic Order of the Golden Dawn**. The rites and rituals of such groups have had some effect on modern **witchcraft**, or **Wicca**, but historical Hermetic magic, always regarded as a highly learned system and limited to a small elite, had little to do with witchcraft in the medieval and early-modern periods.

HERMETIC ORDER OF THE GOLDEN DAWN. Founded in England in 1888, the Golden Dawn was an elite, secret society, along the lines of earlier Masonic and Rosicrucian groups. Unlike those groups, however, the purpose of the society was to promote the study and practice of ritual magic among its members. Although the founders initially claimed that the order was of ancient origin, in fact the rituals and practices of the Golden Dawn were a loose assembly of ancient Greco-Roman, Egyptian, and Hebrew systems of magic and mysticism, along with medieval and modern Christian beliefs. The members of the Golden Dawn could justify such mingling of different belief-systems because they accepted the notion, perhaps most famously articulated in the writings of British anthropologist James Frazer, that all historical religions were built upon a single, underlying mythic system. Such ideas also influenced **Margaret Murray** and others to conceive of historical **witchcraft** as an ancient, pre-Christian fertility cult.

The members of the Golden Dawn, which included such luminaries at W. B. Yeats and the famed occultist **Aleister Crowley**, were not especially interested in witchcraft, which they considered to be a form of low magic. By merging systems of ritual magic into a kind of **neo-pagan** structure of belief, however, the order did help establish a basis for the development of modern witchcraft, or **Wicca**. The principal founder of modern witchcraft, **Gerald Gardner**, was drawn to the sort of occult studies that the Golden Dawn promoted. Significantly, he was inducted by Aleister Crowley into the *Ordo Templi Orientis,* another occult society that Crowley headed after his expulsion from the Golden Dawn.

HERNE THE HUNTER. In Germanic legend, Herne was a male spirit (also given as Herlechin, Harlequin, or Berthold) sometimes thought to lead the **Wild Hunt** instead of the female spirit **Holda** or Berta. He was pictured as wearing an antlered headdress. Christian authorities in the Middle Ages frequently associated him with the **devil**. In modern **witchcraft**, or **Wicca**, he is associated with the **Horned God**.

HERODIAS. In the **Bible**, the wife of Herod who demanded the head of John the Baptist, during the Middle Ages, Herodias was seen as an embodiment of female evil. Nevertheless, her association with **witchcraft** seems quite coincidental. In the Germanic concept of the **Wild Hunt**, a group of spirits was led in nocturnal flight by a female deity most typically named **Holda** or Berta. Authorities writing in Latin typically transformed this deity into the classical **Diana** (although even this was already introducing an error, since it was actually the goddess **Hecate**, closely associated with Diana, who was believed in classical antiquity to lead spirits through the night). Some authorities, however, gave the name Herodias instead, apparently working from the Germanic Ber- (alternately Her-) beginning of the name, but seeking to provide a similar-sounding biblical name instead. The image of the Wild Hunt later became an important basis for the idea of **night flight** of witches to a **sabbath**.

HOBBES, THOMAS (1588–1679). The most important English political philosopher of his day, Hobbes is best known for his extremely important and influential treatise on government, *Leviathan* (1651). He treats **witchcraft** only tangentially in this work, but demonstrates a complete **skepticism** about the reality of witches and witchcraft. For Hobbes, spirits—either angels or **demons**—had no real existence or power in the world. **Biblical** passages referring to such spirits he interpreted metaphorically. Without the real presence of demons in the world, the entire basis for the reality of witchcraft was removed.

HOLDA. A Germanic goddess, also known as Hulda, Holle, Holt, Berta, Bertha, or Perchta, she was associated with fertility, the moon, and the hunt. For these reasons she was often equated by medieval authorities with the classical goddess **Diana**. Holda was believed to lead the **Wild Hunt**, a group of spirits and ghosts who roamed through the night. This Germanic legend became an important basis for the later Christian notions of the **night flight** of witches to a **sabbath**.

HOOPOE. A type of bird, in fact any member of the Upupidae family common in Europe, hoopoes are distinguished in particular by the fanlike crests on their heads. Historically they have long been associated with magic and supernatural powers. The blood of the hoopoe, as well as its brains, tongue, and heart, were all regarded as being particularly efficacious when used in spells, charms, and conjurations, and the hoopoe itself was often used by magicians as a sacrifice when invoking **demons**. Certain modern devotees of magic continue to regard the hoopoe as a sort of totem.

HOPKINS, MATTHEW (?–1647). Born the son of a Puritan minister in Suffolk, Hopkins was a failed lawyer who became, briefly, the most notorious and successful witch-hunter in English history. In less than two years, from 1645 to 1646, he oversaw the executions of no less than 230 witches in southeastern **England**. He declared himself to be England's "Witch-Finder General," and claimed he had been appointed to this post by Parliament. His methods proved too extreme, however, and he quickly found himself faced with criticism and significant opposition from local authorities. His **witch-hunting** activity ended in 1646, as rapidly as it had begun. In 1647, he published a brief treatise entitled *Discoverie of Witches,* defending himself and his procedures. He died in obscurity later that year.

The motivation for Hopkins' zeal in persecuting witches is difficult to access, but might be no more complicated than a desire to salvage an otherwise failed career as a lawyer. Abandoning his legal practice, he determined to make a career as a professional witch-hunter, and announced that for a fee, he and a colleague, John Stearne, would find and eliminate witches in any community that cared to hire them. Hopkins seems to have had no particular expertise in the areas of **witchcraft** or **demonology**, and his knowledge of these subjects was gleaned primarily from **King James'** *Daemonologie.* He first came to fame with a series of trials in **Chelmsford**, Essex, in 1645. Thereafter, his reputation spread, he hired more staff, and conducted numerous trials throughout Essex, Norfolk, Suffolk, and other counties in southeastern England. Although the use of **torture** in cases of witchcraft was forbidden by English law, this prohibition was sometimes ignored, and Hopkins was particularly aggressive in his application of torture to obtain confessions. Such extreme practices helped to rouse opposition to him, however, and brought his short career to an end.

HORNED GOD. In modern **witchcraft**, or **Wicca**, and other forms of **neo-paganism**, the Horned God is the male aspect of the supreme deity, and consort to the **Goddess**. Although the Goddess is generally held to be superior, the Horned God is very important in modern neopagan rituals. The god is often associated with such historical **pagan** deities as the Celtic Cernunnos, the Greek and Roman Pan, and the Celtic and Germanic figure of **Herne the Hunter**. All of these beings were depicted as horned, and often appeared in half-animal forms. Following the theories of **Margaret Murray**, some modern witches believed that historical witchcraft was an actual survival of an ancient, pre-Christian religion, and that during the Middle Ages, Christian authorities had mistakenly (or deliberately) transformed the witches' worship of the Horned God into worship of the Christian **devil**. Murray's theories have long since been disproved, however, and most modern Wiccans see their religion as a creative revival of historical pagan beliefs, not as the continuation of a long, clandestine tradition.

HUMANISM. Describing a program of humanistic studies that developed in Italy in the late 14th and 15th centuries and then spread to the rest of Europe, humanism (the term was actually only coined in the 19th century) is often seen as one of the defining elements of the Italian Renaissance. As a program of study, it stressed attention to the literature of classical antiquity, both Latin and Greek, and placed more value on rhetorical and literary skill than on dialectic logic in argumentation. It developed as an intellectual system in opposition to medieval scholasticism. Regarding **witchcraft**, humanist scholars were often inclined to a certain degree of **skepticism**. This might have been partly because of their natural suspicion of much scholastic thought, which formed the basis for medieval **demonology**. Also, because of their closer attention to ancient texts, humanists often realized that the **Bible** and other ancient sources did not really describe witchcraft as it was conceived in the 15th and 16th centuries. Nevertheless, humanists did not deny the reality of the **devil** or his potential power in the world, and humanism as a system of thought was in no way antithetical to belief in witchcraft.

HUNGARY. *See* EASTERN EUROPE, WITCHCRAFT IN.

– I –

IDOLATRY. Along with **apostasy**, idolatry was considered by most authorities throughout medieval and early-modern Europe to be the main crime entailed in **witchcraft**. Rather than focus on the supposed harm that a witch might achieve through harmful **sorcery** (*maleficium*), first ecclesiastical authorities and then increasingly secular ones as well considered the real evil of witchcraft to lie in the witches' involvement with **demons**. They developed theories that defined how most, if not all, demonic sorcery, such as witches were believed to perform, required that worship be offered to demons, or that they be invoked in some way that set them equal to or above divine power. This was considered idolatry, a serious form of **heresy**. The inquisitor **Nicolau Eymeric** developed an extended and detailed argument about the idolatrous nature of demonic magic in the late 14th century, and thereafter, demonic magic and witchcraft were often classified by authorities as a violation of the first commandment.

IMP. Any type of small **demon** or demonic creature might be called an *imp*. In medieval and early-modern Europe, sorcerers were often thought to keep imps imprisoned in jewels, vials, or glass jars to serve them. Particularly in the **British Isles**, witches were also thought to keep imps in animal form as **familiars**.

INCUBI AND SUCCUBI. In medieval and early-modern Europe, people believed that **demons** could take substantial form and engage in sexual activity with humans. Demons who took male form were called *incubi* and those who took female form were called *succubi*. Such beliefs, especially the belief in seductive, although often also terrible, female demons, are of ancient origins. The ancient Sumerians believed in a terrible spirit called *Ardat Lili* or *Lilitu*, a monstrous female demon with wings and talons who would fly through the night, seduce men, and drink their blood. Such beliefs are also reflected in the Hebrew demon **Lilith** and Greco-Roman creatures **strix** and **lamia**. All of these figures would later contribute to the stereotype of European witchcraft. Witches were themselves thought to engage in sexual activity with demons, especially during the **orgies** held at a witches' **sabbath**. Female witches were often thought to submit sexually to the **devil** himself, whose member was typically described as being ice cold.

Many Christian authorities, especially in the earlier medieval period, were **skeptical** about the real existence of incubi and succubi. They doubted that demons, as spiritual creatures, could assume solid material form in order to engage in sexual intercourse. Such doubts were, for the most part, gradually overcome in the 12th and 13th centuries, as clerical authorities became more concerned about the real power of demons in the world. Notably, the great authority **Thomas Aquinas** developed a full argument to explain how demons could assume solid form, and how they could engage in sexual intercourse with humans. As succubi, Thomas maintained, demons collected semen from human men and were then able to preserve its potency so that later, as incubi, they could impregnate women with it. This theory persisted throughout the period of the major **witch-hunts**.

INFANTICIDE. A major crime historically associated with **witchcraft** has been the killing, in various ways and for various purposes, of babies and small **children**. As far back as classical antiquity, creatures like the **strix** and **lamia** were believed to fly through the night and prey on children. Such nocturnal female monsters later contributed to the stereotype of witchcraft. In medieval and early-modern Europe, witches were thought to kill children in several ways. One standard element of *maleficium*, the harmful **sorcery** witches were thought to perform, was killing and causing disease, especially in children. Witches were also believed to be able to cause miscarriages and abortions of unborn fetuses. The murder of children also played an important role in typical images of the witches' **sabbath**, where witches were thought to use parts of babies' bodies in their magic spells, to sacrifice children to the **devil**, and to **cannibalize** babies as a part of their general feasting and revelry.

One obvious explanation for the longstanding connection of witchcraft with infanticide is the extremely high mortality rate of infants and young children in the pre-modern world. Accusations of witchcraft provided a ready explanation for such misfortune. Historians used to think that **midwives** were frequently accused of witchcraft for this reason, but this theory has since been largely discredited and it now seems clear that in fact very few midwives were accused of witchcraft. Some people still suspect that practitioners of modern witchcraft, or **Wicca**, engage in infanticide, although the ritual murder of children is more often associated with groups practicing **Satanism**. In fact, no Wiccan or Satanist groups engage in or promote any activity like this, and there has never been any substantial, credible evidence that organized groups of any nature exist that focus on the ritualistic abuse or murder of children. Nevertheless, this longstanding myth shows few signs of abating in the modern world.

INNOCENT III, POPE (1160/61–1216). One of the most important popes of the medieval period, reigning from 1198 until 1216, Innocent played a critical role in the introduction of **inquisitorial procedure** to Western Europe. In 1215, the Fourth Lateran Council, under the pope's direction, regularized legal procedures used against heretics, and, importantly, allowed judges to initiate inquests into **heresy** themselves, even when no accuser was present. In following centuries, such procedures would be essential to the spread of **witch-hunts**.

INNOCENT VIII, POPE (1432–1492). In the first year of his pontificate, which lasted from 1484 until 1492, Innocent VIII issued what is sometimes regarded as the most important papal pronouncement concerning **witchcraft**, the bull *Summis desiderantes affectibus* (the title comes from the document's opening words in Latin: "Desiring with Supreme Ardor"). Having been alerted by the papal inquisitors **Heinrich Kramer** and **Jakob Sprenger** to the existence of numerous witches throughout lands of the **German Empire**, the pope expressed his grief that so many Christians had fallen into such grave error and **heresy**, sacrificing their souls to the **devil** and performing harmful **sorcery**, or *maleficium*, in his service. The pope then noted that many local authorities had not given Kramer and Sprenger the assistance they required to conduct their **inquisitions** effectively and root out this particularly terrible error. He commanded that papal inquisitors should have full authority to investigate and prosecute this crime in all territories, and that local authorities should give all necessary assistance and offer no impediments to such action. Although sometimes regarded as marking the official start of **witch-hunting** in Europe, the bull is actually fairly typical of papal pronouncements on sorcery and witchcraft throughout the late-medieval period, at least since the pontificate of **John XXII** in the early 14th century. The bull was later included in the infamous late–medieval witch-hunting manual *Malleus maleficarum*, written by Heinrich Kramer and first printed in 1487, thus greatly enlarging its circulation. Although the bull was first issued several years before the *Malleus*, and was in no way connected to the treatise, its inclusion seemed to lend papal approval to the witch-hunting manual.

INQUISITION. Often regarded as some sort of supreme, repressive legal organ of the church, in fact there never was anything like a coherent and centrally controlled "Inquisition" in medieval Europe. Beginning in the 13th century, there were individual, papally appointed inquisitors who were responsible for helping to combat **heresy**, and in later periods there were certain standing Inquisitions. However, these people and later organizations generally played only a small role in matters of **witchcraft** or **witch-hunting**. Papal inquisitors were important in some of the earliest witch trials in the 15th century, but thereafter, and throughout the period of the great witch-hunts, witchcraft was generally classified as a secular crime and tried in secular courts (albeit courts that were operating according to **inquisitorial procedure**).

The Latin term *inquisitio,* taken in the legal sense, merely meant an inquiry, such that the further clarification *inquisitio haereticae pravitatis* (inquisition into heretical depravity) was needed to define a trial for heresy. Such inquisitions were originally the responsibility of bishops, who were in overall charge of enforcing correct religious observance and belief in their diocese. Owing to the perceived rise in heresy in the 12th and 13th centuries, however, in 1231 **Pope Gregory IX** issued the bull *Ille humani generis,* in which he commissioned the Dominican convent in Regensburg to form an inquisitorial tribunal independent of the local bishop and directly under papal authority. This act is generally taken to mark the creation of "the inquisition" in Europe. However, papal inquisitors, although in theory under the control of Rome, still acted largely as independent agents, and certainly there was no institutional structure or organization that could be called the "Inquisition" at this time.

Inquisitors seem rather quickly to have begun hearing cases involving **sorcery**. However, in 1258, **Pope Alexander IV** specifically forbade papal inquisitors from trying such cases, unless there was clear evidence that the acts of sorcery were also heretical in nature. In practice, this might not have represented much of a limitation on inquisitorial authority because the church assumed that most sorcery relied on the agency of **demons**, and involvement with demons or **pacts** made with them could clearly be construed as heresy. In 1320, **Pope John XXII** specifically ordered the inquisitors of Toulouse and Carcassonne in southern France to take action against any sorcerers who were invoking or worshiping demons as a part of their magical rites. In 1326, John then issued the bull *Super illius specula,* which declared a sentence of automatic excommunication on any sorcerer who invoked demons, worshiped them, or entered into pacts with them. Later that century, in 1376, the inquisitor **Nicolau Eymeric** wrote his *Directorium inquisitorum* (Directory of Inquisitors), in which he proved by theological argument that all magic involving demonic invocation entailed **idolatry**. This was a form of heresy, and therefore subject to inquisitorial authority.

In the 15th century, papal inquisitors played an important role in early witch trials and in the production of some of the earliest literature on witchcraft. The anonymous author of one of the most lurid early accounts, the *Errores Gazariorum* (Errors of the Gazarii—a common term for heretics at the time), was probably an inquisitor. Most famously, **Heinrich Kramer**, author of the infamous *Malleus maleficarum*, was also an inquisitor in southern Germany for several years and conducted many witch trials before he wrote this important treatise on witch-hunting. Despite such important inquisitorial contributions to the emergence of witchcraft, however, one of the basic elements of the crime, namely the practice of harmful sorcery or *maleficium*, had always been under the jurisdiction of secular authorities. Thus witch trials were from the start conducted in both secular and ecclesiastical courts. During the period of the most intense witch-hunting in the 16th and 17th centuries, the majority of trials were conducted in secular courts in most European lands.

It is notable, in fact, that in the lands of **Southern Europe**, where witchcraft remained more often under ecclesiastical jurisdiction, witch-hunts were relatively light and in particular the number of executions for witchcraft was significantly lower than in many other areas. Italy and Spain are also the only two regions of Europe that actually had Inquisitions in the sense of large, centralized, bureaucratic organizations that oversaw the actions of inquisitorial courts. The Spanish Inquisition was founded in 1478 as an instrument of the Spanish royal government, not the pope in Rome. The Holy Office of the Roman Inquisition was founded by Pope Paul III in 1542. Both of these institutions were notably lenient in matters of witchcraft. There are two basic reasons for this. First, inquisitorial courts in general regarded witchcraft as a form of heresy, and traditionally, death sentences were only imposed on recalcitrant heretics. If the accused were willing to confess and formally renounce their errors, then less severe punishment could be imposed. Cases of witchcraft were often somewhat different, because the heresy involved was so extreme, but in general, inquisitorial courts proved more willing to impose lesser sentences than secular ones. Also, the very fact that the Spanish and Roman Inquisitions were large, centralized bureaucracies contributed to their lenience toward witches.

Evidence is clear to show that the most severe witch-hunts took place in regions where local courts had significant autonomy. Local judges were often swept up in the panic that could follow several accusations of witchcraft and therefore allowed certain legal procedures and safeguards (such as those that governed the use of **torture**) to lapse. Centralized courts, on the other hand, were less susceptible to local conditions and tended to stress the proper application of procedure, the careful evaluation of evidence, and so forth. Throughout Europe, in lands where legal systems were largely centralized or at least overseen by a central authority, prosecutions and especially executions for witchcraft were generally low. This was true also for the centralized Inquisitions in Italy and even more so in Spain, where the supreme council in Madrid had very effective control over inquisitorial courts across the country.

INQUISITORIAL PROCEDURE. This refers to a system of legal procedure that came to be used increasingly in European courts of law, both ecclesiastical and secular, after the 13th century, in place of the older **accusatorial procedure**. It was in many ways a more rational procedure than the earlier method, and was based to some extent on the recovery of Roman legal texts and principles of jurisprudence in the course of the 11th and 12th centuries. In terms of the potential to try cases of **sorcery** and **witchcraft**, however, the introduction of inquisitorial procedure had dire consequences. Certain aspects of the accusatorial procedure, above all the potential for punishment of the initial accuser if an accused person was proven innocent, tended to restrict the frequency of accusations for particularly secretive or difficult to prove crimes, of which sorcery was certainly one. Inquisitorial procedure, on the other hand, by placing responsibility for the prosecution of a trial in the hands of the court itself, paved the way for more frequent accusations, and the use of **torture**, allowed under inquisitorial procedure, ensured frequent confession to even the most fantastic crimes.

Under inquisitorial procedure, cases were still often initiated by accusations made by private persons who felt themselves injured or afflicted in some way. However, judges were also given the power to call people before their courts on their own initiative, often based only on some general ill-repute (*infamia*). However cases began, the most important aspect of inquisitorial procedure was that the judges themselves were responsible for the investigation and prosecution of the case. They did this usually by interrogating the accused person and other potential witnesses. For serious crimes, the level of proof needed was testimony from two reliable witnesses or a confession. This was in many respects a far more rational and advanced method of conducting trials than the older accusatorial procedure, which had often relied on trial by ordeal to determine guilt or innocence. However, for crimes like sorcery or witchcraft, judges faced a particular problem in that, because of the secretive and clandestine nature of such acts, reliable witnesses could rarely be found. This meant that much more weight came to rest on the testimony of the accused themselves.

Because it was assumed that people would lie to protect themselves, torture was allowed under inquisitorial procedure in order to obtain a full confession. Judges were fully aware that torture could also be used to produce false confessions, and regulations were put in place to ensure that this did not occur. However, for crimes like witchcraft, which were regarded as particularly terrible, such regulations were often set aside. This was especially true if one or more initial accusations began to produce an atmosphere of panic in the community, to which the judges were often not immune. Thus, inquisitorial procedure facilitated the rise of accusations for witchcraft by eliminating the potential legal repercussions on private individuals for false accusations and by allowing the courts themselves to initiate trials. Also, in cases of witchcraft, inquisitorial procedure provided the courts with a method, one that given the nature of the potential evidence for the crime they were frequently required to use, could virtually ensure conviction. For these reasons, widespread **witch-hunting** would have been practically inconceivable if inquisitorial procedure had not been gradually adopted by almost all European courts by the end of the Middle Ages.

INSTITORIS, HEINRICUS. *See* KRAMER, HEINRICH.

IRELAND. *See* BRITISH ISLES, WITCHCRAFT IN.

ISIDORE OF SEVILLE (ca. 560–636). A major scholar of the Visigothic kingdom in Spain in the seventh century, Isidore's most important work was the 20 volumes of his *Etymologies.* Because he was convinced that most things were best understood by exploring the origins of their names, he organized this work as a study of the roots of words. In fact, it was a virtual encyclopedia of all the knowledge available to him, including a great deal of Roman learning. Isidore did not specifically focus on matters of magic or **witchcraft**, but he preserved much information on these subjects from Roman, Jewish, and early Christian sources. His work was very popular and became a standard reference source and basis for later medieval scholars on all subjects, including magic and the occult.

ITALY. *See* SOUTHERN EUROPE, WITCHCRAFT IN.

– J –

JACQUIER, NICHOLAS (?–1472). A Dominican friar who was active at the **Council of Basel** in 1432 and 1433, Jacquier was later an inquisitor in northern France, where he participated in some witch trials, in Bohemia from 1466 to 1468, and at Lille from 1468 until his death. In 1458, he wrote a treatise entitled *Flagellum haereticorum* *fascinariorum* (Scourge of Heretical Witches). Here, he argued that witches represented a new form of **heresy**, worse than any that had been seen in the past. The famous **canon** *Episcopi's* dismissal of **night flight** as an illusion, for example, did not apply to this new form of heresy. Jacquier joined **Jean Vineti** and **Johannes Hartlieb** in being among the first authorities to systematically address the reality of night flight and the witches' **sabbath**.

JAMES VI and I, KING (1566–1625). King first of **Scotland** (as James VI, 1567–1625) and then later also of **England** (as James I, 1603–1625), James owes his long reign to the fact that his mother, Mary Queen of Scots, was accused of murdering her husband and was forced to abdicate her throne in 1567 in favor of her infant son, then just 13 months old. Regents actually governed the kingdom until 1583 when James took up personal rule. Several years later, the king became directly involved in matters of **witchcraft** with the affair of the **North Berwick Witches**. A group of witches were put on trial in Edinburgh and were, in fact, questioned in the presence of the king. They claimed, among other things, to have tried to murder him by raising **storms** at sea to drown him while he was aboard ship. This case aroused the king's interest in witchcraft, and he began to study the subject. He was alarmed at the **skepticism** about witchcraft expressed in such works as **Reginald Scot's** *Discoverie of Witchcraft* and **Johann Weyer's** *De praestigiis daemonum* (On the Deception of Demons). In response, he wrote his own, far more credulous work, *Daemonologie* (Demonology), first published in 1597. In 1603, Elizabeth I of England died without a direct heir, and James became king of England as well as Scotland. His *Daemonologie* was issued in a new edition, and he ordered copies of Scot's *Discoverie of Witchcraft* to be burned throughout England. A year later, in 1604, Parliament passed a new witchcraft act, strengthening the legislation against witches already passed under Elizabeth I.

James often has been regarded as a severe persecutor of witches. Certainly no other European monarch took so direct an interest in matters of witchcraft, to the extent of producing a treatise on the subject. Nevertheless, the material in *Daemonologie* is not in any way innovative. **Witch-hunting** was quite severe in Scotland in the early years of James' reign, but (aside from the North Berwick case) the king had little direct involvement, and after the 1590s, the number of trials in Scotland began to subside. Likewise in England, although the final and most severe form of the witchcraft act was passed in 1604 under James' rule, earlier monarchs had already established similar legislation. Moreover, the most severe cases of witch-hunting did not occur in England until after James' reign. In all, he seems simply to have shared in the concern over witchcraft widespread in his time, and by the end of his life, in fact, he seems to have become increasingly skeptical about the extent of the danger witches represented.

JEWS. Although often persecuted by Christian authorities in medieval and early-modern Europe, and always marginalized within Christian society, Jews were only rarely accused of being witches. **Witchcraft**, insofar as it was believed to be predicated on a **pact** with the **devil** and the worship of **demons**, was regarded by Christian authorities as a **heresy**, and Jews, as non-Christians, by definition could not be found guilty of heresy. Jews, for their part, shared little of the Christian concern over witchcraft. Judaism did not have as developed a concept of the devil as existed within Christianity, and while Judaism did have elaborate systems of **demonology**, it allowed for the existence of good as well as evil spirits that could be called upon to perform magic, and so not all forms of magical practice were as automatically or thoroughly linked to evil as they were by Christian religious authorities.

In Christian minds, however, Judaism was believed to be very similar to witchcraft in a number of ways, and at times virtually identical to it. Christian authorities typically considered Jews to be a significant threat to the faith, similar to witches, and often conceived of elaborate, conspiratorial plots by Jews to undermine Christian society, just as they suspected that witches were engaged in an organized conspiracy directed by Satan. Christian stereotypes about Jews that had developed in the Middle Ages were often carried over and applied to witches as well. For example, in the earliest documents from the late Middle Ages, secret gatherings of witches are referred to not as **sabbaths** but as synagogues. The image of witches murdering **children** and devouring them also derives partly from earlier anti-Jewish stereotypes. Jews were often accused of murdering Christian children, draining their blood, or eating them in a parody of the Eucharist.

JOAN OF ARC (ca. 1412–1431). Often regarded as one of the most famous victims of accusations of **witchcraft**, Joan was burned at the stake in the city of Rouen in Normandy on May 30, 1431. In fact, although Joan was charged with certain crimes relating to witchcraft, these proved incidental, at best, to her final conviction and execution, which in any event was a foregone conclusion because of the highly politicized nature of her trial during the Hundred Years War fought between the English and the French.

Joan was born in Domrémy in Champagne and began hearing voices while still quite young. She became convinced that these voices were those of the Archangel Michael and Saints Margaret and Catherine, and that they were commanding her to help save France from the invading English. Accepted by the French dauphin, Charles VII, as a genuine messenger of God, she was allowed to lead a force to the relief of the city of Orléans, besieged by the English. She broke the siege and inflicted a major defeat on the English. Slightly over two months later, on July 17, 1429, she was present when Charles VII, having won several other victories, was crowned king in the cathedral of Reims. She led several more campaigns, but in May 1430 she was captured and turned over to the English by their allies the Burgundians. She was put on trial in Rouen, deep in English-held territory.

Joan was accused of a wide variety of crimes and **heresies.** Her voices were assumed by her judges to be demonic, and she was charged with consorting with fairies, summoning **demons**, worshiping them, performing **sorcery**, and making **pacts** with the **devil.** Such charges are certainly similar to those that figured in most cases of witchcraft, but they do not represent a clear accusation of that crime. Moreover the charges of sorcery made against Joan were withdrawn for lack of evidence before her final conviction, which was based entirely on charges of false beliefs and heresy. Nevertheless, for her supposed involvement with demons and her apparently supernatural accomplishments, many contemporary authorities did regard Joan as something very akin to a witch. The early authority **Johannes Nider** included Joan in his discussion of witchcraft in the fifth book of his large treatise *Formicarius* (The Anthill), although he consistently termed her a magician (*maga*) and not a witch (*malefica*).

JOHN XXII, POPE (1244–1334). As one of the most important and powerful popes of the early 14th century, John, who reigned from 1316 until 1334, contributed significantly to the development of ecclesiastical concern over demonic magic. He ordered papal **inquisitors** to begin taking action against suspected demonic **sorcery** because this was deemed to be a form of **heresy**, and he issued a sentence of automatic excommunication against any Christian who practiced such magic. His bull *Super illius specula* remained an important ruling against practitioners of demonic magic for the remainder of the Middle Ages.

Born Jacques Duèse in the French city of Cahors in 1244, John studied both theology and canon law. He came to the papal throne only after a hotly contested election during which the papacy had been vacant for nearly two years. From the very beginning of his pontificate, John was especially concerned with matters of sorcery and demonic magic. He feared that his opponents both within and outside the church were trying to assassinate him through sorcery. In 1317, he had Hugues Géraud, the bishop of Cahors, arrested on such charges, and other arrests were to follow. From 1320 to 1325, charges of sorcery and heresy were brought against many of John's political enemies in Italy, especially members of the Visconti family, the powerful rulers of Milan.

Although it is clear that John often used accusations of sorcery in an entirely cynical way as a political tool, he seems also to have been genuinely concerned about such practices, both because of the perceived threat to his own safety, and because of the heresy involved in dealing with demonic forces. In 1320, he instructed William, Cardinal of Santa Sabine, to order that the papal inquisitors of Toulouse and Carcassonne in southern France begin taking action against anyone who engaged in demonic invocation or sorcery. Later, in 1326, he issued the bull *Super illius specula,* in which he declared a sentence of automatic excommunication on any Christians who invoked or worshiped **demons** in order to perform any kind of magic. Although John was clearly more concerned with learned demonic magic, or **necromancy**, than with common *maleficium* of the sort later associated with **witchcraft**, his rulings formed an important basis for later inquisitorial jurisdiction over cases of witchcraft.

– K –

KNIGHTS TEMPLAR. *See* TEMPLARS.

KRAMER (INSTITORIS), HEINRICH (ca. 1430–1505). A Dominican friar and papal inquisitor, Kramer (the name he used in his German writings; he used Institoris in his Latin works) is best known as the author of the infamous late-medieval **witch-hunting** manual *Malleus maleficarum* (Hammer of Witches), written in 1486 and first printed in 1487. Although he is traditionally listed along with his fellow Dominican **Jakob Sprenger** as the author of this work, much evidence points to Kramer being the sole author.

Before writing his great treatise on witch-hunting, Kramer was active as a papal inquisitor conducting **inquisitions** into **heresy** and **witchcraft** in the southern lands of the **German Empire**. He was appointed to his office in 1474, and in 1484 he and his fellow inquisitor Sprenger were singled out in **Pope Innocent VIII's** bull *Summis desiderantes affectibus*. Concerned over reports of widespread witchcraft and demonic activity coming from Kramer and Sprenger, the pope ordered the inquisitors to proceed against these threats to the faith with all their energies, as well as commanding that all local authorities should aid them in whatever way they could. Although in no way connected to the later *Malleus maleficarum,* this bull was included in printed editions of that book, thereby adding to the treatise's authority.

Especially as it has become increasingly clear that Kramer was the primary author, and in all likelihood the sole author, of the *Malleus maleficarum,* many scholars have sought to link elements of that work to Kramer's own personality. He has been depicted as emotionally disturbed, an almost pathological hater of **women**, and as someone prone to strange sexual fantasies. He was certainly an arrogant and ruthless man who aroused much opposition from local authorities. In 1490, he was censured by the Dominican order for his irregular and excessive activities. In 1500, he was dispatched to combat heresy and witchcraft in Bohemia, where he died.

KYTELER, ALICE (?–1324). A wealthy woman of Kilkenny, **Ireland**, Lady Alice married four husbands, three of whom died under mysterious circumstances. When her fourth husband, John le Poer, began to sicken, several of her children began to accuse her of using **sorcery** to bewitch their fathers into leaving all their wealth to her and her favorite son by her first marriage, William Outlaw. In 1324, the case was taken up by Bishop Richard Ledrede. Ultimately, Alice and a group of accomplices, including one servant who was burned at the stake, were accused of renouncing the Christian faith, worshiping **demons** and sacrificing to them at crossroads, and performing harmful sorcery. Alice supposedly had a demonic **familiar** named Robert or Robin, Son of Art, who would appear to her in the form of a black dog or an Ethiopian. Although the case did not proceed smoothly, since Lady Alice had powerful friends who put up resistance and Bishop Ledrede does not appear to have been a well-liked man, nevertheless eventually Alice was condemned for **heresy**. She only escaped punishment by fleeing to **England**, where she probably spent the rest of her life.

The Kyteler case is the first trial involving harmful sorcery, or *maleficium*, and heretical **diabolism** in Ireland, and no other case would occur until the 17th century. While the case clearly resembles later witch trials in several ways, many aspects of the later witch-stereotype are also clearly absent. Moreover, the case was an isolated event arising out of particular circumstances, not an example of a widespread or developing phenomenon. Thus its place in the overall rise of **witchcraft** and **witch-hunting** in late-medieval Europe is difficult to determine.

– L –

LAMIA. In classical mythology, Lamia was a queen of Libya whom Zeus, the king of the gods, loved. Hera, Zeus' queen, took revenge on Lamia by killing her **children**. She in turn became a monster who roamed the night seeking to kill the children of others. Over time, the individual Lamia became a whole category of **demons** or monsters, all called *lamia* (plural *lamiae*), that preyed on children. They were believed to be **vampires** who sucked the blood from their victims. They contributed to the medieval and early-modern image of the witch as a **woman** who performed evil at night and especially sought to harm babies and small children. The word *lamia* in fact became a common term for witches in many areas of Europe during the era of the major **witch-hunts**.

LANCASHIRE WITCHES. A major witch trial in **England** occurred in 1612 in Lancashire. In all, some 20 people were accused and put on trial, but the case originated with the accusation of an old woman, Elizabeth Sowthern, who was about 80 years old. She not only confessed but also accused another old woman as well as her own granddaughter. From this point, the search for other witches grew. Although the case itself can be seen as fairly typical of English **witchcraft**, it is significant in the records that it produced. The court clerk kept a detailed and semi-official record of the proceedings, and this was subsequently published in 1613 as a chapbook entitled *The Wonderful Discovery of Witches in the County of Lancaster.*

LANCRE, PIERRE DE (1553–1631). A French lawyer and royal official, Lancre was appointed by King Henry IV to investigate **witchcraft** in the Pays de Labourd, a **Basque**-speaking region in the southwest of France. He conducted intense investigations and trials in 1609 and 1610. He then published an extensive account of these trials, *Tableau de l'inconstance de mauvais anges et démons* (Description of the Inconstancy of Evil Angels and Demons) in 1612, as well as later works, *L'incredulité et mescréance du sortilège* (The Incredulity and Misbelief of Witchcraft) and *Du sortilège* (On Witchcraft), in 1622 and 1627 respectively.

Lancre was extremely credulous when it came to accusations of witchcraft. He accepted the testimony of **children**, and many of the accused witches whom he tried were in fact minors. According to his accounts, the Basque lands were the center of the most intense witchcraft in Europe. He believed that huge witches' **sabbaths** were held in this region, with sometimes up to 2,000 witches supposedly attending. Ultimately, he became convinced that almost the entire population of the region, some 30,000 people, including all the local clergy, were tainted by witchcraft. Many accounts state that Lancre executed 600 people during the course of his trials, but this figure is certainly grossly inflated. A more reasonable estimate would be around 80 executions.

LaVEY, ANTON. *See* CHURCH OF SATAN.

LE FRANC, MARTIN (1410–1461). One of the most important French poets of the 15th century, Martin Le Franc included a section on **witchcraft** in his long poem *Le Champion des Dames* (The Defender of Ladies), written between 1440 and 1442. The poem finds its larger context in the late-medieval *querelle des femmes*, the literary discussion of the virtues of **women**. Le Franc wrote *Le Champion* in response to the very misogynistic poem *Roman de la Rose*. In Le Franc's poem, an "Adversary" raises the issue of witchcraft to attack women, noting that far more women than men are accused of this crime. The "Champion" then responds by defending women. In particular, he responds to the accusation of the **night flight** of female witches by arguing from the well-known **canon** *Episcopi* that such flight is only an illusion. He also points out that many learned demonic magicians are men.

Le Franc composed this poem while he was at the **Council of Basel** in the service of Duke Amadeus VIII of Savoy, later elected anti-pope Felix V by the council as a part of its struggle against **Pope Eugenius IV**. The Council of Basel was an important center for the early development and transmission of the idea of witchcraft. Aside from the purely literary influences on *Le Champion des Dames*, Le Franc was certainly also influenced by the environment at the council. His poem stands along with the accounts of the Dominican theologian **Johannes Nider**, the French secular judge **Claude Tholosan**, the Lucerne chronicler **Hans Fründ**, and the anonymous author of the *Errores Gazariorum*, as one of the earliest sources describing the developing idea of witchcraft in the early 15th century.

LELAND, CHARLES (1824–1903). A wealthy American author and amateur anthropologist, Leland devoted his life to studying folklore, magic, and the occult. His major contribution to the emergence of modern **witchcraft**, or **Wicca**, in the 20th century came with the publication of *Aradia, or the Gospel of the Witches* in 1899. While traveling in Italy, Leland claimed to have met a traditional, hereditary witch named Maddalena. She revealed to him that witchcraft was in fact an ancient, **pagan** religion that had been persecuted by religious authorities in the medieval and early-modern periods and driven underground, but which still survived. She claimed to trace her own hereditary powers back to Etruscan roots. She described the beliefs and practices of this religion to Leland, who subsequently published them as *Aradia*. In fact, the doctrines and supposed history outlined in *Aradia* are heavily indebted to 19th-century anthropology and historical studies such as those by Jules Michelet, who argued that historical witchcraft was in fact a form of popular resistance against oppressive religious authorities. Either Leland invented the supposed witch-religion himself or Maddalena simply told her wealthy patron what he wanted to hear. A similar interpretation of historical witchcraft was later advanced in the more influential writings of **Margaret Murray**.

LILITH. In Jewish **demonology**, Lilith was the first wife of Adam but refused to accept the authority God had given him over her and left him. She became a demonic creature who stalked the night, either appearing as a beautiful woman and seeking to seduce men, or trying to kill babies and small **children**. Like other mythological creatures, such as the **lamia** and **strix**, as well as demonic **succubi**, she became an archetype of female evil. As such, she contributed to the later image of the witch, especially to the notions of the female witch as sexually driven and as a murderer of young children. *See also* WOMEN AND WITCHCRAFT.

LOOS, CORNELIUS (1546–1593). A Catholic priest and scholar, Loos was a strong opponent of **witch-hunting** who ultimately suffered condemnation as a **heretic** for his beliefs. Born in Gouda in the Netherlands, Loos studied at Louvain and Liège and then taught at Mainz and **Trier**, which was a center of witch-hunting at the time. He grew increasingly concerned about the nature of the trials taking place and attempted to stop them, writing a treatise *De vera et falsa magia* (On True and False Magic). He not only argued that excessive use of **torture** led to false confessions in witch trials, but also that **demons** could not assume physical bodies to operate in the world. In particular, Loos criticized **Peter Binsfeld**, the suffragan bishop of Trier and a strong proponent of witch-hunting. He was imprisoned on the grounds that failure to accept the reality of **witchcraft** was a **heresy**, his writings were suppressed, and in 1593 he was forced to recant his beliefs. He was then banished to Brussels but refused to remain silent on matters of witchcraft and so was arrested and imprisoned as a relapsed heretic. He probably would have been executed had he not died of natural causes shortly thereafter.

LOUDUN, POSSESSIONS AT. The supposed demonic **possession** of several nuns in a convent at Loudun, **France**, in 1633 and 1634 is among the most notorious cases of possession in early-modern history, made famous again in the 20th century by Aldous Huxley's *The Devils of Loudun*. The case centered on a priest, Father Urbain Grandier. Grandier, an outsider, was appointed to the parish in Loudun and almost immediately began to arouse hostility by seducing local women. In 1630, he was arrested for immorality but, through political connections, was restored to his priestly office. Shortly thereafter another local priest, Father Mignon, and the mother superior and several of the nuns at Loudun hatched a plot to discredit Grandier. The nuns feigned possession and claimed Grandier was responsible.

Required to free the nuns from their possession, which of course he was unable to do, Grandier was eventually imprisoned and subjected to **torture**. He refused to confess to any charges of **witchcraft** or demonic **sorcery**, but was nevertheless burned at the stake in 1634. The entire case was a travesty. Outside investigations found no credible evidence of real possession, and in the course of the events several of the nuns themselves publicly recanted. Ironically, after Grandier's execution, the possessions continued. Either some of the nuns had truly come to believe in the reality of their feigned symptoms or they simply enjoyed the attention that the affair brought to themselves and their convent.

LOVE MAGIC. Producing affection or arousing discord between people, as well as increasing or impeding sexual fertility, have always been among the principal uses to which magic has been put throughout history. In medieval and early-modern Europe, such love magic took the form of a wide variety of popular spells and charms. **Witchcraft** was often strongly associated with the negative aspects of love magic. Witches were thought to be able to arouse enmity, jealousy, and hatred between people. Most especially they were thought to afflict sexual fertility. The harmful **sorcery**, or *maleficium*, that witches performed was believed to be able to cause impotence in men and prevent conception in women. Witches were also thought to cause miscarriages and stillbirths. The infamous **witch-hunting** manual *Malleus maleficarum*, in particular, contains extensive discussion of the sexually destructive aspects of witchcraft.

LUTHER, MARTIN (1483–1546). The primary figure responsible for launching the Protestant **Reformation** in the early 16th century, Luther challenged ecclesiastical authority and traditional medieval theology in many ways. On the question of **witchcraft**, however, he accepted the real existence of witches and all the aspects of medieval theology and **demonology** that underlay the idea of witchcraft. In fact, the great stress he laid on the power of the **devil** to tempt and assail humans might have disposed him to be more concerned about witchcraft than many earlier religious authorities. He never wrote about witchcraft or **sorcery** exclusively, but he did discuss such matters in sermons and biblical commentaries, and he made clear on many occasions that he believed witches were a serious threat to Christian society, and that they needed to be rooted out and destroyed.

LYCANTHROPY. *See* METAMORPHOSIS; WEREWOLVES.

– M –

MALEBRANCHE, NICOLAS (1638–1715). A French philosopher born in Paris, Malebranche studied theology at the university there. In 1660, he entered the Catholic religious order of the Oratorians, intending to pursue his studies of the early church father **Augustine of Hippo**, until he encountered the highly rationalist philosophy of René Descartes. In his major work, *De la recherche de la vérité* (The Search after Truth), published in 1674, Malebranche espoused a near-complete **skepticism** about **witchcraft**. The **devil**, he argued, had very little real power in the world, and so most of the alleged crimes of witchcraft could not be real. When not based on completely false accusations, they arose from delirium, mental instability, and an inability to distinguish delusion from reality on the part of those who confessed to such crimes.

MALEFICIUM. In the broadest terms, the crime of **witchcraft** as it was conceived in late-medieval and early-modern Europe may be said to consist of two elements, the practice of harmful **sorcery**, most often known in Latin as *maleficium,* and the practice of demon-worship, **idolatry**, **apostasy**, and other related heretical elements, usually described collectively as **diabolism**. While diabolism was unique to witchcraft in the Christian West, the practice of harmful sorcery is the defining characteristic of witchcraft, understood in a broader sense, in most cultures around the world.

In the historical European context, *maleficium* could involve any number of harmful acts or crimes performed through sorcery. Typical aspects of *maleficium* included causing disease or death, impeding sexual activity and reproduction in either human beings or livestock, impeding the fertility of crops, bringing pestilence or famine to a region, causing destructive **storms** or hail (or in coastal regions causing storms at sea), committing theft through sorcery, performing **love magic** to arouse either affection or enmity between people, causing pregnant women to miscarry, and killing small **children**. Accusations of *maleficium* most often arose when some otherwise unexplainable misfortune struck an individual, a family, or in some cases an entire community. The misfortune was blamed on the enmity of one or more sorcerers or witches, and by punishing these people, relief could be gained, or at least the assurance that such misfortune would not occur again in the future. Surviving trial records from the period of the great **witch-hunts** show that, in almost all cases, the initial accusation or accusations that sparked a hunt dealt solely with *maleficium*. Most often only in the course of a trial or hunt were elements of diabolism imposed by authorities, either ecclesiastical or secular.

As a crime that supposedly caused real harm, albeit by magical means, *maleficium* fell under the jurisdiction of secular authorities throughout the Middle Ages and early-modern period. When ecclesiastical authorities sought to prosecute a case of witchcraft, they had to bring charges of **heresy** related to elements of diabolism, although this was not typically difficult to do since most authorities held that much, if not all, harmful sorcery was performed by invoking **demons** and offering them sacrifices or worship. During the period of the most intense witch-hunting in the 15th, 16th, and 17th centuries, many secular authorities, as well as ecclesiastical ones, were primarily concerned with the diabolical aspects of witchcraft, not so much with the mere practice of *maleficium*. It is notable that in the **British Isles** and other regions of Europe where witch-hunting was noticeably less severe, elements of diabolism were never fully integrated into the stereotype of witchcraft, and many trials continued to focus exclusively or mainly on *maleficium*. Although still seen as a serious crime and a real threat, harmful sorcery alone could not usually generate the level of panic or fear of widespread diabolical conspiracies needed to launch a full witch-hunt.

MALLEUS MALEFICARUM. Certainly the most famous treatise on **witchcraft** and **witch-hunting** ever written, the *Malleus maleficarum* (Hammer of Witches) was authored by the Dominican inquisitor **Heinrich Kramer** probably in 1486 and was first printed no later than 1487. Since its first publication, the work has generally been attributed to two men, Kramer and his fellow Dominican inquisitor **Jakob Sprenger**. It has long been clear, however, that Kramer was by far the principal author. Strong evidence now exists the Sprenger contributed very little or even nothing to the work aside from his name, which was used to lend authority to the treatise (Sprenger being a theologian educated at the university at Cologne and a prominent figure in the Dominican order). A letter, only discovered in 1972, written by Sprenger's successor in the office of prior of the Dominicans in Cologne, a man who knew Sprenger well, explicitly stated that he had nothing to do with the composition of the *Malleus maleficarum*.

The *Malleus* is written like a scholastic theological treatise. In its contents, however, it reveals itself to be a practical handbook rather than a theoretical work. Much of the material it contains was intended not to convince educated scholars but for use in sermons to inform the public of the dangers of witchcraft and as a guide for those who would be responsible for uncovering and prosecuting this crime. The treatise is composed in three sections. The first part focuses on the nature of witchcraft, describing it as a form of **heresy** that arises because of the evil will of the **devil** and the complicity of human witches. In particular, the *Malleus* argues that **women**, being weak of will and lesser in faith, are far more susceptible to the seductions of the devil than are men, and thus are far more likely to become witches. The author stresses, however (as do all medieval and early-modern religious authorities), that witchcraft is only possible through the tacit permission of God, who allows the devil to tempt and humans to exercise free will. The second section focuses on the activities of witches. Here less attention is given to ideas of **pacts** with **demons** and other elements of **diabolism** inherent in witchcraft, and more focus is laid on the actual harmful **sorcery**, or *maleficium*, that witches perform—killing or causing disease in humans or animals, raising **storms** or hail, afflicting fertility, causing impotence, murdering babies, and so forth—as well as to potential remedies that can be used against such bewitchment. The third section then discusses legal procedures to be used in cases of witchcraft, including a variety of questions to be asked during interrogations of accused witches and directions for the application of **torture**.

The *Malleus maleficarum* has long enjoyed the reputation of being the preeminent piece of literature on witchcraft produced in medieval and early-modern Europe. There is no doubt that the book was very influential, going through numerous printings during the 15th, 16th, and 17th centuries. However, very little research has been done to verify exactly how, where, and when it was regularly employed. Throughout the period of the witch-hunts, the *Malleus* was in no way a definitive source on all aspects of witchcraft, even in Roman Catholic countries and for officials of the church. Later authors did not necessarily agree with the *Malleus* on all points, and later treatises on witchcraft, such as those by the French demonologist **Jean Bodin** and the Jesuit **Martin Del Rio**, enjoyed even greater success and influence. Particularly in the severity of its misogyny and its stress on the essentially female nature of witchcraft the *Malleus* appears to have been unique.

MANDRAKE. A poisonous herb native to the Mediterranean region, mandrake has long been thought to possess magical powers and has been used in a wide variety of spells and potions. The ancient Greeks associated the plant with the semi-divine sorceress **Circe**. The power of the mandrake was attributed to its root, which appears to be a small, human-shaped figure. Supposedly, the mandrake will shriek loudly when uprooted and will kill whoever digs it up. A special procedure for collecting mandrake was therefore developed. A sorcerer or witch would dig up most of the plant but not fully remove it from the ground. A dog was then tied to the plant with a rope, and the human would leave. The dog, trying to follow its master, would pull the mandrake from the ground, whereupon the animal would be struck dead and the human could return to collect the root. Witches were said to pick the root from beneath gallows trees, where it supposedly grew from the blood of hanged criminals. Aside from supposed magical qualities the mandrake is highly toxic. It has therefore frequently been used in a variety of **poisons** and also, in lesser quantities, as an anesthetic for medical purposes.

MAP, WALTER (ca. 1140–1208/10). An English cleric who served as a royal justice under King Henry II, from about 1182, Map recorded various stories, anecdotes, and observations in a work entitled *De nugis curialium* (On the Folly of Courtiers). Here, he included accounts of diabolical **pacts**, demonic activity, **sorcery**, and **heresy**. He described a heretical sect known as *Publicans* or *Patarines,* the members of which gathered secretly to feast, celebrate, and worship a **demon,** who appeared in the form of a large black **cat.** Although Map did not describe them in any way as witches, his account of their activities, and the stereotypes of heretics upon which it drew, would obviously influence the later image of the witches' **sabbath**.

MATHER, COTTON (1663–1728). The son of the important Puritan minister **Increase Mather**, Cotton himself became a leading minister in the Massachusetts colony and was more closely involved in matters of **witchcraft** than was his father. He firmly believed in the reality of witches and the dangerous satanic threat that they supposedly represented. He, therefore, supported witch trials and **witch-hunting** in his sermons and writings. In 1689, he published *Memorable Providences Relating to Witchcraft and Possessions,* recounting the dangers of witchcraft. The book helped to set the stage for the major outbreak of witch-hunting at **Salem**, Massachusetts, in 1692. Once these trials began, Mather met with other Boston ministers to discuss the matter. Although he was concerned about the difficultly in determining a true case of witchcraft, especially when only **spectral evidence** was available, nevertheless Mather, along with the other ministers, encouraged local authorities to seek out and prosecute witches vigorously. In 1693, he wrote *The Wonders of the Invisible World*, justifying his support for the trials in Salem.

Shortly after the trials in Salem, a backlash began to occur against rampant witch-hunting in the New England colonies, and so public opinion began to turn against Mather, who remained firm in his convictions regarding the dangerous threat that witches posed. His reputation suffered, and, among other consequences, this contributed to his being passed over several times for the presidency of Harvard College. In reaction to this perceived insult, Mather began to take an interest in the Connecticut College School, and in 1718 he wrote an impassioned letter to Elihu Yale, urging him to endow this institution, which would thereafter bear his name. The founding of Yale University is surely among the most admirable consequences to be associated, however distantly (it seems Elihu Yale was moved by other pleas for support far more than by Mathers'), with the Salem witch-hunts.

MATHER, INCREASE (1639–1723). A prominent Puritan minister and one of the most important men in colonial Massachusetts in his day, Increase Mather was educated at Harvard and Trinity College, Dublin. He served as a minister in the Church of England until 1661, when he returned to Massachusetts. Alarmed at what he perceived to be a growing religious laxness, and especially by reports of **witchcraft**, in 1684 he published *An Essay for the Recording of Illustrious Providences*. In this work, which did not deal solely with witchcraft, Mather recorded a variety of supernatural occurrences, including demonic activity and demonic **possession**. The book became very popular in the New England colonies. A few years later, in 1692, a series of witch trials took place at **Salem**, Massachusetts. In the wake of these trials, the most severe case of **witch-hunting** seen in **Colonial America**, Mather published a work entitled *Cases of Conscience* in 1693. Here he argued the need for greater caution in prosecuting witchcraft, especially if only **spectral evidence** was available. He concluded, however, in support of all the convictions at Salem. Increase's son **Cotton Mather** was more directly and significantly involved in matters of witchcraft than was his father.

MEDEA. One of the great female sorceresses of classical mythology, Medea was the daughter of the king of Colchis, and a priestess of **Hecate**, the ancient Greek goddess of magic and **witchcraft**. She was also sometimes depicted as related to the other great classical sorceress,

Circe. When the hero Jason came to Colchis in search of the Golden Fleece, Medea fell in love with him and aided him with her magic, which was often dark and murderous. When Jason attained the fleece and fled Colchis, to delay pursuit, Medea performed a spell that involved killing her own brother and dismembering his body. In Greece, she used magic to kill Pelias, the usurper of Jason's kingdom. Later, when Jason fell in love with another princess, Medea gave her a robe as a gift that caused her to burst into flame when she put it on. Medea then killed her own **children** by Jason and fled in a dragon-drawn chariot. In the medieval and early-modern periods, she became a literary archetype of the witch, especially of the notion that witches were motivated by carnal passions.

METAMORPHOSIS. Among the powers that witches were commonly believed to possess was that of metamorphosis, the ability to alter their own shape, usually into that of some kind of animal. In particular, witches were often thought to be able to turn themselves into **werewolves**, and there is a strong historical connection between **witchcraft** and lycanthropy. Authorities in medieval and early-modern Europe differed as to the reality of such transformations, however. For example, **Jean Bodin** accepted its reality, while the *Malleus maleficarum*, following the arguments of **Thomas Aquinas** on the nature and extent of demonic power, held that such changes were just illusions created by **demons** and not real alterations of substance.

MIDWIVES. A great deal of modern scholarship on **witchcraft** maintains that midwives were especially vulnerable to accusations of this crime, and figured prominently in many trials. As healers, they were widely believed to have access to spells for **magical healing** and other occult remedies, and they could easily become suspect of wrongdoing if a birth did not go well. Much feminist scholarship in particular has focused on the idea of the supposed midwife-witch. Observing that midwives occupied one of only a few positions of public power and authority open to **women** in premodern Europe, these scholars have argued that the tarring of midwives with accusations of witchcraft was an attempt by male authorities to reduce or eliminate powerful, independent roles for women in society. Recently, however, the entire premise of such arguments has been called into serious question. Careful study of trial records reveals that very few midwives were ever actually accused of witchcraft. Rather than vulnerable and marginal members of society, they had to be respectable and trusted in order to succeed in their profession. It now seems clear that many historians have been led astray by a few spectacular cases, by the extended reference to midwife-witches in the infamous **witch-hunting** manual *Malleus maleficarum* (noted for a level of misogyny that is not, in fact, present in many other major treatises on witchcraft or **demonology**), and by a tradition of association that originated in the now-discredited work of **Margaret Murray**.

MODERN WITCHCRAFT. *See* WICCA.

MOLITOR, ULRICH (ca. 1442–1507/08). An early author on **witchcraft**, Molitor was born in the southern German city of Constance. He was educated there and at the university at Pavia, where he received his degree in canon law. He served as an official in the episcopal court in Constance and then in the court of Duke Siegmund of Tirol. It was while in the service of the duke that he composed his treatise *De lamiis and phitonicis mulieribus* (Concerning Witches and Women Fortunetellers), completed in 1489. Molitor wrote this work in the form of a dialogue between those who accepted the idea of witchcraft and those who did not, and thereby revealed how this concept was still taking shape and gaining credence in the late 15th century. He concluded, for example, following the tradition of the **canon** *Episcopi*, that witches did not really fly through the night to a **sabbath**, but argued that the nature of their **heresy** remained the same, even if their actions at the sabbath (devil-worship, rejection of the Christian faith, and so forth) were only illusory. Many of his ideas about witchcraft were influenced by the inquisitor **Heinrich Kramer**, who had conducted several witch trials in Tirol, and whose own great treatise on **witch-hunting**, *Malleus maleficarum*, had been published only a few years earlier in 1487.

MONTAIGNE, MICHEL DE (1533–1595). One of the most important French philosophers of the early-modern period, Montaigne exhibited a powerful **skepticism** and uncertainty about the basis of human knowledge in almost every area. His guiding motto was *que sais-je?*

(what do I know?). He did not deny the reality of **witchcraft** outright, but rather argued that, given human nature, it was likely that human deceit or error were involved in most cases of supposed witchcraft. Given this uncertainty, it was generally unwise, he maintained, for authorities to prosecute people as witches.

MORA WITCHES. One of the most severe **witch-hunts** in **Scandinavia** occurred in 1669 in Mora, Sweden. Like the later trials at **Salem**, Massachusetts, which they influenced, the trials at Mora were instigated mainly by the accusations of **children**. In July 1668, a 15-year-old boy accused an 18-year-old girl of stealing children for the **devil**. The next year, a royal commission was appointed to investigate the matter. This investigation, which relied heavily on the testimony of children, uncovered a major supposed diabolic conspiracy. Witches would kidnap children in the night and spirit them away to a **sabbath** held in a mythic location known as Blåkulla. Several hundred children came forward with similar testimony about being kidnapped. Although the case certainly represents a major hunt by Scandinavian standards, the figures in the Mora trials have often been exaggerated. In all, some 60 suspects were interrogated, and 23 people were sentenced to death. These executions also helped to inspire other trials in a panic that spread throughout Sweden, eventually reaching the capital at Stockholm and even into Swedish possessions in Finland.

MORGAN LE FEY. One of the major characters in the legends and literature surrounding the mythic King Arthur of Britain, Morgan le Fey (i.e., Morgan the fairy) is depicted as a powerful sorceress. Although she is either Arthur's sister or half-sister, and although the 15th-century author Thomas Mallory described her as learning her magic in a nunnery, there are elements of pre-Christian supernaturalism about her. Although far removed from the typical image of the witch in late-medieval and early-modern Europe, nevertheless Morgan provided a literary archetype for powerful and threatening female magic.

MURRAY, MARGARET (1863–1963). A British Egyptologist, archeologist, and anthropologist, early in the 20th century, Murray developed the theory that historical **witchcraft** was in fact the remnant of an ancient **pagan** fertility religion. Her ideas were viewed with skepticism in the academic community, but in the 1950s **Gerald Gardner**, the founder of modern witchcraft, or **Wicca**, was inspired by them. Murray, born to British parents in Calcutta, studied Egyptology at the University of London and became a professional academic Egyptologist. She was also interested in anthropology, however, and especially in the history of witchcraft. In 1921, she published her first book on this subject, *The Witch-Cult in Western Europe,* in which she argued that witches really had existed in medieval and early-modern Europe, not as Christian **heretics** or devil-worshipers, but as clandestine practitioners of a pre-Christian fertility religion. She was inspired by the anthropologist James Frazer's theories about fertility cults in his famous book *The Golden Bough* (1890). In her second book on witchcraft, *The God of the Witches* (1931), she traced the history of the **Horned God**, a male pagan fertility deity. She claimed that this horned deity was the basis for the idea of the **devil** presiding over a witches' **sabbath**. Her most radical book, however, was her last, *The Divine King of England* (1954). Here she maintained that every English king from William the Conqueror in the 11th century to **James I** in the 17th was secretly a practitioner of the ancient fertility religion of witchcraft and that the deaths of many important figures in English history could be explained as ritual murders committed by this fertility cult.

Murray never advanced any strong evidence to support her theories, her arguments were based mostly on conjecture and coincidence (and in her final book, at least, on outright conspiracy theories), and her ideas were always controversial in the academic community. Since the publication of her final book in the 1950s, her ideas have been almost completely discredited. However, her theories were an important inspiration for modern witchcraft. In his book *Witchcraft Today,* for which Murray wrote the introduction, Gerald Gardner, the founder of modern witchcraft, maintained that he had discovered a surviving **coven** of traditional, hereditary witches. He claimed that he had been initiated into their ancient religion, which he intended to reintroduce to the modern world. For a time, the idea that witchcraft was a direct survival of an ancient pagan religion was an essential part of Wiccan belief. By the 1990s, however, in the face of mounting historical evidence to the contrary, most Wiccans had abandoned Murray's theory.

– N –

NECROMANCY. Technically referring to a form of **divination** that involves summoning the spirits of the dead, throughout much of the medieval and early-modern periods, necromancy came to mean demonic magic, and specifically a complex, learned form of ritual demonic invocation. Some of this confusion might have arisen from the Christian notion that the spirits of the dead, be they in heaven or hell, could not be summoned to return to earth, and so any sorcerer or diviner claiming to do so was in reality summoning **demons** who merely took the form of a dead person. The famous **Witch of Endor**, for example, who is described in the **Bible** as summoning the spirit of the dead prophet Samuel for King Saul, was widely thought by medieval authorities to have summoned a demon instead.

In the early Middle Ages, ecclesiastical authorities largely dismissed the potential power and reality of demonic magic, believing that demons typically engaged only in deception and illusion. However, in the 12th and 13th centuries, a large number of classical, Jewish, and Arab texts describing learned magical practices were discovered or rediscovered in Western Europe. Some of these systems of magic involved rituals to summon spirits or even explicitly to summon demons. Many European clerics became interested in this new form of learning, and the practice of necromancy began to spread (although still, of course, limited to a small and clandestine group).

Based on learned texts and ancient traditions, necromancy in the later Middle Ages was clearly an elite form of magic restricted to the educated, and often to the clerical, classes. It typically entailed using complex, often quasi-religious ceremonies and rituals to summon and command demons. Such magic was not suited to the masses and could never become widespread. However, it did serve to increase ecclesiastical concern over demonic magic generally. Although many necromancers were in fact clerics of some level, ecclesiastical authorities became concerned that, instead of commanding the demons they invoked, they were worshiping them. By the late 14th century, arguments were established that almost all demonic magic necessarily involved the worship of demons. This belief helped pave the way for the demonization of common harmful **sorcery**, or *maleficium*, and the development of the idea of widespread demonic **witchcraft** in the centuries to come.

NEO-PAGANISM. In the second half of the 20th century, a wide variety of new religious systems emerged, largely based on nature worship and New-Age spirituality, and patterned off of or maintaining a supposed connection to ancient pre-Christian European religions, mainly varieties of Celtic and Norse **paganism**. These are collectively referred to as new- or neo-paganism. Modern **witchcraft**, or **Wicca**, comprises by far the largest segment of the neo-pagan spectrum of movements.

Although by no means adhering to a single unified or coherent system of belief, most forms of neo-paganism share certain basic similarities. They arose after World War II and first began coming to prominence in the 1960s as a response to the notion that the traditional Western religions no longer adequately met modern spiritual needs and were in fact authoritarian and repressive, particularly to **women**. Most neo-pagan groups stress a high degree of individuality and tolerance for individual spiritual pursuits, provided these do not infringe on the rights of others or bring harm to other people. Groups as widely disparate as modern witchcraft and modern **Satanism** adhere to the basic creed, first advanced by the English ritual magician and occultist **Aleister Crowley**: if it harms none, do what you will. Most forms of neo-paganism stress worship and concern for nature, and thus are closely tied to the rise of modern environmentalist ideologies, and many varieties of neo-paganism also place a high emphasis on feminine spirituality, according women an equal if not superior place to men in their systems of belief and practice. Thus, neo-paganism, and especially Wicca, can be seen as related to the growth of modern feminist ideologies since the 1960s and 1970s. Most modern pagans also practice ritual magic in some form and believe in its real efficacy.

NEW ENGLAND. *See* COLONIAL AMERICA, WITCHCRAFT IN.

NIDER, JOHANNES (ca. 1385–1438). A Dominican friar, theologian, and religious reformer, Nider wrote some of the most extensive and important early accounts of **witchcraft** to appear in Europe in the first half of the 15th century. Above all his *Formicarius* (The Anthill—a moralizing dialogue between a theologian and student that takes ants as its organizing image), written mostly in 1437 and early 1438, was very influential. It was printed in seven separate editions from the late 1400s down to 1692, in other words throughout the entire period of the great **witch-hunts**. In addition, it served as an important source of information for the later Dominican **Heinrich Kramer**, author of the *Malleus maleficarum*, first published in 1487. The fifth book of the *Formicarius,* which deals specifically with "Witches and their Deceptions," was printed along with the *Malleus* in some later editions.

Born sometime in the early 1380s in the small town of Isny in Swabia in what is now southern Germany, Nider studied at Cologne and Vienna. He then attended the **Council of Basel**, where he began collecting many contemporary stories and examples of witchcraft that he would include in his *Formicarius*. In that work, he described witchcraft in much the form that it would take throughout the later period of the witch-hunts. Witches were evil sorcerers who performed harmful **sorcery**, *maleficium,* with the aid of **demons**. They attained this power by surrendering themselves to Satan. Gathering at secret nocturnal conventicles (Nider never used the terms synagogue or **sabbath**), they worshiped a presiding demon or the **devil** himself, offered sacrifices to him, desecrated the cross and other religious objects, killed and ate babies and young **children**, and engaged in sexual **orgies**. Nider never described witches as flying to such gatherings, and elsewhere in the *Formicarius* he explicitly denied the reality of **night flight**, although he did not deny the basic power of demons to transport people through the air if they wished.

In another work, the *Preceptorium divinae legis* (Preceptor of Divine Law), Nider attempted to provide a guide to various problems of religious belief and practice based on the Ten Commandments. In this work, he included some important sections on demonic magic and witchcraft under the heading of the First Commandment, which stated that one should not worship any other deities before the one Hebrew, and later Christian, God. Demonic invocation, magic, and witchcraft were thought by medieval theologians to entail the worship of demons and thus constituted **idolatry**.

One particularly important aspect of the witch stereotype that Nider developed was the presumption that **women** were more inclined toward witchcraft than men. In fact, Nider was the first learned authority to advance this position. Although he presented many examples of male witches, he also discussed many female witches. Nider described women as weaker than men in body, mind, and spirit. Thus they were more prone to the seductions and temptations of the devil and submitted more quickly to his service than men. This basic line of argument would become much more pronounced in the extremely misogynist *Malleus maleficarum*.

NIGHT FLIGHT. Witches were widely supposed to have the power to fly through the air. In particular, they were thought to fly to their secret nocturnal gatherings, known as **sabbaths**. They often did so on **brooms**, staves, or occasionally on animals, and this became the standard image of the night flight of witches. The idea of malevolent supernatural beings or of humans empowered by supernatural beings flying through the night and bringing harm to unsuspecting innocents is ancient and widespread, appearing in some form in many human cultures throughout history. In Christian Europe, the idea was codified at least as early as the famous 10th-century **canon** *Episcopi*, and the beliefs upon which the canon was based clearly went back much further, most likely to Germanic notions of the **Wild Hunt**.

The canon *Episcopi* described groups of "wicked **women**, who . . . believe and profess that, in the hours of the night, they ride upon certain beasts with **Diana**, the goddess of the pagans, and an innumerable multitude of women, and in the silence of the night traverse great spaces of earth." The canon went on to state, however, that this belief was entirely false and that such supposed flight was only an illusion created by **demons**. Throughout the Middle Ages, such beliefs were often associated with the practice of **sorcery**, but authorities generally paid them little concern. Only in the 15th century, as the idea of the witches' sabbath began to develop, did the idea of night flight become particularly important. Such flight began to be regarded as the means by which witches would travel to their secret nocturnal gatherings. This meant, however, that if authorities wanted to regard the events of a sabbath as real, night flight also had to be real, and they had to disregard the tradition of the canon *Episcopi*. Some authorities decided that flight must still be an illusion, and so, therefore, must the entire sabbath, but they concluded that accused witches might still be condemned just for believing that they had taken part in such an event. Most authorities, however, were able to argue for the reality of night flight. Because the ability of demons to transport objects through the air was accepted, they argued that although such flight could sometimes be an illusion as stated in the canon *Episcopi*, there was no reason that, in other cases, it could not be entirely real.

There is now much evidence to support the idea that the widespread belief in night flight throughout Europe was at least partially based on the survival, in practice or simply in common folklore, of certain forms of archaic **shamanism**. In many different locations throughout Europe, historians and anthropologists have uncovered ideas of special people or groups of people who were believed to be able to travel at night in spirit form, most often to battle evil spirits in order to ensure fertility for the coming season. The most well-known example of such a group would be the ***benandanti*** of northern Italy. Surviving fragments of such beliefs, misinterpreted by authorities or misremembered by the people themselves, may well have contributed to the concepts of night flight and the witches' sabbath across Europe.

NORTH BERWICK WITCHES. The trials of the so-called North Berwick witches are among the most famous in **Scottish** history, mainly because of the direct participation of the Scottish king, **James VI** (later also **James I** of England). The experience of these trials, held in 1590 and 1591, probably provided the king with important inspiration to write his *Daemonologie* (Demonology), first published in 1597. The trials began when a maid named Gillis Duncan, a resident of the town of Traneten near Edinburgh, began to exhibit certain apparently magical **healing** powers. Her employer was convinced that she must be a witch. She was interrogated and the **devil's mark** was found on her throat. She was imprisoned and forced to implicate other witches from Edinburgh and the surrounding region. These people were also arrested, and several were questioned in the presence of King James VI, who had an interest in matters of **witchcraft** and **demonology**. **Torture** was used, and eventually confessions were extracted. The witches supposedly met at regular **sabbaths** in the town of North Berwick, about 25 miles east of Edinburgh. These gatherings might be attended by as many as 100 witches. In particular, the accused confessed to trying to kill the king by raising a **storm** at sea as he journeyed back from Denmark. The trials of the North Berwick witches helped to inspire an upsurge in other trials around Scotland.

– O –

OBSCENE KISS. The *osculum infame* or obscene kiss refers to the kiss witches were often thought to have to give the **devil** on his buttocks or anus as a sign of their homage and subservience to him while he presided over a witches' **sabbath**. A kiss was a typical sign of reverence in medieval society, and a kiss on the anus symbolized the profound inversion and obscenity entailed in **witchcraft**. Similar actions such as kissing **demons** or animals (the devil was often thought to preside over a sabbath in animal form) had earlier been attributed to medieval heretical groups.

OBSESSION. *See* POSSESSION.

OINTMENTS. Supposedly magical ointments might consist of almost any grease-like substance spread over the body or some object. Historically, witches were thought to use ointments in many of their magical operations. The two chief uses of ointments were as **poison** to kill people or cause disease, and for **night flight**. Witches were commonly thought to know many recipes, often supposedly learned from the **devil** in the context of a witches' **sabbath**, for making poisonous ointments that they would then spread on peoples' skin to injure or kill them. Witches were also often thought to anoint themselves or various instruments such as **brooms** with other ointments in order to fly. Use of such ointments has led to speculation on the part of some scholars that at least some aspects of witchcraft can be attributed to the use of hallucinogenic compounds. Recipes for certain ointments supposedly used by witches are recorded in treatises on **witchcraft**. Some of these would clearly be toxic. Others, if spread on the skin, could produce a trance-like state and delusions of flight.

ORGIES. In medieval and early-modern Europe, witches were thought to be sexually driven and sexually promiscuous people. One of the main features in descriptions of the witches' **sabbath** was the participation of witches in sexual orgies with each other and with **demons** who were also present at these gatherings. The notion of people gathering in secret and engaging in wild, orgiastic rites was a common element of medieval clerical diatribes against most forms of **heresy**, carried over and applied also to witches when the concept of a diabolically organized, heretical cult of witches developed in the late Middle Ages. Certain aspects of the stereotype might have derived from surviving descriptions of ancient **pagan** fertility festivals, such as the Roman **Bacchanalia**. Within modern **witchcraft**, or **Wicca**, certain groups perform some rituals nude (*skyclad,* as it is often termed). This is thought to reduce inhibitions within the group and promote the flow of magical energies. Some critics of Wicca, however, fixate on such practices and continue to associate modern witchcraft with sexual immorality.

– P –

PACTS, DEMONIC. The notion of a pact with **demons** or with the **devil**, either explicit or tacit, was for Christian authorities in medieval and early-modern Europe an essential element of most forms of **sorcery**, and this was one of the central crimes entailed in **witchcraft**. The roots of the Christian notion of the demonic pact are found in the **Bible**, chiefly Isaiah 28:15, given in the early-modern King James' Version as, "We have made a covenant with death and with hell we are at agreement." The medieval Latin Vulgate actually uses the word pact: "... *et cum inferno fecimus pactum.*" Early church fathers such as Origen (185–254) and **Augustine of Hippo** (354–430) began to link the performance of sorcery and **divination** to pacts made with demons. Augustine in particular viewed the entire world in terms of a struggle between demonic and divine power, and he contrasted the evil of demonic magic starkly with the good and salvational power of divine miracle in his famous *City of God* and other works. His notions of demonic pacts would form the essential foundation on which all later Western Christian thought on this subject was based.

For much of the early Middle Ages, Christian authorities seem to have been relatively less concerned about real demonic power in the world than they would later become, although Augustine's notions of demonic pacts did enter into official ecclesiastical canon law at this time. Around the 12th century, Christian authorities became increasingly concerned about demonic activity. In the 13th century, the great theologian **Thomas Aquinas** began to develop the notion of the demonic pact and its connections to demonic sorcery to a further extent. By the end of the 14th century, the theologian and inquisitor **Nicolau Eymeric** developed a detailed argument proving that all demonic sorcery necessarily involved the agreement and cooperation of demons. Sorcerers had to worship these demons and form pacts with them, either explicitly or implicitly, and so were guilty of terrible **idolatry** and **heresy**.

When the full stereotype of European witchcraft finally developed in the 15th century, the pact with the devil was central to the entire concept of how witchcraft supposedly operated. Typically at a **sabbath**, new witches were thought to be required to renounce their faith and swear loyalty to the devil. Increasingly, accounts came to describe a formal, written agreement signed by the witch, often in blood. The notion of a pact made with the devil in order to attain wealth, power, or worldly pleasure also existed outside of the stereotype of witchcraft. Probably the most famous story of a human entering into a pact with the devil is that of the German magician **Faust**.

PAGANISM. Historically used by Christian religious authorities to refer to any form of polytheistic religious belief, in contrast to the three main monotheistic religions of the West—Christianity, Islam, and Judaism—the term *paganism* derives from the Latin *pagus*, meaning the countryside, and *paganus*, meaning rustic people, generally. In late antiquity, as Christianity became the dominant religion in the Roman world, it was initially centered in the cities, and so early Christians began to use the term *pagan* to describe those who held to the older, polytheistic religions of the ancient world. During the Middle Ages, Celtic, Germanic, and Slavic tribes that had not yet converted to Christianity were labeled *pagans*. There is no evidence of any direct connection between historical **witchcraft** and paganism in any form. However, in the late 19th and early 20th centuries, certain professional and amateur scholars, most notably the British Egyptologist and anthropologist **Margaret Murray**, advanced the argument that historical witchcraft actually represented the covert but direct survival of pagan religion into the Christian era. Encountering pagan rituals still practiced among the common people, Christian authorities supposedly condemned these practices as devil-worship and thus created the stereotype of witchcraft and cults of witches gathering at ritual **sabbaths**.

Although certain elements of the historical stereotype of witchcraft were clearly influenced by the remnants of some ancient, pre-Christian practices, for example the **shamanistic** fertility rites practiced by the northern Italian *benandanti*, the notion that pagan religiosity survived intact throughout the medieval and early-modern periods never found any firm support and has long since been discredited in historical scholarship. Nevertheless, such notions were crucial to the development of modern witchcraft, or **Wicca**. The early founders of this movement, following the arguments of Margaret Murray, believed or at least claimed they believed that they had rediscovered an authentic, ancient, pagan religion. Even within Wicca, this view has since largely been abandoned, however, and most modern witches, along with practitioners of other variants of modern **neo-paganism**, recognize that they are developing new religious systems creatively based on ancient, pagan models.

PARACELSUS (PHILIPPUS AUREOLUS THEOPHRASTUS BOMBAST VON HOHENHEIM) (1493–1541). A Swiss physician and **alchemist**, Paracelsus was never involved in any aspect of **witchcraft**, and he was in fact **skeptical** of much magic based on incantation and ritual demonic invocation. He did, however, believe strongly in what might be called *natural magic*. That is, he believed that occult properties and powers existed in natural substances and throughout the natural world, including the stars and planets. Magicians, sorcerers, and **cunning men and women**, he felt, often knew how to employ these natural properties for magical **healing** or for other purposes. Using such practices, common healers often excelled educated physicians in the effectiveness of their remedies.

After studying medicine in Vienna and Italy, Paracelsus traveled extensively throughout Europe. Originally going by his given name of Theophrastus, he eventually took the name Paracelsus to denote his connection to the famous ancient Roman physician Celsus. He gained a considerable reputation as a healer. His acerbic personality, however, guaranteed that he was never popular, and he rarely stayed in one position for very long.

PENTAGRAM. The pentagram or pentacle, a five-pointed star usually inscribed within a circle, is an important religious symbol for modern **witchcraft**, or **Wicca**. The five points of the star are typically interpreted as representing the divine, or alternately humanity, in harmony with the four natural elements. This symbol has little association with historical witchcraft. Magical circles of various sorts, often with stars or other occult symbols inscribed within them, were frequently employed to perform ritual magic, especially ritual demonic magic or **necromancy**, in the medieval and early-modern periods. The use of such symbols was then revived in the modern era by occult groups such as the **Hermetic Order of the Golden Dawn**. An inverted pentagram (with a single point of the star facing down as opposed to the Wiccan pentagram in which the single point faces up) has also been adopted as the symbol of **Baphomet** by the modern **Church of Satan**, and this or similar symbols are frequently used by many groups practicing modern **Satanism**.

PERKINS, WILLIAM (1555–1602). A major English authority on **demonology**, **witchcraft**, and **witch-hunting**, Perkins was a fellow of Christ's College at Cambridge. His major work, *Discourse on the Damned Art of Witchcraft,* was published posthumously in 1608 and soon surpassed even the *Daemonologie* of **King James I** to become the standard authority on matters of witchcraft in **England** in the 17th century. Perkins relied heavily on the **Bible** for his condemnation of witchcraft, but drew relatively little from earlier, continental authorities, with the notable exception of **Nicholas Rémy**, on whom he relied heavily

PICCO DELLA MIRANDOLA, GIANFRANCESCO (1469–1533). A nephew of the more famous Renaissance philosopher Giovanni Picco della Mirandola, Gianfrancesco was also a Renaissance **humanist** by training. He did not, however, share in the **skepticism** about **witchcraft** that some humanists showed. In 1523, he was present for several witch trials in Bologna, and from this experience he wrote *Strix sive de ludificatione daemonum* (Strix, or the Deceptions of Demons—**strix** was a term for witches at this time). In this dialogue, several characters debate about the reality of witchcraft and then question an actual witch. In the end, the skeptical character in the dialogue is convinced of the error of his position and accepts the reality of witchcraft. Written in Latin, the work was translated into Italian as early as 1524.

POISON. Historical witches were often accused of using poisons to harm or kill others. In some cases, people accused of **witchcraft** may in fact have been skilled herbalists capable of producing very dangerous poisons. The root of the **mandrake** plant, for example, often associated with witchcraft, could be very toxic. More often, however, the supposed link between witchcraft and poisoning was more fantastic. Witches were often described as receiving various poisons, along with other magical **ointments**, from the **devil** at a witches' **sabbath**. They would use these poisons to kill or injure people at the devil's command.

POLAND. *See* EASTERN EUROPE, WITCHCRAFT IN.

POSSESSION, DEMONIC. Referring to cases where a **demon** or the **devil** has supposedly entered a person's body and taken control over physical actions and to some extent the mind and personality, possession, and its near equivalent obsession, in which demons were thought to afflict people from outside of their bodies, was often associated with **witchcraft**. Witches were believed to be able to send demons to afflict people whom they wished to harm. In cases of possession, they often employed some item of bewitched food to convey the demonic spirit into the person. According to some authorities, apples were particularly useful for this sort of activity. In cases of obsession, the demon was sometimes thought to appear, visible only to the person it was afflicting, in the form of the witch herself. This formed a basis for some cases of **spectral evidence**.

During the Middle Ages, the church prescribed **exorcism** as a remedy for possession. The basis for the power of exorcism, as for possession itself, is found in the **Bible**, primarily the New Testament passages in Matthew 8:28–32, Mark 5:2–13, and Luke 8:27–33, in which Christ encounters a possessed man (or two possessed people in Matthew's account) and frees him by commanding the demons to enter a herd of swine, which then drown themselves. In early Christianity, possession, and more so obsession, was often thought to be a sign of holiness. Much early Christian **demonology** was developed in the deserts of Egypt by hermit monks who frequently believed themselves to be assailed by and in spiritual conflict with demons. By the later Middle Ages and the early-modern period, possessed people were often thought to have been victims of witchcraft. Perhaps the most famous such case occurred in a convent in the French town of **Loudun** where several nuns claimed to have been possessed because of the **sorcery** of a local priest. The charges were false and in fact were politically motivated, and the whole affair was a ruse, but the priest was, nevertheless, eventually burned at the stake. Another famous case linking possession to witchcraft occurred in **Salem**, Massachusetts, where a major **witch-hunt** began when several young girls began to exhibit signs of possession, obsession, and bewitchment.

Throughout the period of the witch-hunts, exorcism remained a common remedy for possession in Catholic lands. In Protestant countries, where the clergy had abandoned the formal rite of exorcism, people resorted to prayer. In addition, to free themselves from supposed demonic assault, people often turned to a variety of common spells and charms that could be acquired from **cunning men and women**. The causes of possession could vary, from outright deception as in the Loudun case, and possibly in the case of Salem as well, to real mental illness or dementia. Authorities did recognize that some cases of apparent possession might be caused by such factors, and many **skeptical** authorities, such as **Johann Weyer**, argued that many aspects of witchcraft and demonic activity were in fact signs of physical diseases and should be treated medically, not spiritually.

PRICKING. A method of detecting witches during the period of the major European **witch-hunts** was to prick the skin of suspects with a needle or some sharp object. Witches were often thought to have dead areas of skin that would not bleed and were insensitive to pain. Such an area of flesh was evidence of the **devil's mark**, a spot where the **devil** had branded the witch in his service. The process of pricking was especially humiliating because it required the suspected witch, usually a **woman**, to disrobe before authorities. Such marks were generally thought to be located on very private and thus easily concealed areas of the body, such as near the genitalia, although they could be found anywhere and were even thought to move around the body.

PROTESTANT REFORMATION. *See* REFORMATION.

– R –

REFORMATION. The Protestant Reformation of the 16th century and the Catholic Counter-Reformation that occurred to some extent in response to the Protestant challenge contributed to the fear of **witchcraft** in Europe in complex ways. Although Protestant leaders like **Martin Luther** and **Jean Calvin** rejected many aspects of medieval theology and canon law, they did not challenge any of the basic notions of medieval **demonology** on which the idea of diabolical witchcraft rested. In fact, many Protestant leaders were acutely concerned about the power of the **devil** to assail human beings on earth. In Calvinist Scotland, for example, and especially in Puritan **New England**, the severity of the **witch-hunts** was at least partly caused by the profound concern of religious leaders over demonic and diabolic threats to their communities. Severe witch-hunts also took place in Catholic lands, however, and there were many Protestant lands where witch-hunting was relatively mild, so concern over witchcraft was clearly not linked exclusively to any one religious confession.

The social and political conflicts that emerged out of the Reformation, and especially the bloody religious wars that gripped Europe in the 16th and 17th centuries, seem to have contributed to witch-hunting only indirectly. That is, there is no clear correlation between confessional strife and frequency of witch trials, although confessional conflict certainly added to the general level of social instability that, in turn, might have led to increased concern over witchcraft and facilitated witch-hunting. The increased attention to issues of morality and concern over personal and communal religious belief that arose in this period caused by both the Protestant and Catholic Reformations also certainly helped to create a general atmosphere in which the fear of witches and witch-hunting could flourish.

RÉMY, NICHOLAS (1530–1612). An important French demonologist who claimed personally to have condemned over 900 witches in trials during a 10-year period in Lorraine, Rémy is the author of *Daemonolatreiae* (Demonolatry), first published in 1595. This became one of the major treatises on **witchcraft** and **demonology** of the 17th century, ranking in importance with those of **Jean Bodin** and **Martin Del Rio**. The authority of Rémy's treatise was augmented by the author's extensive personal experience with witches and in conducting witch trials.

Born at Charmes in Lorraine, Rémy came from a family of lawyers and in his turn went to study law at the university in Toulouse. After serving in Paris from 1563 until 1570, he became Lieutenant General of his native *département* of Vosges in Lorraine. Shortly thereafter, he became privy councilor to the duke of Lorraine. It was in this period that Rémy claimed to have sentenced over 900 witches, although this number cannot be confirmed from surviving records and he himself only mentions 128 witches by name. He began to become concerned about witchcraft, apparently, in 1582, when his oldest son died only shortly after Rémy had refused alms to an old beggar woman. Convinced that she was a witch who had murdered his son, he put her on trial. In 1591, he was appointed attorney general of Lorraine and was able to influence the prosecution of witches in the entire region. In 1592, an epidemic struck the city of Nancy, and Rémy left for an extended stay at a country estate, where he began composing the treatise based on his experiences.

RENAISSANCE. *See* HUMANISM.

RUSSIA. *See* EASTERN EUROPE, WITCHCRAFT IN.

– S –

SABBATH, WITCHES'. As conceived by both religious and secular authorities in the late-medieval and early-modern periods, **witchcraft** entailed membership in a heretical, explicitly diabolic cult. Authorities were thus convinced that witches gathered at secret, typically nocturnal assemblies, where they would summon **demons** or Satan himself, offer up their worship, receive instructions, and engage in a variety of nefarious and horrific activities. Most aspects of the witches' sabbath (also known early on as a *synagogue*) were clearly derived from long-standing medieval stereotypes concerning **heresy** and heretical cults, and some stereotypes concerning **Jews**, although these stereotypes were of course modified and some elements were unique to the witches' sabbath. Perhaps the most notable unique element was the concept of **night flight**, that is, that witches would fly on certain nights to very large gatherings, often held on remote mountain peaks. The concept of the sabbath was crucial to the development of **witch-hunting** because it implied that witches did not act alone, but rather as part of a large, diabolically organized conspiracy, and that any accused witch could be expected, indeed often required, to identify other witches.

The idea of the sabbath developed in the 15th century. At this time, ecclesiastical authorities, especially inquisitors, were taking a major interest in demonic magic and **sorcery**. Demonic magic had always been associated with heresy. By the late 14th century, the inquisitor **Nicolau Eymeric** provided the definitive theological argument that demonic magic necessarily entailed the worship of demons and was thus always heretical. It was, therefore, natural for authorities to begin associating stereotypical heretical behavior with witches. All of the sources on witchcraft from the early 15th century included some mention of the notion that witches were members of diabolical cults that met in secret. The most explicit in these terms was the ***Errores Gazariorum*** (Errors of the Gazarii), a brief tract that referred to such gatherings as synagogues, and described them in horrible detail. By 1458, the inquisitor **Nicholas Jacquier**, in his *Flagellum haereticorum fascinariorum* (Scourge of Heretical Witches), was using the term *sabbath.*

Descriptions of the witches' sabbath could vary, but certain general characteristics were almost always present. Witches would gather in secret at night. They would most typically fly to a sabbath on **brooms**, staves, or other common items, although some authorities, especially early on, denied the reality of such flight. In this, they followed the tradition of the **canon *Episcopi*,** which stated that such night flight was only an illusion caused by demons. Following this argument, these authorities then had to maintain that the entire experience of the sabbath was only an illusion. For most authorities, however, the horrors of a sabbath were terribly real. At these gatherings, witches would invoke their demonic master, often summoning the **devil** himself, who would typically appear in the form of a black **cat**, **goat**, or other animal. Witches would then formally renounce their Christian faith and offer him their worship, usually symbolized by the *osculum infame* or **obscene kiss** on the devil's buttocks or anus. They would also engage in feasts, dancing, and other revels, culminating in indiscriminate sexual **orgies** with each other and with the attendant demons. Sources typically revel in relating how men coupled with men and women with women, and even members of the same family with one another—brothers with sisters, and mothers and fathers with sons and daughters. The murder of babies and young **children** also typically played an important part in the sabbath. Witches either killed and ate these children as part of their feasts, boiled down the bodies to make magical powders, potions, and **ointments**, or they did both. The size of a sabbath could vary from a small group of 10 or 20 witches (there is no historical evidence for the supposedly traditional **coven** of 13) to huge gatherings ranging up to several thousand witches. Perhaps the greatest sabbath was that supposedly celebrated each April 30 on *Walpurgisnacht* on the peak of the Brocken in the Harz Mountains in Germany.

The sabbath obviously was meant to symbolize a complete inversion of every imaginable aspect of natural order—religious, sexual, social, and familial norms were all horrifically subverted. Most of the aspects of the sabbath—worship of the devil in animal form, the obscene kiss, desecration of religious artifacts, sexual orgies, etc.—were drawn directly from earlier medieval stereotypes about gatherings of heretical cults. The murder and **cannibalism** of babies was often associated with both heretics and Jews in the Middle Ages. There is some credible evidence that aspects of the sabbath, especially night flight, were derived from common folk beliefs. Thus, the sabbath may in part represent the remnants of archaic **shamanism**, belief in nocturnal spirit battles, and other fertility rites evident in many areas of Europe. The most direct roots of the sabbath, however, seem clearly to lie in the linkage between demonic magic and the heretical worship of demons, as well as in standard Christian stereotypes of heretical and non-Christian groups.

SALAZAR FRIAS, ALONSO DE (ca. 1564–1635). A cleric and inquisitor in Spain, in 1609, Salazar Frias was appointed to the regional inquisitorial tribunal in Logroño in the **Basque lands** in northern Spain. Numerous witch trials had been conducted at Logroño, resulting in many hundreds of confessions and convictions. Salazar Frias, however, expressed considerable **skepticism** regarding the procedures used in these trials, and was gravely concerned that convictions were being obtained from inconclusive evidence and forced confessions. The *Suprema,* the central council of the Spanish **Inquisition** in Madrid, directed him to undertake an inspection of the courts throughout the region for which his tribunal was responsible. In an investigation in 1611 and 1612, he confirmed his suspicions that many witch trials were being conducted improperly. As a result of his report, the *Suprema* issued a directive to all inquisitorial tribunals throughout Spain, instructing them to enforce stricter procedures in witch trials conducted under their jurisdiction. This careful application of proper legal procedure helped to reduce significantly the number of witch trials, and especially the number of convictions and executions for **witchcraft**, in Spanish lands. *See also* INQUISITORIAL PROCEDURE.

SALEM, WITCHCRAFT AT. The most severe, important, and certainly most famous case of **witch-hunting** in **Colonial America** took place in the summer of 1692 at Salem, Massachusetts. The panic started when some young girls began to exhibit strange symptoms after playing at fortune telling, and ended with 19 people executed by hanging and one being pressed to death. Two more of the accused died while in jail, and a total of more than 100 people were imprisoned. Although witch trials were by no means unknown in New England in the 17th century, the events at Salem were extremely severe given the overall size of the population involved. The 20 executions constitute well over half of all executions for **witchcraft** in the New England colonies for the entire century.

This major outbreak of witch-hunting began when several young girls, including the daughter of the minister of Salem Village, Samuel Parris, began to play at **divination**, trying to learn the identities of their future husbands. Shortly thereafter they began to exhibit nervous symptoms that the people of Salem took to be evidence of demonic **possession** and bewitchment. The symptoms grew worse and spread to other girls and young women. Under questioning, the girls accused three women—Sarah Goode, Sarah Osborne, and a West Indian slave named Tituba—of having bewitched them. Goode and Osborne denied the charges, but Tituba, for reasons unknown, confessed to having had dealings with the **devil**. In the wake of this confession, fear grew and accusations multiplied, spreading from Salem Village to the larger Salem Town and coming to the attention of clergy in Boston, where **Cotton Mather** and other leading ministers debated the matter. They expressed caution and the need for reliable evidence. Mather was especially concerned about the reliance on **spectral evidence**, in which victims claimed to have seen the spectral shape of a witch, invisible to others, tormenting them. Nevertheless, these ministers did nothing to halt the trials and in fact encouraged local authorities to root out all potential witches. The first execution took place on June 10, 1692, and the last on September 22.

After the executions, however, the severity of the hunt created a backlash. Many people became concerned about the use of evidence in the trials, and **skepticism** about the girls' initial accusations grew. Ultimately, even **Increase Mather**, the father of Cotton Mather, preached the need for restraint in witch trials, arguing that it was better for a true witch to go free than for an innocent person to be killed. Because of this backlash, the trials at Salem effectively marked the end of witch-hunting in New England.

SANDERS, ALEX (1926–1988). The self-proclaimed "King of the Witches," Alex Sanders was an important figure in the early development of modern **witchcraft**, or **Wicca**, in England. He founded the so-called Alexandrian tradition of witchcraft, which differed from the Gardnerian tradition derived from the founder of modern witchcraft, **Gerald Gardner**.

According to Sanders' own account, his grandmother was a hereditary witch, that is, one whose knowledge of witchcraft had been passed down through her family. When he was seven, she initiated him into the ancient religion of the witches. His later writings on witchcraft, however, reveal the strong influence of the writings of Gerald Gardner and others in the Gardnerian tradition. Sanders claimed that these similarities were because Gardner himself had taken many elements from hereditary witchcraft, and that he, Sanders, actually represented a more genuine tradition. Sanders sought publicity to an even greater extent than Gardner did, and he helped to generate much media interest in Wicca in the late 1960s and 1970s. Although Alexandrian witchcraft is rather clearly derived from the original Gardnerian tradition, Sanders introduced some important new elements. He stressed ritual magic much more than Gardner did, and developed more formal and elaborate rites. Some have referred to the Alexandrian tradition as "high church" witchcraft.

SANTERÍA. Like **Voodoo,** Santería is a syncretistic religion in which **African** spirits and deities have been assimilated with Roman Catholic saints and other religious figures. Santería developed first among African slaves brought to the Americas and forced to convert to Catholicism. The religion is now widespread in many parts of Latin America and also in North American cities with large Hispanic populations. Many people see no conflict or difficulty in practicing Santería and Catholicism together. In Santería, deities are known as *orishas.* They are powerful and sometimes capricious in nature. The sacrifice of animals to the *orishas* is a major element of the religion. Typical sacrifices include chickens and roosters, pigeons and doves, and even **goats** and pigs. **Cats** and dogs are often rumored to be used when casting harmful spells. Especially in the United States, this practice arouses strong opposition from people who suspect that these animals are tortured before they are killed, or who fear that pets might be stolen for sacrifice.

Santería is infused with magical practices. The *orishas* can be propitiated to heal illness or injury, to provide good luck, to incite love, or for many other positive purposes. Practitioners of harmful magic or **witchcraft** supposedly also exist, however. These people are often known as *mayomberos* or "black witches." These witches are regarded similarly to how supposed witches were seen during the period of the major European **witch-hunts.** They are entirely evil creatures who frequent graveyards and often employ parts of dead bodies in their spells. The principal tool of the *mayomberos* is a magical cauldron known as a *nganga,* in which such parts can be mixed with other magical ingredients. *Mayomberos* are often considered to be in league with the **devil**.

SATANISM. Referring to the worship of Satan, the Christian **devil,** Satanism has long been associated with **witchcraft.** In the medieval and early-modern periods, Christian authorities, both ecclesiastical and secular, assumed that all witches were in league with Satan. They were guilty of **heresy, idolatry,** and **apostasy**, having supposedly renounced the true faith and offered worship to the devil instead, most notably at secret nocturnal gatherings known as witches' **sabbaths.**

In exchange for this worship, the devil taught them magical arts and gave them power to command **demons** and to perform *maleficium*, harmful **sorcery**, at his direction. Although it is entirely possible that some individuals during the period of the great **witch-hunts** actually did worship Satan, there is absolutely no evidence that most accused witches did so, or that any large, organized Satanist groups ever existed. Rather, the supposed worship of the devil, along with attendance at sabbaths, sexual **orgies**, the murder and **cannibalism** of **children**, and the possession of demonic **familiars** (collectively often referred to as **diabolism**) were largely creations of ecclesiastical and secular authorities forced on people in the course of trials, often through the use of **torture**.

In the modern period, Satanism can have two meanings. Again, it can refer to the supposed worship of the Christian devil. Allegations of the existence of Satanist groups worshiping the devil through animal or human sacrifice, often involving the kidnapping, sexual molestation, and frequently the murder of babies and young children, occur regularly throughout the Western world. Many of the activities detailed in such allegations—secret gatherings of a conspiratorial cult worshiping the devil, performing obscene rites, and harming children—are very reminiscent of historical accusations of witchcraft. No credible evidence has ever been uncovered, however, that any such large, organized form of Satanism really exists.

Modern Satanism can also refer to actual, organized, and open Satanist groups, the largest and most famous of which is the **Church of Satan**, founded in San Francisco in the 1960s. These groups, however, do not really worship Satan in the sense of the actual Christian devil, perceived to be the incarnation of all evil and immorality. Rather, such groups reject the Christian moral structure entirely and idealize instead principles of personal freedom, individuality, and pleasure (often specifically carnal pleasure), which they believe Christianity has wrongly condemned and associated with evil. Such groups actually adhere to their own strict, although non-Christian, moral code, and absolutely forbid the use of animal, let alone human, sacrifice or any form of non-consensual sexual activity, such as the sexual molestation of children.

Neither form of modern Satanism is an aspect of modern witchcraft, or **Wicca**. Actual Satanist groups like the Church of Satan share some basic similarities with modern witchcraft. Both are marked by a rejection of Christianity and both practice and believe in the real efficacy of some forms of magic. Otherwise, however, modern Satanism and modern witchcraft have nothing to do with one another, and indeed the two groups generally have little respect for one another (it should be noted that modern, organized Satanism is an extremely small movement, much smaller than the large and growing number of Wiccan groups). Modern witches are, of course, also sometimes still associated with the other supposed aspects of Satanism—worshiping the devil, killing children, and so forth. Such practices are completely antithetical to modern witchcraft, however, and insofar as there is no credible evidence that any organized groups practice this form of Satanism, there is certainly no evidence that any Wiccan groups do.

SCANDINAVIA, WITCHCRAFT IN. Scandinavia experienced significantly less **witch-hunting** than did the lands of the **German Empire** immediately to its south. As elsewhere in Europe, belief in harmful **sorcery** was widespread in the Scandinavian countries— Denmark, which during this period also ruled Norway, and Sweden, which controlled much of Finland. Yet all told, there were less than 2,000 executions for **witchcraft** in Scandinavian lands. One of the major factors holding down the number of witch-hunts seems to have been a late and incomplete acceptance of the full stereotype of witchcraft, which included **diabolism** as well as the practice of *maleficium*, or harmful sorcery. In addition, the use of **torture** was limited in Scandinavia, although by no means totally restricted.

Perhaps not surprisingly, Denmark, the country closest to the Germanic heartland of the witch craze, experienced the most severe hunts, with around 1,000 executions, a significant number for a country with such a small population (slightly over half a million people). In addition, hunts began there around the middle of the 16th century, earlier than in other regions of Scandinavia. Still the severity of the hunts was limited. In 1547, a law was passed declaring that the testimony of certain criminals, including those guilty of performing sorcery, could not be used to convict others, and this obviously reduced the potential for individual accusations of witchcraft to grow into large hunts. In addition, the application of torture was forbidden until after a death sentence had been passed. In Norway, hunts were even less severe, with only about 350 executions for witchcraft. Most convictions were for *maleficium,* particularly raising **storms** at sea, and did not include much evidence of diabolism, although demonic **pacts** and demonic magic were certainly not unknown.

In Sweden, too, charges of witchcraft generally focused more on *maleficium* than diabolism. Witch trials began in the second half of the 16th century, but less than 500 people were executed in Sweden and Swedish-controlled Finland. Nevertheless, the potential for large hunts did exist. The most severe broke out in 1668 in the north of Sweden and eventually spread to much of the country, including parts of Finland. The panic lasted until 1676, when the central Court of Appeal in Stockholm began to take a more direct role in investigating the evidence (rather than simply confirming convictions as it had done earlier). All told, more than 200 people were executed, making this by far the most severe phase of the witch-hunts in Sweden, although still mild compared to some of the major hunts elsewhere in Europe.

SCOT, MICHAEL (ca. 1175–1235). A scholar in the service of the German emperor Frederick II, Scot was interested in magic and occult learning, especially in systems of **astrology**. He devised categories of permissible and impermissible magic and **divination**, and he wrote about and described methods of demonic invocation, although he was careful to condemn such practices. Despite this care, he developed a dark reputation as a powerful demonic sorcerer, something that often developed around medieval scholars with interests in the occult.

SCOT, REGINALD (1538–1599). One of the earliest and fullest skeptics of **witchcraft,** Scot published his important *Discoverie of Witchcraft* in 1584. It was at the time one of only a handful of books written on the subject in the English language. Scot was born into the landed gentry in Kent and attended Oxford University but did not stay to receive a degree. He was briefly a member of Parliament but lived mostly as a country gentleman. His interest in witchcraft seems to have arisen from pure intellectual curiosity and not from any practical experience or professional involvement. This might help to explain his extreme **skepticism** on the subject.

In his *Discoverie,* Scot went beyond mere criticism of the procedures and methods of witch trials, to which many other critics of **witch-hunting** limited themselves both before and after him. Instead, he attacked the very basis of the idea of witchcraft: the witches' **pact** with the **devil** in exchange for the ability to perform demonic **sorcery**. Scot maintained that the devil had no real power in the physical world, and so even those who truly believed themselves to be witches were incapable of performing any of the acts for which they were held guilty. In fact, Scot felt that most people convicted for witchcraft were either entirely innocent but were victims of trial procedures, especially the use of **torture**, that virtually guaranteed conviction, or they were senile or deluded in some way. There were some witches, he maintained, who did work real harm, but they did so through natural means such as **poison** and not through supernatural demonic powers. Also there were some frauds who claimed to have supernatural power for their own gain. In his skepticism, and especially in his arguments about possible natural and especially medical causes for witchcraft, he was influenced by another skeptical writer, **Johann Weyer**.

SCOTLAND. *See* BRITISH ISLES, WITCHCRAFT IN.

SEXUALITY AND WITCHCRAFT. Historically, **witchcraft** has always been viewed as a highly sexually charged act. Throughout the era of the great **witch-hunts**, witches were commonly thought to engage in sexual activity with **demons** in the form of **incubi and succubi**. Sexual **orgies** were a centerpiece of the witches' **sabbath**, and as a sign of their subservience and degradation, witches were often thought to have sex with the **devil** himself. Many authorities considered that sexual lust and the desire for carnal pleasures were among the chief reasons people became witches, and this was also thought to be one of the reasons that far more **women** became witches than did men. Women were generally considered to be weaker than men, more driven by their appetites and lusts, and far more susceptible to carnal temptations. Sexual relations with demons or the devil were not, however, thought to be pleasurable in most cases, and the sexual organs of these creatures were generally described as being as cold as ice. Sexuality also plays an important role in modern witchcraft, or **Wicca**, although here in an entirely positive way. Much Wiccan belief centers on aspects of natural fertility, and sexual energy, properly channeled, is thought to play an important part in many magical rituals.

SHAMANISM. An aspect of many ancient religious systems, shamanism describes a variety of practices in which individuals enter an ecstatic state and believe that they are able to encounter and interact with spirits and spiritual forces. In recent years, increasing evidence has been uncovered linking certain aspects of historical **witchcraft** to shamanism. The elements of **night flight** and communion with spiritual forces that characterized the witches' **sabbath** were at least partly grounded in recollections of older religious beliefs and practices—the Roman **Bacchanalia** festivities or the Germanic concept of the **Wild Hunt**, for example—that were probably themselves rooted in archaic shamanistic practices. The most famous example of shamanistic practices interacting with Christian notions of witchcraft was the case of the Italian *benandanti*. In the modern period, practitioners of modern witchcraft, or **Wicca**, and other forms of **neo-paganism** sometimes incorporate aspects of shamanism into their beliefs and rituals.

SIMON MAGUS. In the **Bible**, the most famous magician in the New Testament is Simon Magus of Samaria, who is described encountering Peter and John, the apostles of Christ, in Acts 8:9–24. When Simon sees that they can bestow the spirit of God on someone by laying on their hands, he offers them money to receive this power, but Peter refuses him. In apocryphal biblical literature, the rivalry between Simon Magus and the apostle Peter, also called Simon Peter, was amplified. In the so-called Acts of Peter, for example, Simon uses his magic to simulate bringing a dead man back to life, but only Peter is able to truly revive him. Then Simon announces that he will fly up to heaven, but at a word from Peter, he comes crashing to the earth. Later medieval commentators made clear that Simon Magus was being born aloft by **demons** that Peter was able to dispel. In the Middle Ages, Simon Magus became the archetype of the demonic magician or necromancer, and ideas about **necromancy** served as an important basis for later notions of diabolical **witchcraft**.

SKEPTICISM. **Witchcraft** beliefs were never uniform across Europe, and there were always people, including some authorities, who were skeptical of elements of the witch stereotype, the conduct of witch trials, or even of the entire concept of witchcraft. Many authorities were doubtful of the reality of certain aspects of witchcraft, most notably **night flight**. Here authorities could follow the tradition of the early **canon** *Episcopi*, which stated that such flight was only a delusion caused by the **devil**. Since witches were typically assumed to fly to large gatherings known as **sabbaths**, some authorities then argued that the entire experience of the sabbath must also be illusory. Such skepticism, however, had little effect on the overall course of **witch-hunting**, because authorities could still condemn people for believing that they had engaged in the diabolic worship and other horrors of the sabbath, even if these were considered to be only illusory.

Another level of skepticism, which can be termed legal skepticism, focused on the procedures of witch trials, especially the virtually unrestricted use of **torture** in many areas. Some authorities realized that these procedures could be used to ensure that anyone accused of witchcraft would confess, and therefore could be convicted, regardless of actual guilt or innocence. They therefore sought to restrict or eliminate witch trials, although they did not deny the basic possibility of the reality of witchcraft. Perhaps the most famous example of such a skeptic was the German Jesuit **Friedrich Spee**. Such isolated thinkers had little effect on the overall course of the persecution of supposed witches, but more widespread legal skepticism in the late 17th and 18th centuries was an important factor in the curtailment of witch-hunting across much of Europe even before the general belief in witchcraft began to decline.

Of course, there were always some people who were fully skeptical of the reality of witchcraft. Authors like **Johann Weyer**, **Reginald Scot**, and **Balthasar Bekker** denied that the devil had such extensive power over the physical world, or that human beings could enter into **pacts** with **demons**. They thus undermined the very foundations of the idea of witchcraft as it was conceived in medieval and early-modern Europe. Although important, however, such thinkers were always a decided minority and often themselves faced persecution because of their more liberal ideas. *See also* HOBBES, THOMAS; LOOS, CORNELIUS; MALEBRANCHE, NICOLAS; MONTAIGNE, MICHEL DE; PARACELSUS; SALAZAR FRIAS, ALONSO DE.

SORCERY. The term *sorcery* is frequently used as a synonym or near-synonym for magic or **witchcraft**. While the meanings of these words are often vague and certainly overlap, some distinctions can be drawn. First, sorcery is often used to describe low magic, that is, common or unlearned magic. Sorcery is supposedly performed by simple words or actions, whereas forms of high or learned magic are supposedly performed by complex and highly ritualized verbal formulas and ceremonies. In Europe during the medieval and early-modern periods, complex, ritualized demonic magic was often termed **necromancy** and was thought to be quite distinct from common sorcery or witchcraft. Sorcery can also carry implications of negative or harmful magic. In this sense, of connoting simple (or low) and harmful magic, the term *sorcery* is very close to the term *witchcraft*. It is worth noting that the English word *sorcery* derives from the French *sorcellerie*, which means both sorcery and witchcraft. Likewise, the common Latin term to describe harmful sorcery during the Middle Ages and early-modern period, *maleficium*, also came to mean *witchcraft*.

Nevertheless, the concept of sorcery can be usefully distinguished from witchcraft in several ways. First, sorcery does not always carry the connotation of negative or harmful magic. Sorcery can sometimes be used to describe positive forms of magic, such as **magical healing** or magical means of prognostication and **divination**. Some scholars, notably anthropologists studying **African witchcraft**, have distinguished sorcery from witchcraft by arguing that sorcery involves certain performed actions (spoken words or gestures) along with the use of certain material objects to obtain desired supernatural effects while witchcraft draws on some inherent power found in the witch herself. Under this definition, anyone can learn to be a sorcerer, but one must be born a witch. This distinction, while useful when applied to African and other societies, is not as helpful when applied to medieval or early-modern Europe. During the period of the great **witch-hunts**, witches were believed actively to learn how to perform witchcraft from **demons** or from the **devil**, and anyone could become a witch. But witches were also regarded as being in certain ways inherently evil and corrupt because of the **pacts** they made with the devil and their **apostasy** from the true faith.

SOUTHERN EUROPE, WITCHCRAFT IN. The lands of Southern Europe, Spain and Italy, each had a long association with the black arts. Some of the earliest true witch trials in Europe had occurred in Italy, including a trial at Rome in 1426 and one at Todi in 1428. In Spain, it was long rumored that secret schools operated to train pupils in black magic at Toledo and Salamanca (although the training here was more along the lines of learned, ritual demonic magic, or **necromancy**, and not **witchcraft**). Nevertheless, although belief in witchcraft and demonic **sorcery** was widespread, the **witch-hunts** in these lands were relatively mild, especially when one considers the number of executions that the trials produced. In Italy, where the hunts were more severe, probably around 1,000 witches were executed. For comparison, consider the fact that in **Scandinavia**, probably around the same number of witches were executed in Denmark alone, which had a population less than 1/20th that of Italy. In the **British Isles**, England and Scotland, where the combined population numbered about half of Italy's, authorities executed at least 50 percent more witches. Witch-hunts were even more limited in Spain, with only around 300 executions, and virtually no executions took place in Portugal.

The single greatest cause of the limited severity of witch-hunting in southern lands was clearly the presence of large, bureaucratic, and highly centralized ecclesiastical **Inquisitions**. Although papally appointed inquisitors had operated in Europe since the mid-13th century and were in theory answerable to Rome, in fact throughout the Middle Ages they had never been part of any overall, centralized organization. In the early-modern period, in the lands of Southern Europe, such organizations first came into existence. The Spanish Inquisition was created in 1478 as a national institution under the control of the Spanish king, not the pope in Rome. From a supreme council in Madrid, the Inquisition closely controlled the operation of numerous regional tribunals. Similarly, the Holy Office of the Roman Inquisition was founded in 1542 by Pope Paul III to supervise and control the operation of other inquisitorial tribunals throughout Italy (with varying degrees of success—the Inquisition in Venice was notoriously independent).

The existence of these Inquisitions helped to restrain witch-hunting activity in several ways. First, as has been shown to be true of large, centralized judicial structures elsewhere, the Inquisitions were less inclined to panicky reactions based on local fears of witchcraft and were more concerned with matters of procedure and the careful accumulation and weighing of evidence. It is significant to note that charges of **diabolism** in connection to witchcraft, although rooted in Christian **demonology** and theological principles, were largely absent from trials conducted in southern lands. The major exception was the severe outbreak of witch-hunting in the **Basque lands** in northern Spain from 1609 to 1614, in which highly detailed accounts of diabolical **sabbaths** emerged. Nevertheless, the courts in Spain and Italy rarely forced confessions of diabolic activity on the accused, as often happened in northern lands. **Torture** was only rarely applied, and almost always under strict procedural controls. Also, in the absence of clear evidence of diabolism, the courts of the Inquisitions were extremely hesitant to impose death sentences. The accused might still be convicted of performing sorcery of some sort, but this was often regarded as a matter for more lenient punishment, the object being to correct error and eliminate superstition, not to eradicate a perceived satanic threat to Christian society. Although secular courts in Spain and Italy seem to have been slightly harsher in matters of witchcraft than inquisitorial courts, when such matters came under their jurisdiction they in general appear to have followed the model set by the Inquisitions of careful consideration of evidence and adherence to procedure rather than blind panic.

SPAIN. *See* BASQUE LANDS, WITCHCRAFT IN; SOUTHERN EUROPE, WITCHCRAFT IN.

SPANISH INQUISITION. *See* INQUISITION.

SPECTRAL EVIDENCE. Given the inherent secrecy in all aspects of the crime of **witchcraft**, finding substantial evidence on which convictions could be based was always a problem for authorities. The best evidence, of course, was the confession of the accused themselves, usually obtained through **torture**. Another possible form of evidence, however, was spectral evidence, in which other people testified to having seen the spectral image of the witch. Such evidence might be supplied by another accused witch, who would testify to having seen someone in attendance at a witches' **sabbath** (many authorities maintained that witches traveled to sabbaths only in spirit), or by victims who would testify to having seen the form of a witch tormenting them. Many authorities argued that, although these specters might not be the witch herself, God would never allow the **devil** or a **demon** to impersonate an innocent person while working evil. Others, however, were very **skeptical** of such testimony, and throughout the period of the **witch-hunts**, spectral evidence was never generally held to be as reliable as confession. Perhaps the most famous case of spectral evidence occurred at **Salem**, Massachusetts, where a number of young girls who exhibited symptoms of **possession** testified that they were often tormented by witches in spectral forms that only they could see.

SPEE, FRIEDRICH (1591–1635). A German Jesuit and important opponent of **witchcraft** prosecutions, Spee is the author of *Cautio criminalis* (A Warning for Prosecutors), a major work denouncing the frequent conviction of innocent people for witchcraft and the use of excessive **torture** to elicit confessions from anyone accused. Although Spee certainly serves as an example of **skepticism** about witchcraft, his could be called a *legal skepticism*. That is, given the abuses of procedure he typically witnessed in witch trials, he came to realize that most of the people accused of the crime were innocent but were nevertheless convicted on flimsy evidence or coerced confessions. He never denied the potential reality of witchcraft or the power of **demons** and the **devil** in the world.

Spee was born in Kaiserswerth in the Rhineland and attended the Jesuit college in nearby Cologne. He entered the Jesuit order in 1611 and then studied at Würzburg and Mainz. In 1627, he returned to Würzburg as a professor of theology. In the late 1620s, Würzburg and nearby **Bamberg** were centers of particularly severe **witch-hunting**. Spee was appointed to hear the final confessions of condemned witches in prison. Initially fully convinced of the real threat of witchcraft, in the course of hearing these confessions, Spee realized that most if not all of the condemned people were innocent, and that if fair legal procedures had been properly applied, they would never have been convicted. He also recognized that, because witches were believed to be members of a satanic cult, convicted witches were forced to name accomplices. Because the legal procedures in place at the time ensured that these people too would almost certainly be convicted, he feared that ultimately witch-hunting might spiral completely out of control and threaten entire communities.

In 1631, Spee published the *Cautio criminalis* anonymously, although within the Jesuit order his authorship was widely known. The book focused on a sharp critique of the legal procedures of witch trials. It never denied the potential reality of witchcraft. Nevertheless, given the ease of false conviction, Spee ultimately came to believe that there were very few real witches in the world. Even this somewhat limited critique of witch trials roused considerable opposition from many proponents of witch-hunting, including many within the Jesuit order.

SPINA, ALFONSO DE (ca. 1420–1491). A Franciscan friar who converted from Judaism, Alfonso de Spina was a theologian at the university at Salamanca, and was the personal confessor to King Juan II of Castile. Just prior to his death, he was appointed bishop of Thermopolis. Around 1459, he wrote a treatise entitled *Fortalicium fidei* (Fortress of the Faith), in which he discussed various threats to the faith, including **heretics**, **Jews**, Saracens, and **demons**. In the section on demons, he also discussed **witchcraft**. Although Alfonso de Spina was not the first clerical authority to describe witchcraft in the 15th century, and his treatment of this subject was more moderate than some, his work, printed in the 1460s, became the first published treatise to deal with witchcraft.

SPINA, BARTOLOMMEO (ca. 1475–1546). A prominent Dominican friar and theologian, Spina studied in Bologna and Padua. He eventually became Master of the Sacred Palace in Rome, the chief theologian to the pope, and he was appointed by Pope Paul III to consider the important theological questions raised at the Council of Trent. He wrote several works arguing for the reality of **witchcraft** and the real danger that witches represented. His major work in this area was his *Questio de strigibus* (Concerning Witches), written in 1523.

SPRENGER, JAKOB (ca. 1436/38–1495). Traditionally listed as one of the authors of the infamous late-medieval **witch-hunting** manual *Malleus maleficarum* (Hammer of Witches), Sprenger was a Dominican friar, theologian, and papal inquisitor active in the **German Empire** in the later 15th century. He was born in or around the city of Basel and studied in Cologne, where in 1475 he received his doctorate in theology. He then taught and served in several offices at the university in Cologne. He was also an important figure within the Dominican order. In 1472, he became prior of the Dominicans in Cologne, an office he held until 1482, when he was relieved in order to be able to undertake other duties as a papal inquisitor. From 1481, he conducted numerous **inquisitions** into **heresy** and **witchcraft** in the Rhineland, and later more generally across southern Germany. In this capacity, he worked with **Heinrich Kramer**, and it was to these two inquisitors specifically that **Pope Innocent VIII** directed his bull *Summis desiderantes affectibus*, ordering all local authorities to assist them in their pursuit of witches. In 1488, Sprenger was named to the office of Provincial of the Dominican province of Teutonia, a position second only to the Master General of the entire order in that region.

Although he is typically listed as an author, along with Heinrich Kramer, of the *Malleus maleficarum,* there is much evidence to suggest that Sprenger had little or even nothing to do with the writing of this treatise on witchcraft. The strongest piece of evidence, only discovered in 1972, is a letter written by Sprenger's successor in the office of prior in Cologne, Servatius Fanckel. Fanckel knew Sprenger well and explicitly stated that he was in no way involved in writing the *Malleus.* Because Fanckel was, in fact, an admirer of that work, there is no reason to suppose that he had any motive to downplay any actual involvement Sprenger might have had. It seems likely that Sprenger's identification as an author of the *Malleus* arose because of his association with Kramer. As Sprenger's reputation as a theologian and prominent Dominican was greater than Kramer's, the addition of his name to the work could only add to its authority.

STAMFORD WITCHES. At the same time as the major **witch-hunt** in **Salem**, Massachusetts, was occurring, a smaller panic occurred in Stamford, Connecticut, leading to much different results. In the spring of 1692, a servant girl named Katherine Branch began to suffer from fits, and she accused a respected local matron, Elizabeth Clauson, of bewitching her. Eventually, five other people were implicated as well. One fled to neighboring New York and three others were quickly cleared of all charges. Clauson and another woman, Mercy Disborough, came under more severe scrutiny, but eventually Clauson was freed. Disborough was convicted and sentenced to death, but was later reprieved. Unlike in Salem, at Stamford authorities were **skeptical** of the accusations from the start, and no large panic ever developed within the community as a whole.

STARHAWK (1951–). An important figure in modern **witchcraft**, also known as **Wicca**, Starhawk is an American witch, feminist, peace activist, and author. She has dedicated most of her life to teaching, developing rituals, working within various organizations, and spreading knowledge of Wicca and of **neo-paganism** more generally to as broad an audience as possible. Her most important work is her book *The Spiral Dance*, a reflection on and statement of Wiccan principles, practices, and beliefs. The book, originally published in 1979, the same year as **Margot Adler**'s influential *Drawing Down the Moon*, has been reissued in 10th- and 20th-anniversary editions.

Born into a Jewish family, Starhawk was raised in a strongly religious household and by her own assessment was a devoutly religious child. As she grew, however, she became deeply concerned with what she saw as the severely limited role allowed to **women** in traditional Judaism. Already by the time she entered college at the University of California at Los Angeles, she had been exposed to various forms of neo-pagan beliefs and felt herself drawn toward this form of religiosity. While in college, she was exposed more fully to Wicca. She was attracted especially to the religion's focus on worship of the **Goddess** and to the elevated place it allowed to women. Upon graduating, she briefly entered UCLA's film school, but soon set about writing and traveling. Eventually, she began to work on what would become *The Spiral Dance*, an account of Wiccan pseudo-history, beliefs, and practices. Starhawk's lyrical and evocative writing seemed to capture the essence of Wiccan religiosity, highlighting especially the compatibility of Wicca with feminist and environmentalist concerns. The success of her book helped to spark a surge in the overall success of Wicca as a growing religious movement. The book became an essential Wiccan text, supplanting to some degree the writings of the founder of modern witchcraft, **Gerald Gardner**, especially in America, where feminist and environmentalist elements within Wicca were more developed than in Great Britain and elsewhere.

Starhawk herself eschews any "authoritative" role in the Wiccan or larger neo-pagan traditions. Although she has been a member of several groups and **covens**, she has also developed and practiced her beliefs alone. Much of her knowledge and inspiration, she claims, comes from her own dreams and trance experiences. She adheres to most standard elements of the Wiccan tradition, however, as developed by Gerald Gardner and others. She is particularly credulous of the claim that modern witchcraft is a direct descendant of historical European witchcraft, which was supposedly an ancient, pre-Christian fertility religion, demonized and brutally persecuted by the Christian church (in *The Spiral Dance*, she originally claimed that around 9,000,000 people were executed for witchcraft in medieval and early-modern Europe, although in later editions she has been forced to admit that this figure is "probably high"). This interpretation of historical witchcraft was largely developed in the late-19th and early-20th centuries, most famously by the British Egyptologist and amateur anthropologist **Margaret Murray**. Murray's theories have since been completely discredited, and many modern witches now maintain that their religion is not a direct survival of ancient **pagan** beliefs, but rather a deliberate recreation of imagined forms of ancient religion. Starhawk herself, in later editions of *The Spiral Dance*, argues that Wiccan beliefs are not dependent on any real historical tradition for their validity. Nevertheless, she does persist in maintaining that the supposed history of the Wiccan faith as a truly ancient pagan religion is essentially true, if not necessarily accurate in all details.

STORMS AND STORM RAISING. Affecting the weather and raising destructive storms was believed to be a common element of harmful **sorcery**, or *maleficium*, in Europe throughout the medieval and early-modern periods, and is a standard element of harmful magic around the world. Such weather magic was deemed particularly appropriate to witches and other demonic sorcerers by Christian authorities because, in Christian theology, **demons** were spiritual, airy creatures and could easily manipulate the element of air. The very earliest sources on **witchcraft** describe witches raising storms, especially lightning and hail, which could destroy crops and cause widespread damage to property across entire regions. The early authority **Johannes Nider** gave an account of a witch performing a demonic invocation and then having the demon raise a storm with lightning and hail, and the ***Errores Gazariorum*** (Errors of the Gazarii), another early source, described witches flying high into the Alps to chip off large blocks of ice from the mountains. They then let this ice fall as hail. One of the most famous examples of weather-working witchcraft came in the case of the **North Berwick Witches**, who supposedly raised several storms at sea in order to drown the Scottish king **James VI**.

STRAPPADO. One of the most common means of **torture** used on witches and others in the later Middle Ages and early-modern period was the strappado (from the Latin *strappare,* to pull). The wrists of a prisoner were bound behind his or her back with a rope attached to a pulley. He was then hoisted into the air. Often weights were attached to the prisoner's feet to increase the weight on the arms and shoulders, which frequently dislocated, causing extreme pain. The prisoner was then left hanging in this position while being interrogated by authorities. To increase the pain, the prisoner could be raised to a significant height and then dropped suddenly to within a few inches of the floor, exerting tremendous, sudden pressure on the arms and shoulders.

STRIX (STRIGA). In classical mythology, *striges* (the plural of *strix* or *striga*) were malevolent nighttime monsters. The Latin *strix* literally meant screech-owl, and the *striges* were believed to be birdlike creatures with great talons. They preyed especially on sleeping men and **children**. With men, they often turned themselves into beautiful women and had sexual intercourse (thereby showing a relation to **succubi**) before killing them. They were also **vampires**, sucking the blood from their victims. The image of the *strix* contributed to the later Christian idea of witches as **women** who flew at night and often murdered babies and young children. The word also became a term for witch in the medieval and early-modern periods.

SUCCUBI. *See* INCUBI AND SUCCUBI.

SUMMIS DESIDERANTES AFFECTIBUS, **BULL.** *See* INNOCENT VIII, POPE.

SWIMMING. A common, although by no means universal or universally accepted, method for identifying witches, swimming involved binding a suspected witch and immersing her in water. If she immediately floated to the surface, she was judged to be guilty. If she managed to remain submerged for some period of time, she was deemed to be innocent. The procedure operated on the theory that water was a pure element and would reject any guilty person, causing them immediately to float. Thus, the witch was bound not to prevent her from swimming to the surface, but from deliberately keeping herself submerged. Although some people could drown in the process of proving their innocence, normally the accused was not required to remain submerged for very long. Swimming was never fully accepted by authorities as a proper method of proof. It derived from notions of trial by ordeal that had been employed in early-medieval Europe but that were increasingly abandoned by courts with the steady adoption of **inquisitorial procedure** beginning in the 12th century. Throughout the later period of the **witch-hunts**, authorities often challenged the legitimacy of swimming, and it was banned in many areas, although this did not necessarily end its use entirely.

SWITZERLAND, WITCHCRAFT IN. Even more than the lands of the **German Empire**, to which all of the Swiss Confederation belonged at the beginning of the period of the **witch-hunts**, Switzerland can lay claim to being the real heartland of the European witch craze. Some estimates put the number of executions for **witchcraft** at around 5,000 for this relatively small region, while other estimates range as high as 10,000. Even taking the lowest of these figures, well over twice as many witches were executed per capita in Switzerland than in German lands. Moreover, Switzerland experienced some of the earliest witch-hunts in Europe in the early 15th century, and also some of the latest. The last execution for witchcraft in Europe to receive full and unquestioned legal sanction took place in the canton of Glarus in Switzerland in 1782. Because of this long duration, however, and because of the intense political, religious, and even linguistic disunity of Swiss lands, the overall patterns of witchcraft persecution in Switzerland are difficult to discern, if indeed any overall pattern can be said to exist.

The Swiss Confederation was comprised of a patchwork of independent cantons, some containing a sizeable area and some little more than city-states, some highly urbanized and some extremely rural. Some regions, like Geneva and Basel, were cosmopolitan centers of intellectual and economic activity, while others, especially in the high Alps, were relatively cut-off and backward. In general, it can be said that this fragmentation itself no doubt contributed to the severity of many Swiss witch-hunts. Local courts, free from external control and subject to the intense local fears, as well as the social and economic pressures that might drive a hunt, were often very inclined to pursue and promote accusations of witchcraft to the fullest extent possible. On the other hand, larger, more centralized and bureaucratic legal structures tended to emphasize strict adherence to proper legal procedure and careful consideration of evidence, which in turn inhibited the potential for a witch-hunt to get out of hand. Although some regions of Switzerland experienced relatively light witch-hunting, others experienced some of the most intense and destructive hunts that occurred in Europe.

– T –

TEMPLARS. The Knights of the Temple of Solomon, or Knights Templar, were a crusading, military order during the Middle Ages. The Templars originated around 1120 in the Holy Land as a small group of knights dedicated to defending pilgrims. The order quickly grew in size and popularity, until the knights in the Holy Land were supported by a large Templar network spread across Western Europe. The Templars acquired vast amounts of land, usually through pious donations. After the fall of Acre, the last Christian outpost in the Holy Land, in 1291, the Templars no longer had a clear purpose, and their great wealth aroused opposition to the order. In 1307, the Templars in **France** were arrested on the order of King Philip IV. The charges ranged from **heresy** and sodomy to worshiping **demons**, but in reality the arrests were motivated by Philip's desire to disband the order and seize its tremendous wealth and property. **Torture** was applied, however, and confessions were extracted, although many Templars later recanted. Under pressure from the French, in 1312 Pope Clement V officially suppressed the order, and in 1314 the Grand Master of the order, Jacques de Molay, was burned at the stake.

The Templars were never charged with **witchcraft**, and even charges of demonic **sorcery** did not figure significantly in their final condemnation. However, the dynamics of their arrest and trial, especially the use of torture to extract clearly false confessions, was reminiscent of later witch trials, and the trial of the Templars is often seen as foreshadowing in certain respects the persecution of witches that was to come.

THOLOSAN, CLAUDE (?–ca. 1450). The exact years of Claude Tholosan's life are unknown, but he served as chief magistrate of Briançonnais, the region around Briançon in Dauphiné, from 1426 until 1449. He was a layman and a secular official, although highly educated and clearly familiar with ecclesiastical canon law as well as certain aspects of theology. In the early 15th century, the Alpine regions of Dauphiné were the location of some of the earliest witch trials in European history, and in his capacity as chief judge, Tholosan personally conducted numerous trials for **witchcraft**. Around 1436, he wrote a treatise *Ut magorum et maleficiorum errores manifesti ignorantibus fiant* (That the Errors of Magicians and Witches May be Made Clear to the Ignorant), based on his own experiences trying witches. Unknown for many years and only rediscovered in the late 1970s, this treatise takes it place beside the works of **Johannes Nider**, **Hans Fründ**, **Martin Le Franc**, and the anonymous *Errores Gazariorum* (Errors of the Gazarii), as one of the most important early pieces of literature on witchcraft. It is particularly significant because, of all these early accounts, this is the only one for which the author had certain first-hand experience with supposed witches.

Tholosan described witchcraft in terms fairly close to what would become the standard stereotype. Witches performed harmful **sorcery**, *maleficium*, through the agency of **demons**; they renounced their faith and worshiped Satan; they were members of a secret sect and gathered at regular secret meetings to worship the **devil** and engage in activity that would come to typify the witches' **sabbath** (although Tholosan, as most other early authorities, denied the reality of **night**

flight to the sabbath). As a lay judge, Tholosan was also concerned to justify secular authority over the crime of witchcraft, which he did by equating the **apostasy** of witches to a kind of treason or *lèse-majesté* against God, which the secular prince, as the representative of divine justice and order on earth, was required to combat.

TINCTORIS, JOHANNES (ca. 1400–1469). Born in Tournai, Tinctoris studied theology at the university in Cologne, where he became dean of the arts faculty, then later dean of the theological faculty and ultimately rector of the university. Sometime before 1460, he returned to Tournai, where around that year he wrote a *Tractatus de secta vaudensium* (Treatise on the Sect of Witches), based on sermons he had delivered.

TORQUEMADA (TURRECREMATA), JUAN DE (1388–1468). A Spanish prelate and uncle of the more famous Tomás de Torquemada, who was chief inquisitor of the **Spanish Inquisition** in the late 15th century, Juan de Torquemada spent most of his life in Rome. In a commentary on canon law written around 1450, he addressed the notion of the **night flight** of witches as described in the **canon** *Episcopi*, asserting that such flight was entirely an illusion and a deception of **demons**.

TORTURE. The legal use of torture to extract confessions in court cases has a long history in Europe. The controlled use of torture was justified under ancient Roman law. For most of the early Middle Ages, legal torture was not widely used. Rather, under the **accusatorial procedure**, guilt or innocence was often determined by judicial ordeal, or in some cases trial by combat, both of which theoretically left the determination in the hands of God, who would ensure that the just party prevailed. With the gradual rediscovery of Roman law in the 11th and 12th centuries, and especially with the increasing use of **inquisitorial procedure**, torture also returned to use.

Torture was typically applied in cases of crimes where evidence and witnesses were lacking. **Heresy** was one such category of crime, since it involved errors of belief for which there might be no external evidence. Likewise heretical demonic **sorcery** and ultimately **witchcraft** were deemed crimes that often required torture to prosecute. Since there was often no external evidence or reliable witnesses in a case of witchcraft, a witch's own confession was the best means to secure a conviction. Controls were placed on the legal use of torture. It was only supposed to be applied once (although a single session of torture could be suspended and then continued at a later date), only for a limited time, and all confessions extracted under torture had to be verified by the accused later. Authorities were fully aware, and concerned about, the potential for torture to produce false confessions.

Especially in cases of witchcraft, however, the limits and controls on the use of torture were often ignored. Witchcraft was considered a *crimen exceptum*, an exceptional crime that, because of its severity, had to be prosecuted to the fullest extent possible. Moreover, judges and legal officials themselves would often become caught up in the panic that could surround a large **witch-hunt**. Many authorities were convinced that the **devil** made witches particularly insensitive to pain or prevented them from freely confessing, and so extraordinary measures could be justified against them. Many other authorities, however, were concerned about the potential for unrestricted torture to wring a confession out of almost any innocent person. This **skepticism** about the use of torture led to much of the early criticism of witch trials and opposition to witch-hunting. *See also* STRAPPADO.

TRANSVECTION. *See* NIGHT FLIGHT.

TRIER, WITCH-HUNTS AT. A series of severe witch trials took place in the archbishopric of Trier, which was also an independent principality within the **German Empire**, over the course of about 12 years, from 1582 to 1594. The trials were largely directed by the suffragan bishop of Trier, **Peter Binsfeld**, under the overall authority of Prince-Archbishop Johann von Schönenburg. Binsfeld would later write an important treatise on **witchcraft** intended mainly to justify the trials at Trier. The accusations of witchcraft seem to have been sparked by years of inclement weather, poor harvests, and economic suffering in the region. The initial trials were conducted in secular court under the direction of the senior civic judge and vice-governor of the city, **Dietrich Flade**. Unfortunately, Flade was less enthusiastic about **witch-hunting** than were the religious authorities, and ultimately he came to be suspected of witchcraft himself. He was tried and executed in 1589. The trials also aroused the opposition of the theologian **Cornelius Loos**, who wrote a treatise expressing his **skepticism** about witchcraft and the methods used in witch-hunting. Binsfeld took action against him as well. The treatise was suppressed, and Loos was banished to Brussels.

TRIMETHIUS, JOHANN (1462–1516). A Benedictine monk, abbot of Sponheim and later of St. Jacob's in Würzburg, Trimethius wrote two works dealing, at least in part, with **witchcraft**. In 1508, he discussed witchcraft in his *Liber octo questionum* (Book of Eight Questions), in response to questions put to him by the German emperor Maximilian I, several of which concerned witches. In the same year, he also wrote *Antipalus maleficiorum* (Testimony of Witches) at the request of the Elector of Brandenburg, which was dedicated fully to explicating the evils of witchcraft.

– V –

VALIENTE, DOREEN (1922–). An early member of the movement of modern **witchcraft**, or **Wicca**, in England, Valiente was the chief disciple of the founder of modern witchcraft, **Gerald Gardner**. In the mid-1950s, she co-authored with him many of the basic Wiccan rituals and texts that shaped the development of the new religion. She also founded her own **coven**, which soon broke away from Gardner's overall control.

Born in London, Valiente became very interested in occultism and considered herself to have psychic abilities. She was introduced to Gerald Gardner, and in 1953 she was initiated by him into his coven. Gardner claimed that modern witchcraft was a direct survival of an ancient, pre-Christian, **pagan** fertility religion; that he himself had been initiated into a coven of traditional, hereditary witches; and that he had learned of the rituals, practices, and beliefs of witchcraft from them. Valiente accepted all these claims, although from her own explorations of occultism, she recognized that many aspects of the practices Gardner described were based on other modern writings, such as those of the famous ritual magician and occultist **Aleister Crowley**.

From 1954 until 1957, Valiente collaborated with Gardner on re-working the so-called **Book of Shadows**, the key text of Wiccan rituals. In particular, she worked to reduce those elements that were clearly drawn from Crowley and other occultist sources, to emphasize the role of the **Goddess**, and to shape witchcraft more into a modern **neo-pagan** religion. Eventually tiring of Gardner's overbearing influence, in 1957 Valiente formed her own coven and broke with Gardner. She has continued to publish on the principles and practices of Wicca in the years since.

VAMPIRES. There are two major connections between vampiric creatures and **witchcraft**. In classical mythology, creatures called *lamiae* and *striges* were monsters who haunted the night. *Lamiae* were thought to attack and kill **children**, often sucking their blood. *Striges* were bird-like creatures (the Latin *strix* means screech-owl) that also sucked blood. They appear to have provided an early basis for the later medieval and early-modern stereotype of witches as murderers of children who flew through the night. In some regions of Europe during the period of the **witch-hunts**, both *lamia* and *strix* (or *striga*) were used as terms for witch. In addition to this association, another connection between witchcraft and vampirism took shape in Hungary and other areas of the Balkans in the 18th century. Here it appears that popular belief in vampires gradually took over some of the social and cultural functions that belief in witchcraft had filled. As official willingness to prosecute witches declined, accounts of vampirism rose, and vampires came to be seen as a cause for much otherwise unexplainable misfortune, as witches had been earlier.

VINETI, JEAN (?–ca. 1475). A Dominican friar, Vineti was first a professor of theology at the university in Paris and then an **inquisitor** at Paris and later at Carcassonne in the south of **France**. Around 1450, he wrote a treatise *Contra daemonum invocatores* (Against Invokers of Demons), in which he addressed the subject of **witchcraft**. Vineti was very credulous and was one of the first authorities, along with **Nicholas Jacquier** and **Johannes Hartlieb**, to present an extended argument against the tradition of the **canon *Episcopi*** that the **night flight** of witches to a **sabbath** was only an illusion. Vineti maintained that both night flight and the sabbath itself were entirely real.

VISCONTI, GIROLAMO (?–1477 or 1478). A member of the princely family of Milan, Girolamo became a Dominican friar. In 1448, he was appointed to be a professor of logic at the university in Milan, and from 1465 until his death, he was the Dominican provincial, or head of the order, in the province of Lombardy. Sometime around 1460, he wrote *Lamiarum sive striarum opusculum* (Little Book on Witches—*lamia* and *strix* both being words that meant witch in Italy at this time). Here he argued both for the reality of witches and for the **heretical** nature of **witchcraft**, placing them under the jurisdiction of clerical **inquisitions**.

VOODOO. Developing originally among the slave populations of the Caribbean region, primarily in Haiti, Voodoo is a religion that consists of a complex blend of Christian and native African elements. In this syncretism, it is similar to **Santería**. The word *Voodoo* derives from the West African *vodu*, meaning spirit or deity. It can alternately be given as *Voudou* or *Vodoun*, and practitioners generally prefer this latter term, as *Voodoo* or the even worse corruption *Hoodoo* are often seen as carrying pejorative connotations, denoting some sort of system of black magic devoid of any religious meaning. In fact, it is incorrect to equate Voodoo purely with harmful magic, although such **sorcery** does have a place within the overall religious system of Voodoo.

The basis of Voodoo is worship of the *loa*, spirits that can exercise power in the world. Practitioners believe in the single great creator-god of Christianity, but also maintain that there are numerous other powerful spirits in the world. The *loa* represent a mixture of Christian saints and angels along with traditional African spirit-deities. The Catholic Church generally equates the *loa* with **demons** and sees Voodoo as a corruption of Christianity. Believers, however, regard it as an enrichment of Christianity and themselves as absolutely faithful Christians. The *loa* are neither wholly good nor entirely evil, and so humans can access their power for a variety of purposes. Harmful sorcery and other practices akin to **witchcraft** certainly have a place in the system of Voodoo. A particularly evil form of sorcery is the creation of zombies, animated corpses that will serve the sorcerer who creates them. The *loa* also serve, however, as benign spirits, and people pray to them for protection from harmful sorcery.

Ideas of evil sorcery within Voodoo share many elements in common with historical ideas of harmful magic and witchcraft in Europe, and probably derive partly from European influence along with traditional elements of **African witchcraft**. Sorcerers are often thought to carry babies and young **children** off to secret gatherings where they kill and devour them, or they break into homes at night and suck the blood from children while they sleep. They are also often believed to use magic **ointments** that they rub on their bodies in order to fly, just as historical European witches were often thought to do.

– W –

WALDENSIANS. Followers of a man named Valdes, a rich merchant in Lyon in the late 12th and early 13th centuries, the Waldensians became the most widespread and enduring of all medieval heretical groups. Seeking to lead an "apostolic life" of poverty and preaching, as described in Christ's instructions to his disciples in the **Bible**, the Waldensians were condemned by the medieval church for refusing to accept episcopal and papal authority (first the archbishop of Lyon and then Pope Alexander III refused to allow them, as untrained laymen, to preach), and the movement was branded a **heresy**. Waldensianism nevertheless persisted as a widespread movement in southern **France**, the **German Empire**, and Italy for the remainder of the Middle Ages. Waldensian groups eventually developed a number of unorthodox doctrines and practices, but they were never particularly associated with the practice of demonic **sorcery**. Then, in the 15th century, in the western Alpine regions of Savoy, Dauphiné, and certain cantons in western **Switzerland**, several trials that began as **inquisitions** into Waldensian heresy shifted into some of the first **witch-hunts** in Europe. In the French-speaking regions of these territories, the word for Waldensian, *Vaudois*, became an early term for witches, and certain documents described the supposed satanic sect of witches as ". . . *heresim illorum haereticorum modernorum Valdensium*"—the heresy of the new Waldensian heretics. There is, however, no credible evidence to suggest that actual Waldensian practice ever involved the worship of the **devil** or the practice of demonic magic.

WALPURGISNACHT. The night of April 30, prior to the feast day of Saint Walpurga (on May 1), Walpurgisnacht was widely believed throughout Germanic and Scandinavian lands to be a time of particular celebration and revelry for witches. On this night, witches were believed to fly to remote mountaintops to participate in great witches' **sabbaths.** The most famous of these supposedly took place on the peak of the Brocken in the Harz Mountains in northern Germany. Walpurgisnacht coincided with Celtic and Germanic spring fertility festivals, and the supposed revels of witches associated with this day may have derived at least partly from **pagan** religious celebrations later demonized by Christian authorities.

WARLOCK. Because, historically, most witches were thought to be **women**, an alternate term, warlock, is sometimes used in modern writings to designate a male witch. The word derives from an Old English term for an oath-breaker or traitor. By the mid-15th century, it had become associated with witchcraft, although it carried no gender connotations and could be used for either male or female witches. There seems to be no particular historical basis for the modern application of the term only to men. Among practitioners of modern witchcraft, or **Wicca**, the term *warlock* is little used. Male practitioners prefer to be called *witches* or *Wiccans*, just as female practitioners are.

WEATHER MAGIC. *See* STORMS AND STORM-RAISING.

WEREWOLVES. The belief in lycanthropy, the ability of certain people to transform themselves or be transformed into wolves, is ancient. In Christian Europe during the medieval and early-modern periods, many learned demonologists took the issue of lycanthropy quite seriously. Like **witchcraft**, transformation into a werewolf was regarded not just as a potentially harmful supernatural feat, but also as a sin against God, a willful abandonment of the divinely ordained human form and spirit. In many regions, suspected werewolves were often tried in much the same manner as were witches. In addition, witches were sometimes described as transforming themselves into wolves. Most authorities agreed that no such physical transformation of the human body could actually take place. However, a **demon** or the **devil**

might closely superimpose the form of a wolf over the real body of a witch. Alternately, the transformation might simply be a demonic illusion or deception.

WEYER, JOHANN (1515–1588). A physician and scholar, Weyer was one of the first important opponents of **witch-hunting**. Not only did he argue that from a legal standpoint many witch trials were deeply flawed, but he also maintained on theological and physiological grounds that much supposed **witchcraft** was impossible, or at least could not be the work of human witches. Nevertheless, he did not deny the reality or power of **demons** or of the **devil**, and so could not fully undermine the basic foundations on which the idea of witchcraft rested.

Born in Brabant in the Netherlands, Weyer grew up in a merchant family. At the age of 15 he went to live and study with Heinrich Cornelius **Agrippa** von Nettesheim. It was probably Agrippa who first introduced Weyer to the Neoplatonic and **Hermetic** traditions of learned Renaissance magic. After leaving Agrippa, Weyer studied medicine at Paris and Orléans and then returned to the Low Countries as a practicing physician. He married and in 1550 took up the post he held for the rest of his life as the personal physician to the duke of Cleves, whose court was centered at Düsseldorf. Sometime after taking this position, he began to become concerned with the matter of witchcraft. Witch trials were at that time on the rise in the entire region of the lower Rhine. In response to this occurrence, Weyer produced his most important work, *De praestigiis daemonum* (On the Deceptions of Demons), first published in 1563. Here he went beyond the sort of judicial **skepticism** about witch trials that was already present in his day, namely that most prosecutions for witchcraft were improperly conducted and seriously flawed and thus often resulted in false convictions. Rather he denied the very possibility of witchcraft itself.

Weyer did not seek to deny the real existence or power of demons. Instead he argued that demons could not be compelled by human beings to perform the sorts of acts that formed the basis of accusations of witchcraft. Drawing on his expertise as a physician, he demonstrated that many cases of witchcraft or demonic **possession** were better explained by medical conditions, such as senility or insanity.

He also attacked the concept of the demonic **pact** between a witch and the devil or a lesser demon. Viewing this pact as a contract, he set out to prove that legally it could not exist. According to Roman law, which formed the basis for most European law codes at this time, a valid contract required good faith (*bona fides*) from both parties, and could not be entered into with malicious intent. Obviously, argued Weyer, no good faith could be expected from the devil.

Weyer's arguments, while powerful and logically coherent, did little to convince the many proponents of the witch-hunts that their cause was unjust, or that the crime they opposed had no basis in reality. His writings aroused great controversy and were fiercely attacked by almost every later authority on witchcraft and **demonology**. As Weyer never made any attempt to deny the basic existence of the devil and his demons, or their power, he left his later opponents an obvious point from which to launch their attacks. Still, the extent to which he did deny the reality of witchcraft makes him virtually unique among early opponents of the witch-hunts.

WICCA. An alternate term for modern **witchcraft**, *Wicca* is the preferred term among many modern witches (or Wiccans). Wicca is an Old English word for witch or more accurately sorcerer, but modern Wiccans who prefer the word generally do so because it now carries none of the negative stereotypes attached to the terms witch and witchcraft. It should be noted, however, that many practitioners of modern witchcraft staunchly maintain the use of the words witch and witchcraft and insist that they will reclaim these words from the negative connotations that they now carry.

Modern witchcraft originated in the 1950s. The father of the movement, and for all intents and purposes the founder of modern witchcraft, was the Englishman **Gerald Gardner**. In 1939, Gardner, a student of various esoteric religions, supposedly joined a **coven** of witches in England. He claimed that this group was a remnant of an ancient **pagan** religion practicing rites that had been preserved from the distant past. During the medieval and early-modern periods, this religion had been persecuted by Christian authorities as demonic witchcraft, but in fact the religion was older than Christianity and had nothing to do with either the Christian god or the Christian **devil**. Fearing that the religion was now on the verge of dying out, in 1954

Gardner declared its existence and its principles openly in his book *Witchcraft Today*. In maintaining that modern witchcraft was a direct survival of an ancient pagan religion, Gardner was following the theories of **Margaret Murray.** Murray's thesis has since been completely debunked, and there is no credible evidence that historical witchcraft was rooted in some clandestine pre-Christian religion, or that modern witchcraft has any links to such a religion. It is now clear that Gardner simply invented most of the tenets of modern witchcraft from his earlier studies of world religions.

Modern witchcraft is by no means a single, unified, or cohesive faith. There is no one central organization to govern beliefs and practices. The original form of witchcraft created by Gardner, now known as Gardnerian witchcraft, is only one among many different forms (although all forms follow at least the basic principles that Gardner established). In general, witches are organized into groups called covens. These are presided over by a high priestess assisted by a high priest. Most forms of modern witchcraft give **women** an equal or even a superior place to men in the religion. Similarly, the supreme Wiccan deity is dual, taking the form of the **Goddess** and the God (often known as the **Horned God**). Of the pair, the Goddess is generally held to be superior and is strongly associated with the earth and nature. Modern witchcraft stresses a respect for the natural world, and modern witches worship the Goddess and God in a variety of ceremonies, often conducted outdoors. Practitioners of modern witchcraft also believe that they can perform a variety of magical spells, but always with the strict understanding that they should never use their power to bring harm or misfortune to others.

Because of the prominent place given to the Goddess and to women practitioners, modern witchcraft quickly drew the attention of many feminists, who wanted to see in it an essentially feminine religion in contrast to the perceived patriarchal structures of traditional Western religions. In 1979, the American witch **Starhawk** published her book *The Spiral Dance,* which more than any other work marked the successful fusion of the formal structures and beliefs of witchcraft from the Gardnerian tradition with the notion of witchcraft as an expression of essential female spirituality. Especially in America, where the tradition of feminist witchcraft is stronger than in Britain, this book in large part replaced Gardner's *Witchcraft Today* to become the basic statement of the religion. Also in 1979, the journalist and practicing witch **Margot Adler** published her book *Drawing Down the Moon.* This was the first systematic study of the beliefs and origins of modern witchcraft. In it, Adler rejected the Gardnerian notion that modern witchcraft was a direct survival of a real, pre-Christian religion. Instead, she recognized (as do most Wiccans today) that this pseudo-history would be better regarded as a foundational myth, and she argued that this realization in no way weakened the force or value of modern witchcraft as a religion.

WILD HUNT. In Germanic and Celtic legend, the Wild Hunt consisted of a band of ghosts or spirits who would ride through the night. The hunt was usually led by a divine or semi-divine figure, either female, often called **Holda** or Berta, or male, often called **Herne the Hunter.** In Christian Europe during the Middle Ages, authorities often transformed the female leader of the Wild Hunt into the classical goddess **Diana**, herself a goddess of hunting whom Christian authorities regarded as a **demon**. In addition, the belief developed that groups of **women**, instead of the spirits of the dead, would ride with Diana. The most famous expression of this belief is found in the 10th century **canon** *Episcopi.* Although condemned by the canon as mere demonic deception, this belief was an important basis for the later notions of **night flight** and the witches' **sabbath.**

WILLIAM OF MALMESBURY (ca. 1095–1142). A well-known chronicler and historian, William of Malmesbury wrote two important accounts of the history of England up to the 12th century. In his history of the kings of England, *Gesta regum,* written around 1140, he included a brief account of the **Witch of Berkeley**, which later became very famous and circulated also outside of William's history for the remainder of the Middle Ages and into the early-modern period.

WITCH BOTTLE. A form of protective charm common especially in England, a witch bottle consisted of a small glass bottle made for a victim of bewitchment by another witch or **cunning man or woman.** Often some strands of the victims's hair, urine, or nail clippings were placed inside the bottle. Bottles could be used in a variety of ways. If buried under the hearth or threshold of a house, they were believed to undo harmful spells cast against that home or its residents. They might be smashed or thrown into a fire to strike back against the witch who had supposedly cast the original spell, causing her pain or death. They could also be hung near doors, windows, and chimneys to protect a home from any potential **witchcraft**.

WITCHCRAFT. The term *witchcraft* can be, and historically has been, used to denote a variety of supposed practices. Most broadly, witchcraft refers to relatively simple forms of common or low magic (as opposed to learned or high magic, which is typically very complex and ritualistic, and is limited to an educated elite) used to harmful effect. In this sense, witchcraft is largely synonymous with **sorcery**. In Europe during the medieval and early-modern periods, the Latin term for harmful sorcery, *maleficium*, was also the most common term for *witchcraft*. Taken to mean simply the practice of such sorcery, witchcraft can be said to have existed in almost every human society throughout history. Some anthropologists differentiate witchcraft from sorcery by labeling as sorcery any common magical practices that supposedly operate through certain words or gestures, or through certain material objects. Witchcraft, on the other hand, supposedly operates through some power inherent in the witch herself. Thus, sorcery is a learned skill while witchcraft is an innate characteristic. This distinction, however, does not pertain to witchcraft as defined during the period of the major European **witch-hunts**.

During the period of the major witch-trials in Western Europe in the 16th and 17th centuries, witchcraft was widely conceived to involve the practice of harmful sorcery, *maleficium*, which operated through demonic forces. Witches learned to perform such sorcery from **demons** or from the **devil**, to whom they swore their allegiance. Such sorcery was not the only element of witchcraft in this period, however, and in many respects it was not the most important element. Witchcraft was also believed to involve profound **diabolism**. In exchange for magical powers, witches abandoned the Christian faith and gave their worship to the devil instead. They entered into **pacts** with demons and gathered as members of organized cults at secret, nocturnal **sabbaths**. Here, witches were believed to desecrate sacred items, such as the cross and Eucharist, to murder and **cannibalize** small **children**, and to engage in sexual **orgies** with each other and with attendant demons. For most Christian authorities, the **apostasy** and **idolatry** entailed in this image of witchcraft were far worse crimes than whatever harmful sorcery witches might work. This conception of witchcraft only appeared in Europe late in the Middle Ages, primarily in the early 15th century. Being so closely bound up with specifically Christian notions of theology and **demonology**, witchcraft in this sense obviously cannot be said to have existed in any other world culture.

In the 20th century, witchcraft came to take on yet another meaning. Self-styled modern witches conceive of witchcraft as a religious system, based on pre-Christian, **pagan** models. Although some modern witches maintain that there is a connection between their practices and historical witchcraft in Europe, they have sought to distance themselves from the historically negative connotations of witchcraft, and thus modern witchcraft is often referred to as **Wicca** (an Old English term for sorcery) instead. Modern witchcraft does involve certain magical practices that modern witches believe to have real power.

WITCH DOCTOR. *See* CUNNING MEN AND WOMEN.

WITCH-HUNT. Although **witchcraft** can with some justification be seen as an almost perennial aspect of numerous pre-modern human cultures, and although witches were uniformly regarded within these cultures as evil and socially harmful individuals who needed to be punished or often eradicated, witch-hunting in the historical sense is limited to a specific period and place. In Europe, the full notion of diabolical witchcraft, that is, of the witch as someone who not only practiced harmful **sorcery**, *maleficium*, against others, but who did so by means of **demons** and demonic power, and in league with the **devil**, only emerged in the early 15th century. In this new conception of witchcraft, the witch was not regarded as an individual practitioner of evil, but was believed to be a member of a **heretical** sect. Witches were thought to gather at regular nocturnal assemblies known as witches' **sabbaths** where they would commit **idolatry** and **apostasy** by worshiping demons and surrendering their souls to the devil in exchange for magical powers. The belief that witches were members of a secret, conspiratorial, diabolical cult provided the necessary basis for true witch-hunts, that is, series of connected witch trials that fed off each other and resulted in numerous executions.

The first real witch-hunts took place in the 15th century, mostly located in lands in and around the western Alps. The period of major witch-hunting, however, occurred later, in the 16th and 17th centuries. Reliable figures for many regions are lacking, but across Europe probably around 100,000 people were put on trial for witchcraft during these centuries, and probably around 50,000 were executed. The frequency and severity of witch-hunting varied widely from region to region and from year to year across Europe. Nevertheless, some generalizations can be made. Central Europe, above all the lands of **Switzerland** and the **German Empire**, were clearly the heartland of the witch-hunts. Some of the earliest, as well as some of the latest, witch trials took place in Switzerland, and over half of all executions for witchcraft, around 30,000, took place in German lands. In other regions of Europe, witch-hunting was less intense. In **Southern Europe**, for example, witch-hunting was kept under control mainly by the Roman and Spanish **Inquisitions**, while in the **British Isles**, witch-hunts were made more difficult because of certain legal controls and the fact that the notion of fully diabolical witchcraft described above never gained wide credence and most accusations of witchcraft continued to focus on simple *maleficium*.

Across Europe, witch-hunting seems to have been most widespread in those regions where effective, centralized legal bureaucracies were lacking. Witch-hunting depended to a large extent on a relatively localized atmosphere of panic, and large, distant bureaucracies tended to act more slowly and with greater caution. Most witch-hunts began with an accusation of *maleficium* made against some individual. A trial would be held, and in many cases the process ended there, with the conviction (or, less often, acquittal) of a single suspected witch. Because witches were believed to be members of diabolical cults, however, often an accused witch was required by her judges to name other witches. If she proved reluctant, **torture** could be used. Also, a single witch trial could encourage other people in the same locality to make further accusations. Often the process would still remain relatively contained and would end with only a few executions, producing what might be called a *mid-level hunt*. In some cases, however, the level of fear and panic generated in a community that felt itself to be under attack by diabolical forces could spiral entirely out of control. Especially if the officials in charge of the legal proceedings shared in the local panic, new accusations could be generated almost indefinitely. With the liberal use of torture, confessions could be extracted from virtually anyone accused, and so there was no natural stop to the string of convictions and executions that could take place. Such major hunts typically ended only when accusations came to be leveled against socially and politically powerful people, such as priests and ministers, civic officials, and their wives. Faced with the possibility of convicting such people, magistrates would finally realize that the process was out of control and put an end to the hunt. *See also* BAMBERG WITCH TRIALS; BASQUE LANDS, WITCHCRAFT IN; CHELMSFORD WITCHES; MORA WITCHES; NORTH BERWICK WITCHES; SALEM, WITCHCRAFT AT; STAMFORD WITCHES; TRIER, WITCH-HUNTS AT.

WITCH'S MARK. Also known as a witch's teat, a witch's mark could be any small mark, mole, wart, or bodily protuberance (including an actual third nipple) supposedly used by witches to suckle their demonic **familiars**, who were thought to crave human blood. In those areas where belief in the witch's mark prevailed, accused witches would be stripped and thoroughly searched, and almost any bodily mark or blemish could be seen as evidence of witchcraft. In the absence of any clear mark, scars might be seen as evidence of an attempt to cut off or remove the mark.

WOMEN AND WITCHCRAFT. Throughout the period of the **witch-hunts** in Europe, the vast majority of people accused of this crime, and an even greater percentage of those convicted and executed for it, were women. In most regions of Europe, the number of accused witches who were women typically exceeded 75 percent of total accusations, and in some regions the figure rose to well over 90 percent. From at least the 15th century down to modern times, **witchcraft** has been particularly, although by no means exclusively, associated with women, so much so that alternate terms, such as **warlock**, are sometimes used to describe male witches.

The strong association of witchcraft with women has many historical roots. During the period of the witch-hunts, Christian authorities, both ecclesiastical and secular, regarded witches as servants of Satan, guilty of worshiping **demons**, **apostasy** from the faith, and member-ship in a conspiratorial, diabolic cult. Because both **biblical** and clas-sical Greek and Roman traditions supported the notion that women were inferior to men physically, mentally, and spiritually, authorities could easily turn to such standard ideas of female weakness to ex-plain why women were more susceptible than men to the deceptions and seductions of the **devil**. The first authority to employ such argu-ments to explain the predominance of female witches was the 15th-century Dominican theologian **Johannes Nider**. Shortly thereafter, the French poet **Martin Le Franc** presented a strongly gendered de-piction of witchcraft in his long poem *Le Champion des Dames* (The Defender of Ladies). Later in that century, the infamously misogynist treatise on witch-hunting, *Malleus maleficarum* (Hammer of [Fe-male] Witches), expanded this line of argument to its fullest extent and declared confidently, "all witchcraft comes from carnal lust, which in women is insatiable." Nevertheless, before accepting too readily the notion that the misogyny of learned, particularly clerical, authorities lies entirely at the root of the association of witchcraft with women, it should be noted that no later treatise on witchcraft was as fully misogynist as the *Malleus maleficarum,* and in fact many learned **demonologists** and later theorists of witchcraft devoted rela-tively little attention to the gendered nature of the crime. Also, it is clear that the number of women being accused of **sorcery** and witch-craft began to rise substantially even before learned theorists first took note of this fact.

Although early trial records are of course sketchy and many have not survived, from 1300 to 1350, over 70 percent of those accused in sorcery trials seem to have been men. In the second half of the 14th century, however, the percentage of men accused fell to 42 percent while women took over the majority with around 58 percent. In the first half of the 15th century, when Nider and Le Franc wrote, already 60 to 70 percent of those accused in sorcery or witch trials were women. Rather than being imposed by ideologically driven authori-ties, the predominance of women accused of witchcraft seems to have arisen naturally from the accusations. This would support the notion that throughout pre-modern Europe, as in many traditional so-cieties, women were often associated more than men with the prac-tice of common, everyday magic, and especially with harmful sorcery. In particular, women frequently performed various forms of magical **healing**, and the power to heal was often believed to be closely related to the power to harm.

Once the stereotype of the female witch became established, many other factors contributed to the more frequent prosecution of women than men for this crime. Most basically, women—especially old women, widows, or the unmarried—were socially marginalized and legally weak or powerless in pre-modern European society. Many modern scholars, especially feminist historians, have argued that witch-hunts were a powerful device employed, either consciously or unconsciously, by authorities to suppress and discipline women who did not, in one way or another, conform to the roles prescribed for them by an essentially patriarchal society. There is certainly some truth to this argument, but again care must be taken when determining to what extent, and certainly to what degree deliberately, authorities alone were responsible for targeting women as witches.

In modern witchcraft, or **Wicca**, the status of women has been entirely reversed from the historical stereotype of witchcraft. As a system of religious belief, Wicca propounds a complete equality between male and female, and exhibits a great respect especially for female generative powers. The religion identifies both a god (often known as the **Horned God**) and a **Goddess**, who represents nature and the earth. In theory, these deities are equal, but in practice an emphasis often falls on the Goddess. As Wicca spread in the 1960s and 1970s, some elements of the movement became closely associated with the feminism of that period. A key figure here was the influential Wiccan author **Starhawk**. Many practitioners are drawn to Wicca, at least in part, because of the positive emphasis it places on women, as opposed to what they perceive as the patriarchal and repressive nature of more traditional Western religions.

Bibliography

This bibliography, as this dictionary as a whole, focuses primarily on the phenomenon of witchcraft in Christian Europe during the medieval and early-modern periods, and above all on the age of the great European witch-hunts from the 15th through the 17th centuries. The historical development of witchcraft in Europe, however, was shaped by traditions of magic—and by legal, intellectual, and social responses to magic—stretching back to the early Christian period and even into classical antiquity. Likewise, historical witchcraft has continued to exert a powerful influence on the modern world, being appropriated into modern occultist, neo-pagan, and Satanist movements, among others. Thus literature covering magic and witchcraft for virtually the full span of Western history is included here. The basic organization of the bibliography is chronological, with some sections and subsections arranged thematically. Systems of harmful magic similar to historical European witchcraft are prevalent in many other world cultures, and scholars taking an anthropological approach to the study of witchcraft have often made comparisons between the European and non-European aspects of this phenomenon. Therefore, a section on non-European witchcraft, focusing particularly on studies of African systems of magic and supernatural power, is also included, primarily for comparative purposes.

The history of witchcraft has been a subject of scholarly attention for well over a century. Many early studies, however, are now of little use. Scholars in the 19th and early 20th centuries, steeped in the traditions of the Enlightenment, were often dismissive of earlier "superstitions," or sought simply to condemn, rather than to understand, the phenomenon of witch-hunting in Europe. Other scholars fell (and some continue to fall) into an alternate trap—that of overly romanticizing earlier beliefs and practices, and trying to shape them into some grander or more appealing design than they actually represented. Most notable in this regard was the British Egyptologist and amateur anthropologist Margaret Murray, who wrote several books on European witchcraft in the first half of the 20th century. Drawing to some extent on popular anthropological and historical theories of the time, Murray constructed a fanciful account of historical witchcraft as a genuine, clandestine survival of pre-Christian popular religion. Although thoroughly debunked by more recent scholarship, the Murray thesis continues to exert a sway over certain modern approaches to historical witchcraft, especially within the movement of modern witchcraft, or Wicca.

In more recent years, and especially since the 1970s, the historical study of witchcraft has blossomed. Taking into account developments in social and cultural history, the rise of gender studies, and the concerns of post-modern textual critiques, scholars have approached witchcraft from almost every conceivable angle. Yet the subject remains as interesting, and in many ways as intractable, as ever. With every new approach, new questions pose themselves. Because of this floresence, this bibliography is limited largely to works from the last several decades. Earlier works are included only if they have proven particularly seminal for later research.

Scholarship on witchcraft is a truly international effort. Every country in Europe experienced witchcraft and witch-hunting to some extent, every country has produced its own scholarship, and important and innovative work has appeared in almost every European language. Aside from the many major studies in German or French, one thinks, most recently, of the work being done on Dutch and Hungarian witchcraft. As the present volume is intended for an English-speaking audience, English-language scholarship has been preferred as much as possible. However, especially for regional studies, scholarship in other languages is essential.

Although a great deal of scholarly attention has been focused on witchcraft, still the field is dominated by narrow studies rather than broad syntheses. The emphasis of the bibliography is on books, which are typically more easily available and which are more often addressed to (or at least accommodating of) general readers, but a large number of scholarly articles are also listed. Where several articles have been published in a single volume, to save space and avoid needless pedantry, only the full volume is listed. To readers looking to begin their investigations or interested in a general overview, the following suggestions can be made. Probably the best survey of the entire history of magic and witchcraft in the Western world is Jeffrey Russell's *A History of Witchcraft*. Richard Kieckhefer's *Magic in the Middle Ages* is the best survey for that period, culminating in a consideration of the emergence of diabolic witchcraft and witch-hunting, which actually only appeared at the end of the Middle Ages. Brian Levack's *The Witch-Hunt in Early Modern Europe* is the standard English-language survey of the period of the witch-hunts proper. An excellent and readily available collection of primary sources in translation, covering the entire medieval and early-modern period, is Alan Kors and Edward Peters, eds., *Witchcraft in Europe 400–1700*. The six volumes of *Witchcraft and Magic in Europe*, edited by Bengt Ankarloo and Stuart Clark, promise to be the most complete and detailed survey of the entire historical development of witchcraft in Western civilization from the ancient world to the 20th century. Each volume, arranged chronologically, contains three to four long pieces by various experts on particular periods or issues. Each of these books also has extensive bibliographies to guide further research.

ORGANIZATION

I. Primary Sources: Collections and Translations
   1. Modern Editions and Translations
   2. Edited Source Collections
II. General Studies
   1. General Surveys
   2. Bibliographical and Historiographical Surveys
   3. Encyclopedias and Reference Sources
III. Witchcraft in the Ancient World
IV. Witchcraft in Medieval and Early-Modern Europe
   1. Late Antiquity and Early Middle Ages
   2. The Middle Ages
   3. The Era of the Witch-Hunts
   4. The Witches' Sabbath
   5. Witchcraft, Medicine, and Disease
   6. Women, Gender, and Witchcraft
   7. Magic and Occult Science in the Era of the Witch-Hunts
V. Witchcraft in Medieval and Early-Modern Europe: Regional Studies
   1. British Isles
   2. Colonial America
   3. Eastern Europe
   4. France and the Low Countries
   5. German Lands
   6. Italy, Portugal, and Spain
   7. Scandinavia
   8. Switzerland
VI. The Devil and Demonology, Possession and Exorcism
VII. Theorists of Witchcraft, Treatises and Literature on Witchcraft
VIII. Witchcraft in Art
IX. Witchcraft in the Modern World
   1. Magic and Superstition after the Witch-Hunts
   2. Modern Wicca, Neo-Paganism, and Satanism
X. Non-European Witchcraft, Anthropological and Comparative Studies

I. PRIMARY SOURCES:
COLLECTIONS AND TRANSLATIONS

1. Modern Editions and Translations

Bouget, Henry. *An Examen of Witches*. Ed. Montague Summers. Trans. E. A. Ashwin. 1929. Reprint, New York: Barnes and Noble, 1971.

Copenhaver, Brian P. *Hermetica: The Greek Corpus Hermeticum and the Latin Asclepius in a New English Translation with Notes and Introduction*. Cambridge: Cambridge University Press, 1992.

Davidson, L. S., and J. O. Ward, eds. *The Sorcery Trial of Alice Kyteler: A Contemporary Account (1324) Together with Related Documents in English Translation, with Introduction and Notes*. Binghamton, N.Y.: Medieval and Renaissance Texts and Studies, 1993.

Del Rio, Martin. *Investigations into Magic*. Ed. P. G. Maxwell-Stuart. Manchester, Eng.: Manchester University Press, 2000.

Guazzo, Francesco Maria. *Compendium Maleficarum*. Ed. Montague Summers. Trans. E. A. Ashwin. 1929. Reprint, New York: Barnes and Noble, 1970.

Hopkins, Matthew. *The Discovery of Witches*. Ed. Montague Summers. London: Cayme, 1928.

Kramer, Heinrich. *The Malleus Maleficarum of Heinrich Kramer and James Sprenger*. Trans. Montague Summers. 1928. Reprint, New York: Dover, 1971.

———. *Malleus Maleficarum von Heinrich Institoris (alias Kramer) unter Mithilfe Jakob Sprengers aufgrund der dämonologischen Tradition zusammengestellt*. Ed. André Schnyder. Göppingen, Ger.: Kümmerle, 1991. *Kommentar zur Weidergabe des Erstdrucks von 1487*. Göppingen, Ger.: Kümmerle, 1993.

———. *Malleus maleficarum 1487 von Heinrich Kramer (Institoris): Nachdruck des Erstdruckes von 1487 mit Bulle und Approbatio*. Ed. Günter Jerouschek. Hildesheim, Ger.: Georg Olms, 1992.

Mammoli, Domenico, ed. *The Record of the Trial and Condemnation of a Witch, Mattueccia di Francesco, at Todi, 20 March 1428*. Res Tudertinae vol. 14. Rome: n.p., 1972.

Rémy, Nicholas. *Demonolatry*. Ed. Montague Summers. Trans E. A. Ashwin. 1930. Reprint, Secaucus, N.J.: University Books, 1974.

Scot, Reginald. *The Dicoverie of Witchcraft*. Ed. Montague Summers. 1930. Reprint Washington, D.C.: Kaufman and Greenberg, 1995.

Spee, Friedrich von. *Cautio Criminalis, or a Book on Witch Trials*. Trans. Marcus Heller. Charlottesville, Va.: University of Virginia Press, 2003.

Weyer, Johann. *On Witchcraft: An Abridged Translation of Johann Weyer's De praestigiis daemonum.* Ed. Benjamin G. Kohl and H. C. Erik Midelfort. Trans. John Shea. Ashville, N.C.: Pegasus Press, 1998.

———. *Witches, Devils, and Doctors in the Renaissance: Johann Weyer, De Praestigiis Daemonum.* Ed. George Mora. Binghamton, N.Y.: Medieval and Renaissance Texts and Studies, 1991.

2. Edited Source Collections

Behringer, Wolfgang, ed. *Hexen und Hexenprozesse.* 3rd ed. Munich: Deutscher Taschenbuch, 1995.

Betz, Hans Dieter, ed. *The Greek Magical Papyri in Translation, including the Demotic Spells.* 2nd ed. Chicago: University of Chicago Press, 1992.

Boyer, Paul, and Stephen Nissenbaum, eds. *The Salem Witchcraft Papers: Verbatim Transcripts of the Legal Documents of the Salem Witchcraft Outbreak of 1692.* 3 vols. New York: Da Capo Press, 1977.

———. *Salem-Village Witchcraft: A Documentary Record of Local Conflict in Colonial New England.* 2nd ed. Boston: Northeastern University Press, 1993.

Gager, John G., ed. *Curse Tablets and Binding Spells from the Ancient World.* Oxford: Oxford University Press, 1992.

Gibson, Marion. *Early Modern Witches: Witchcraft Cases in Contemporary Writing.* London: Routledge, 2000.

Hall, David D., ed. *Witch-Hunting in Seventeenth Century New England: A Documentary History, 1638–1693.* 2nd ed. Boston: Northeastern University Press, 1999.

Hansen, Joseph, ed. *Quellen und Untersuchungen zur Geschichte des Hexenwahns und der Hexenverfolgung im Mittelalter.* 1901. Reprint, Hildesheim, Ger.: Georg Olms, 1963.

Hill, Frances. *The Salem Witch Trials Reader.* New York: Da Capo Press, 2000.

Kors, Alan, and Edward Peters, eds. *Witchcraft in Europe, 400–1700: A Documentary History.* 2nd ed. Philadelphia: University of Pennsylvania Press, 2001.

Larner, Christina, Cristopher Hyde Lee, and Hugh V. McLachlan, eds. *Source-Book of Scottish Witchcraft.* Glasgow: SSRC Project on Accusations and Prosecutions for Witchcraft in Scotland, 1977.

Lea, Henry Charles. *Materials Toward a History of Witchcraft.* Ed. Arthur C. Howland. 3 vols. Philadelphia: University of Pennsylvania Press, 1939.

Luck, Georg, ed. *Arcana Mundi: Magic and the Occult in the Greek and Roman Worlds.* Baltimore, Md.: Johns Hopkins University Press, 1985.

Mandrou, Robert, ed. *Possession et sorcellerie au XVIIe siècle: Textes inédits.* Paris: Hachette, 1979.

Maxwell-Stuart, P. G., ed. *The Occult in Early Modern Europe: A Documentary History*. New York: St. Martin's Press, 1999.

Ostorero, Martine, Agostino Paravicini Bagliani, and Kathrin Utz Tremp, eds. *L'imaginaire du sabbat: Edition critique des textes les plus anciens (1430 c.–1440 c.)*. Lausanne, Switz.: Université de Lausanne, 1999.

Rosen, Barbara, ed. *Witchcraft in England, 1558–1618*. Amherst, Mass.: University of Massachusetts Press, 1991.

II. GENERAL STUDIES

1. General Surveys

Ankarloo, Bengt, and Stuart Clark, eds. *Witchcraft and Magic in Europe*. 6 vols. Philadelphia: University of Pennsylvania Press, 1999–2003 (vol. 1: *Biblical and Pagan Societies*; vol. 2: *Ancient Greece and Rome*; vol. 3: *The Middle Ages*; vol. 4: *The Period of the Witch Trials*: vol. 5: *The Eighteenth and Nineteenth Centuries*; vol. 6: *The Twentieth Century*).

Behringer, Wolfgang. *Hexen: Glaube, Verfolgung, Vermarktung*. Munich: Beck, 1998.

Breslaw, Elaine G., ed. *Witches of the Atlantic World: A Historical Reader and Primary Sourcebook*. New York: New York University Press, 2000.

Caro Baroja, Julio. *The World of the Witches*. Trans. O. N. V. Glendinning. Chicago: University of Chicago Press, 1965.

Daxelmüller, Christoph. *Zauberpraktiken: Die Ideengeschichte der Magie*. Düsseldorf, Ger.: Albatros, 2001.

Dülmen, Richard van, ed. *Hexenwelten: Magie und Imagination vom 16.–20. Jahrhundert*. Frankfurt: Fischer, 1987.

Franklyn, Julian. *Death by Enchantment: An Examination of Ancient and Modern Witchcraft*. New York: Putnam, 1971.

Hoyt, Charles Alva. *Witchcraft*. 2nd ed. Carbondale, Ill.: Southern Illinois University Press, 1989.

Lehmann, Arthur C., and James F. Myers. *Magic, Witchcraft and Religion: An Anthropological Study of the Supernatural*. Stanford, Calif.: Stanford University Press, 1985.

Levack, Brian P., ed. *Articles on Witchcraft, Magic and Demonology*. 12 vols. New York: Garland, 1992 (vol. 1: *Anthropological Studies of Witchcraft, Magic, and Religion*; vol. 2: *Witchcraft in the Ancient World and the Middle Ages*; vol. 3: *Witch-Hunting in Early Modern Europe: General Studies*; vol. 4: *The Literature of Witchcraft*; vol. 5: *Witch-Hunting in Continental Europe: Local and Regional Studies*; vol. 6: *Witchcraft in England*; vol. 7: *Witchcraft in Scotland*; vol. 8: *Witchcraft in Colonial America*; vol. 9: *Possession and Exorcism*; vol. 10: *Witchcraft, Women, and Society*; vol. 11: *Renaissance Magic*; vol. 12: *Witchcraft and Demonology in Art and Literature*).

———. *New Perspectives on Witchcraft, Magic, and Demonology*. 6 vols. New York: Garland, 2001 (vol. 1: *Demonology, Witchcraft, and Religion*; vol. 2: *Witchcraft in Continental Europe*; vol. 3: *Witchcraft in the British Isles and New England*; vol. 4: *Gender and Witchcraft*; vol. 5: *Witchcraft, Healing, and Popular Diseases*; vol. 6: *Witchcraft in the Modern World*).

Maxwell-Stuart, P. G. *Witchcraft: A History*. Charleston, S.C.: Tempus, 2000.

Muchembled, Robert, ed. *Magie et sorcellerie en Europe du Moyen Age à nos jours*. Paris: Colin, 1994.

Ravensdale, Tom, and James Morgan. *The Psychology of Witchcraft: An Account of Witchcraft, Black Magic, and the Occult*. New York: Arco, 1974.

Russell, Jeffrey Burton. *A History of Witchcraft: Sorcerers, Heretics and Pagans*. London: Thames and Hudson, 1980.

Schwaiger, Georg, ed. *Teufelsglaube und Hexenprozesse*. 4th ed. Munich: Beck, 1999.

Wilson, Stephen. *The Magical Universe: Everyday Ritual and Magic in Pre-Modern Europe*. London: Hambledon, 2001.

2. Bibliographical and Historiographical Surveys

Barstow, Anne. "On Studying Witchcraft as Women's History: A Historiography of the European Witch Persecutions." *Journal of Feminist Studies in Religion* 4 (1988): 7–19.

Behringer, Wolfang. "Neue Historische Literatur: Erträge und Perspektiven der Hexenforschung." *Historische Zeitschrift* 249 (1989): 619–40.

Crowe, Martha J., ed. *Witchcraft: Catalogue of the Witchcraft Collection in the Cornell University Library*. Millwood, N.Y.: KTO Press, 1977.

Franz, Günther, and Franz Irsigler, eds. *Methoden und Konzepte der historischen Hexenforschung*. Trier, Ger.: Spee, 1998.

Gijswijt-Hofstra, Marijke. "Recent Witchcraft Research in the Low Countries." In *Historical Research in the Low Countries*, ed. N. C. F. van Sas and Els Witte. The Hague: Nederlands Historisch Genootschap, 1992, 23–34.

Melton, J. Gordon. *Magic, Witchcraft, and Paganism in America: A Bibliography*. New York: Garland, 1982.

Midelfort, H. C. Erik. "Recent Witch Hunting Research, or Where Do We Go from Here?" *Papers of the Bibliographical Society of America* 62 (1968): 373–420.

———. "Witchcraft, Magic and the Occult." In *Reformation Europe: A Guide to Research*, ed. Steven Ozment. St. Louis, Mo.: Center for Reformation Research, 1982, 183–209.

Monter, E. William. "The Historiography of European Witchcraft: Progress and Prospects." *Journal of Interdisciplinary History* 2 (1972): 435–51.

Purkiss, Diane. *The Witch in History: Early Modern and Twentieth-Century Representations*. London: Routledge, 1996.

Whitney, Elspeth. "International Trends: The Witch 'She' / The Historian 'He': Gender and the Historiography of the European Witch-Hunts." *Journal of Women's History* 7 (1995): 77–101.

3. Encyclopedias and Reference Sources

Golden, Richard, et al., eds. *Encyclopedia of Witchcraft: The Western Tradition*. Santa Barbara, Calif.: ABC-Clio, forthcoming.

Greenwood, Susan. *The Encyclopedia of Magic and Witchcraft: An Illustrated Historical Reference to Spiritual Worlds*. London: Lorenz, 2001.

Grimassi, Raven. *Encyclopedia of Wicca and Witchcraft*. St. Paul, Minn.: Llewellyn 2000.

Guiley, Rosemary Ellen. *The Encyclopedia of Witches and Witchcraft*. 2nd ed. New York: Checkmark, 1999.

Lewis, James R. *Witchcraft Today: An Encyclopedia of Wiccan and Neopagan Traditions*. Santa Barbara, Calif.: ABC-Clio, 1999.

Newall, Venetia. *The Encyclopedia of Witchcraft and Magic*. London: Hamlyn, 1974.

Pickering, David. *Cassell's Dictionary of Witchcraft*. London: Cassell, 1996.

Robbins, Rossell Hope. *The Encyclopedia of Witchcraft and Demonology*. New York: Crown, 1959.

III. WITCHCRAFT IN THE ANCIENT WORLD

Abusch, Tzvi. *Babylonian Witchcraft Literature: Case Studies*. Atlanta, Ga.: Scholars Press, 1987.

———. "The Demonic Image of the Witch in Standard Babylonian Literature: The Reworking of Popular Conceptions by Learned Exorcists." In *Religion, Science, and Magic in Concert and in Conflict*, ed. Jacob Neusner, Ernest S. Frerichs, and Paul Virgil McCracken Flesher. Oxford: Oxford University Press, 1989, 27–58.

———. "An Early Form of the Witchcraft Ritual *Maqlû* and the Origin of a Babylonian Magical Ceremony." In *Lingering over Words: Studies in Ancient Near Eastern Literature in Honor of William L. Moran*, ed. Tzvi Abusch, John Huehnergard, and Piotr Steinkeller. Atlanta, Ga.: Scholars Press, 1990, 1–67.

——. "Mesopotamian Anti-Witchcraft Literature: Textes and Studies, Part I: The Nature of *Maqlû*, Its Character, Divisions, and Calendrical Setting." *Journal of Near Eastern Studies* 33 (1974): 251–62.

Aune, D. E. "Magic in Early Christianity." In *Aufsteig und Niedergang der römischen Welt* II.23.2, ed. Wolfgang Haase. Berlin: Walter de Gruyter, 1980, 1507–57.

Barb, A. A. "The Survival of Magic Arts." In *The Conflict Between Paganism and Christianity in the Fourth Century*, ed. Arnaldo Momigliano. Oxford: Clarendon, 1963, 100–25.

Bernand, André. *Sorciers grecs*. Paris: Fayard, 1991.

Brenk, Frederick E. "In the Light of the Moon: Demonology in the Early Imperial Period." In *Aufsteig und Niedergang der römischen Welt* II.16.3, ed. Wolfgang Haase. Berlin: Walter de Gruyter, 1986, 2068–2145.

Clerc, Jean-Benoît. *Homines Magici: Etude sur la sorcellerie et la magie dans la société romaine impériale*. Bern: Peter Lang, 1995.

Cryer, Frederick H. *Divination in Ancient Israel and Its Near Eastern Environs: A Socio-Historical Investigation*. Sheffield, Eng.: Journal for the Study of the Old Testament Press, 1994.

Dickie, Matthew W. "Heliodorus and Plutarch on the Evil Eye." *Classical Philology* 86 (1991): 17–29.

——. *Magic and Magicians in the Greco-Roman World*. London: Routledge, 2001.

Faraone, Christopher A. "An Accusation of Magic in Classical Athens." *Transactions of the American Philological Association* 119 (1989): 149–60.

——. *Ancient Greek Love Magic*. Cambridge, Mass.: Harvard University Press, 1999.

——. "Binding and Burying the Forces of Evil: Defensive Use of 'Voodoo' Dolls in Ancient Greece." *Classical Antiquity* 10 (1991): 165–205.

——. "Deianira's Mistake and the Demise of Heracles: Erotic Magic in Sophocles' *Trachiniae*." *Helios* 21 (1994): 115–35.

Faraone, Christopher A., and Dirk Obbink, eds. *Magika Hiera: Ancient Greek Magic and Religion*. Oxford: Oxford University Press, 1991.

Finkel, Irving L. "Necromancy in Ancient Mesopotamia." *Archiv für Orientforschung* 29–30 (1983–84): 1–17.

Frankfurter, David. "The Magic of Writing and the Writing of Magic: The Power of the Word in Egyptian and Greek Traditions." *Helios* 21 (1994): 189–221.

Garrett, Susan R. *The Demise of the Devil: Magic and the Demonic in Luke's Writings*. Minneapolis, Minn.: Fortress Publishing, 1989.

Graf, Fritz. *Magic in the Ancient World*. Trans. Franklin Philip. Cambridge, Mass.: Harvard University Press, 1997.

——. "The Magician's Initiation." *Helios* 21 (1994): 161–77.

————. "Medea, the Enchantress from Afar: Remarks on a Well-Known Myth." In *Medea: Essays on Medea in Myth, Literature, Philosophy, and Art*, ed. James J. Claus and Sarah Iles Johnston. Princeton, N.J.: Princeton University Press, 1997, 27–43.

Janowitz, Naomi. *Magic in the Roman World: Pagans, Jews and Christians.* London: Routledge, 2001.

Jeffers, Ann. *Magic and Divination in Ancient Palestine and Syria.* Leiden: Brill, 1996.

Luck, Georg. *Hexen und Zauberei in der römischen Dichtung.* Zurich: Artemis, 1962.

Meyer, Marvin, and Paul Mirecki, eds. *Ancient Magic and Ritual Power.* Leiden: Brill, 1995.

Michalowski, Piotr. "On Some Early Sumerian Magical Texts." *Orientalia* n.s. 54 (1985): 216–25.

Ogden, Daniel. *Greek and Roman Necromancy.* Princeton, N.J.: Princeton University Press, 2001.

Pinch, Geraldine. *Magic in Ancient Egypt.* Austin, Tex.: University of Texas Press, 1995.

Rabinowitz, Jacob. *The Rotting Goddess: The Origin of the Witch in Classical Antiquity.* New York: Autonomedia, 1998.

Reiner, Erica. *Astral Magic in Babylonia.* Philadelphia: American Philosophical Society, 1995.

Remus, Harold E. "Magic or Miracle: Some Second-Century Instances." *Second Century* 2 (1982): 127–56.

Rollins, S. "Women and Witchcraft in Ancient Assyria (c. 900–600 B.C.)." In *Images of Women in Antiquity*, ed. Averil Cameron and Amélie Kuhrt. Detroit, Mich.: Wayne State University Press, 1983, 34–45.

Schäfer, Peter, and Hans G. Klippenberg, eds. *Envisioning Magic: A Princeton Seminar and Symposium.* Leiden: Brill, 1997.

Scobie, Alex. "Strigiform Witches in Roman and Other Cultures." *Fabula* 19 (1978): 74–101.

Smith, Jonathan Z. "Towards Interpreting Demonic Powers in Hellenistic and Roman Antiquity." *Aufsteig und Niedergang der römischen Welt* II.16.1, ed. Wolfgang Haase. Berlin: Walter de Gruyter, 1978, 425–39.

————. "The Evil Eye in Mesopotamia." *Journal of the Near Eastern Society* 51 (1992): 19–32.

————. "The Wisdom of the Chaldaeans: Mesopotamian Magic as Conceived by Classical Authors." In *East and West: Cultural Relations in the Ancient World*, ed. Tobias Fischer-Hansen. Copenhagen: Museum Tusculanum, 1988, 93–101.

Thomsen, Marie-Louise. *Zauberdiagnose und Schwarze Magie in Mesopotamien.* Copenhagen: Carsten Niebuhr Institute for Ancient Near Eastern Studies, 1987.

Ulmer, Rivka. *The Evil Eye in the Bible and Rabbinic Literature*. Hoboken, N.J.: KTAV Publishing House, 1994.

Walters, Stanley D. "The Sorceress and Her Apprentice: A Case Study of an Accusation." *Journal of Cuneiform Studies* 23 (1970–71): 27–38.

Ward, John O. "Women, Witchcraft and Social Patterning in the Later Roman Lawcodes." *Prudentia* 13 (1981): 99–118.

IV. WITCHCRAFT IN MEDIEVAL AND EARLY-MODERN EUROPE

1. Late Antiquity and Early Middle Ages

Brown, Peter. "Sorcery, Demons and the Rise of Christianity: From Late Antiquity into the Middle Ages." In Peter Brown, *Religion and Society in the Age of St. Augustine*. New York: Harper and Row, 1972, 119–46.

———. "Society and the Supernatural: A Medieval Change." *Daedalus* 104.2 (1975): 133–51.

Dukes, Eugene D. *Magic and Witchcraft in the Dark Ages*. Lanham, Md.: University Press of America, 1996.

Flint, Valerie I. J. *The Rise of Magic in Early Medieval Europe*. Princeton, N.J.: Princeton University Press, 1991.

Janowitz, Naomi. *Icons of Power: Ritual Practice in Late Antiquity*. University Park, Pa.: Pennsylvania State University Press, 2002.

Markus, Robert A. "Augustine on Magic: A Neglected Semiotic Theory." *Revue des études augustiniennes* 40 (1994): 375–88.

Meens, Rob. "Magic and the Early Medieval World View." In *Community, the Family, and the Saint: Patterns of Power in Early Medieval Europe*, ed. Joyce Hill and Mary Swan. Turnhout, Bel.: Brepols, 1998, 285–95.

Murray, Alexander. "Missionaries and Magic in Dark-Age Europe." *Past and Present* 136 (1992): 186–205.

Riché, Pierre. "La magie à l'époque carolingienne." *Comptes rendus des séances de l'Académie des Inscriptions et Belles-lettres* 1 (1973): 127–38.

Schäfer, Peter. "Jewish Magical Literature in Late Antiquity and the Early Middle Ages." *Journal of Jewish Studies* 41 (1990): 75–91.

Smelik, K. A. D. "The Witch of Endor: 1 Samuel 28 in Rabbinic and Christian Exegesis till 800 A.D." *Vigiliae Christianae* 33 (1979): 160–79.

Thee, Francis C. R. *Julius Africanus and the Early Christian View of Magic*. Tübingen, Ger.: Mohr, 1984.

Ward, John O. "Witchcraft and Sorcery in the Later Roman Empire and the Early Middle Ages: An Anthropological Comment." *Prudentia* 12 (1980): 93–108.

2. The Middle Ages

Bailey, Michael D. "From Sorcery to Witchcraft: Clerical Conceptions of Magic in the Later Middle Ages." *Speculum* 76 (2001): 960–90.

Barber, Malcolm. *The Trial of the Templars*. Cambridge: Cambridge University Press, 1978.

Blauert, Andreas, ed. *Ketzer, Zauberer, Hexen: Die Anfänge der europäischen Hexenverfolgungen*. Frankfurt: Suhrkamp, 1990.

Bologne, Jean-Claude. *Du flambeau au bûcher: Magie et superstition au Moyen Age*. Paris: Plon, 1993.

Boudet, Jean-Patrice. "La genèse médiévale de la chasse aux sorcières: Jalons en vue d'une relecture." In *Le mal et le diable: Leurs figures à la fin du Moyen Age*, ed. Nathalie Nabert. Paris: Beauchesne, 1996, 34–52.

Cohn, Norman. *Europe's Inner Demons: The Demonization of Christians in Medieval Christendom*. Rev. ed. Chicago: University of Chicago Press, 2000.

Habiger-Tuczay, Christa. *Magie und Magier im Mittelalter*. Munich: Diederichs, 1992.

Hansen, Joseph. *Zauberwahn, Inquisition und Hexenprozess im Mittelalter und die Entstehung der grossen Hexenverfolgung*. 1900. Reprint, Aalen, Ger.: Scientia, 1964.

Harmening, Dieter. "Magiciennes et sorcières: La mutation du concept de magie à la fin du Moyen Age." *Heresis* 13–14 (1989): 421–45.

———. *Superstitio: Überlieferungs- und theoriegeschichtliche Untersuchungen zur kirchlich-theologischen Aberglaubensliteratur des Mittelalters*. Berlin: Schmidt, 1979.

———. *Zauberei im Abendland: Vom Anteil der Gelehrten am Wahn der Leute: Skizzen zur Geschichte des Aberglaubens*. Würzburg, Ger.: Köningshausen & Neumann, 1991.

Harvey, Margaret. "Papal Witchcraft: The Charges against Benedict XIII." In *Sanctity and Secularity: The Church and the World*, ed. Derek Baker. Oxford: Blackwell, 1973, 109–16.

Jones, William R. "Political Uses of Sorcery in Medieval Europe." *The Historian* 34 (1972): 670–87.

Kieckhefer, Richard. "Avenging the Blood of Children: Anxiety over Child Victims and the Origins of the European Witch Trials." In *The Devil, Heresy and Witchcraft: Essays in Honor of Jeffrey B. Russell*, ed. Alberto Ferreiro. Leiden: Brill, 1998, 91–109.

———. "Erotic Magic in Medieval Europe." In *Sex in the Middle Ages: A Book of Essays*, ed. Joyce E. Salisbury. New York: Garland, 1991, 30–55.

———. *European Witch Trials: Their Foundations in Popular and Learned Culture, 1300–1500*. Berkeley, Calif.: University of California Press, 1976.

———. *Forbidden Rites: A Necromancer's Manual of the Fifteenth Century.* University Park, Pa.: Pennsylvania State University Press, 1998.

———. "The Holy and the Unholy: Sainthood, Witchcraft, and Magic in Late Medieval Europe." *Journal of Medieval and Renaissance Studies* 24 (1994): 355–85. Reprinted in *Christendom and Its Discontents: Exclusion, Persecution, and Rebellion, 1000–1500*, ed. Scott L. Waugh and Peter D. Diehl. Cambridge: Cambridge University Press, 1996, 310–37.

———. *Magic in the Middle Ages.* Cambridge: Cambridge University Press, 1989.

———. "The Specific Rationality of Medieval Magic." *American Historical Review* 99 (1994): 813–36.

Lecouteux, Claude. *Fées, sorcières et loups-garous au Moyen Age.* Paris: Imago, 1992.

Maier, Anneliese. "Eine Verfügung Johannes XXII. über die Zuständigkeit der Inquisition für Zaubereiprozesse." *Archivum Fratrum Praedicatorum* 22 (1952): 226–46. Reprinted in Anneliese Maier, *Ausgehendes Mittelalter: Gesamelte Aufsätze zur Geistesgeschichte des 14. Jahrhunderts.* 3 vols. Rome, 1964–77, 2:59–80.

Manselli, Raoul. *Magia e stregoneria nel medio evo.* Turin: Giappichelli, 1976.

Murray, Alexander. "Medieval Origins of the Witch-Hunt." *The Cambridge Quarterly* 7 (1976): 63–74.

Peters, Edward. *The Magician, the Witch, and the Law.* Philadelphia: University of Pennsylvania Press, 1978.

Rose, Elliot. *A Razor for a Goat: Problems in the History of Witchcraft and Diabolism.* 1962. Reprint, Toronto: University of Toronto Press, 1989.

Russell, Jeffrey Burton. "Medieval Witchcraft and Medieval Heresy." In *On the Margin of the Visible: Sociology, the Esoteric, and the Occult*, ed. Edward A. Tiryakian. New York: Wiley, 1974, 179–89.

———. *Witchcraft in the Middle Ages.* Ithaca, N.Y.: Cornell University Press, 1972.

Russell, Jeffrey B., and Mark W. Wyndham. "Witchcraft and the Demonization of Heresy." *Mediaevalia* 2 (1976): 1–21.

Tucker, Elizabeth. "Antecedents of Contemporary Witchcraft in the Middle Ages." *Journal of Popular Culture* 14 (1980): 70–78.

3. The Era of the Witch-Hunts

Ankarloo, Bengt, and Gustav Henningsen, eds. *Early Modern European Witchcraft: Centres and Peripheries.* Oxford: Oxford University Press, 1990.

Barry, Jonathan, Marianne Hester, and Gareth Robert, eds. *Witchcraft in Early Modern Europe: Studies in Culture and Belief*. Cambridge: Cambridge University Press, 1996.

Bechtel, Guy. *Le sorcier et l'Occident: La destruction de la sorcellerie en Europe des origines aux grands bûchers*. Paris: Plon, 1997.

Becker, Gabriele, et al. *Aus der Zeit der Verzweiflung: Zur Genese und Aktualität des Hexenbilds*. Frankfurt: Suhrkamp, 1976.

Behringer, Wolfgang. "Kinderhexenprozesse: Zur Rolle von Kindern in der Geschichte der Hexenverfolgung." *Zeitschrift für historische Forschung* 16 (1989): 31–47.

———. "Weather, Hunger and Fear: Origins of the European Witch-Hunts in Climate, Society and Mentality." *German History* 13 (1995): 1–27.

Ben-Yehuda, Nachman. "The European Witch Craze of the Fourteenth to Seventeenth Centuries: A Sociologist's Perspective." *American Journal of Sociology* 86 (1980): 1–31.

———. "Problems Inherent in Socio-Historical Approaches to the European Witch-Craze." *Journal for the Scientific Study of Religion* 20 (1981): 326–38.

———. "Witchcraft and the Occult as Boundary Maintenance Devices." In *Religion, Science, and Magic in Concert and in Conflict*, ed. Jacob Neusner, Ernest S. Frerichs, and Paul Virgil McCracken Flesher. Oxford: Oxford University Press, 1989, 229–60.

Bever, Edward. "Old Age and Witchcraft in Early Modern Europe." In *Old Age in Pre-Industrial Society*, ed. Peter N. Sterns. New York: Holmes and Meier, 1982, 150–90.

Blécourt, Willem de. "Witch Doctors, Soothsayers and Priests: On Cunning Folk in European Historiography and Tradition." *Social History* 19 (1994): 285–303.

Briggs, Robin. *Witches and Neighbors: The Social and Cultural Context of European Witchcraft*. 2nd ed. New York: Viking, 2002.

Clark, Stuart. "Inversion, Misrule and the Meaning of Witchcraft." *Past and Present* 87 (1980): 98–127.

———. *Thinking with Demons: The Idea of Witchcraft in Early Modern Europe*. Oxford: Clarendon, 1997.

Clark, Stuart, ed. *Languages of Witchcraft: Narrative, Ideology and Meaning in Early Modern Culture*. New York: St. Martin's Press, 2001.

Currie, Elliott P. "Crimes without Criminals: Witchcraft and Its Control in Renaissance Europe." *Law and Society Review* 3 (1968): 7–32.

Eliade, Mircea. "Some Observations on European Witchcraft." *History of Religions* 14 (1975): 149–72. Reprinted in Mircea Eliade, *Occultism, Witchcraft, and Cultural Fashions: Essays in Comparative Religions*. Chicago: University of Chicago Press, 1976, 69–92.

Hoak, Dale. "The Great European Witch–Hunts: A Historical Perspective." *American Journal of Sociology* 88 (1983): 1270–74.

Honegger, Claudia, ed. *Die Hexen der Neuzeit: Studien zur Sozialgeschichte eines kulturellen Deutungsmusters*. Frankfurt: Suhrkamp, 1978.

Horsley, Richard A. "Further Reflections on Witchcraft and European Folk Religion." *History of Religions* 19 (1979): 71–95.

———. "Who Were the Witches? The Social Roles of the Accused in the European Witch-Trials." *Journal of Interdisciplinary History* 9 (1979): 689–715.

Klaits, Joseph. *Servants of Satan: The Age of the Witch Hunts*. Bloomington, Ind.: Indiana University Press, 1985.

Larner, Christina. "*Crimen Exceptum*? The Crime of Witchcraft in Europe." In *Crime and the Law: The Social History of Crime since 1500*, ed. V. A. C. Gatrell, Bruce Lenman, and Geoffrey Parker. London: Europa, 1980, 49–75.

———. *Witchcraft and Religion: The Politics of Popular Belief*. Ed. Alan Macfarlane. Oxford: Blackwell, 1984.

Levack, Brian. "The Great Witch-Hunt." In *Handbook of European History, 1400–1600: Late Middle Ages, Renaissance, and Reformation*, 2 vols., ed. Thomas A. Brady Jr., Heiko A. Oberman, and James D. Tracy. Leiden: Brill, 1994–95, 2:607–40.

———. *The Witch-Hunt in Early Modern Europe*. 2nd ed. London: Longman, 1995.

Maxwell-Stuart, P. G. *Witchcraft in Europe and the New World, 1400–1800*. New York: Palgrave, 2001.

Midelfort, H. C. Erik. "Were There Really Witches?" In *Transition and Revolution: Problems and Issues of European Renaissance and Reformation History*, ed. Robert M. Kingdon. Minneapolis, Minn.: Burgess, 1974, 189–205.

———. "Witch Hunting and the Domino Theory." In *Religion and the People, 800–1700*, ed. James Obelkevich. Chapel Hill, N.C.: University of North Carolina Press, 1979, 277–88, 323–25.

Monter, E. William. "French and Italian Witchcraft." *History Today* 30 (November 1980): 31–35.

———. *Ritual, Myth and Magic in Early Modern Europe*. Athens, Ohio: Ohio University Press, 1983.

Monter, E. William, ed. *European Witchcraft*. New York: Wiley, 1969.

Muchembled, Robert. *Le roi et le sorcière: L'Europe des bûchers (XVe-XVIIe siècle)*. Paris: Desclée, 1993.

———. *Le sorcière au village: XVe-XVIIIe siècle*. Paris: Gallimard, 1979.

Nugent, Donald. "The Renaissance . . . of Witchcraft." *Church History* 40 (1971): 69–78.

Oldridge, Darren, ed. *The Witchcraft Reader*. London: Routledge, 2002.

Oplinger, Jon. *The Politics of Demonology: The European Witchcraze and the Mass Production of Deviance*. London: Associated University Presses, 1990.

Quaife, G. R. *Godly Zeal and Furious Rage: The Witch in Early Modern Europe*. New York: St. Martin's Press, 1987.

Scarre, Geoffrey. *Witchcraft and Magic in 16th and 17th Century Europe*. 2nd ed. Atlantic Highlands, N.J.: Humanities Press, 2001.

Scribner, Robert W. "Magic, Witchcraft, and Superstition." *Historical Journal* 37 (1994): 219–30.

———. "The Reformation, Popular Magic, and the 'Disenchantment of the World.'" *Journal of Interdisciplinary History* 23 (1992–93): 475–94.

Segl, Peter, et al. *Hexenglaube und Hexenverfolgungen: Eine kritische Bilanz*. Augsburg, Ger.: Akademie-Publikationen, 1989.

Stephens, Walter. *Demon Lovers: Witchcraft, Sex, and the Crisis of Belief*. Chicago: University of Chicago Press, 2002.

———. "Incredible Sex: Witches, Demons, and Giants in the Early Modern Imagination." In *Monsters in the Italian Literary Imagination,* ed. Keala Jewel. Detroit, Mich.: Wayne State University Press, 2001, 153–76.

Thurston, Robert W. *Witch, Wicce, Mother Goose: The Rise and Fall of the Witch Hunts in Europe and America*. New York: Longman, 2001.

Trevor-Roper, H. R. *The European Witch-Craze of the Sixteenth and Seventeenth Centuries and Other Essays*. New York: Harper, 1969.

4. The Witches' Sabbath

Bailey, Michael D. "The Medieval Concept of the Witches' Sabbath." *Exemplaria* 8 (1996): 419–39.

———. *Ecstasies: Deciphering the Witches' Sabbath*. Trans. Raymond Rosenthal. New York: Pantheon, 1991.

Ginzburg, Carlo. "The Witches' Sabbat: Popular Cult or Inquisitorial Stereotype?" In *Understanding Popular Culture: Europe from the Middle Ages to the Nineteenth Century*, ed. Steven L. Kaplan. Berlin: Mouton, 1984, 39–51.

Jacques-Chaquin, Nicole, and Maxime Préaud, eds. *Le sabbat des sorciers, XVe–XVIIIe siècles*. Grenoble, France: Millon, 1994.

Klaniczay, Gábor. "Der Hexensabbat im Spiegel von Zeugenaussagen in Hexen-Prozessen." *Zeitschrift für Kulturwissenschaften* 5 (1993): 31–54.

Paravicini Bagliani, Agostino, Kathrin Utz Tremp, and Martine Ostorero. "Le sabbat dans les Alpes: Les prémices médiévales de la chasse aux sorcières." In *Sciences: Raison et déraisons*. Lausanne, Switz.: Payot, 1994, 67–89.

Tschacher, Werner. "Der Flug durch die Luft zwischen Illusionstheorie und Realitätsbeweis: Studien zum sog. Kanon Episcopi und zum Hexenflug." *Zeitschrift der Savigny-Stiftung für Rechtsgeschichte* 116, Kan. Abt. 85 (1999): 225–76.

5. Witchcraft, Medicine, and Disease

Andreski, Stanislav. "The Syphilitic Shock: A New Explanation of the 'Great Witch Craze' of the 16th and 17th Centuries in the Light of Medicine and Psychiatry." *Encounter* 58 (1982): 7–26.

Estes, Leland. "The Medical Origins of the European Witch Craze: A Hypothesis." *Journal of Social History* 17 (1983): 271–84.

Geyer-Kordesch, Johanna. "Whose Enlightenment? Medicine, Witchcraft, Melancholia and Pathology." In *Medicine in the Enlightenment*, ed. Roy Porter. Amsterdam: Rodopi, 1994, 113–27.

Harner, Michael J. "The Role of Hallucinogenic Plants in European Witchcraft." In *Hallucinogens and Shamanism*, ed. Michael J. Harner. Oxford: Oxford University Press, 1973, 125–50.

King, L. S. "Friedrich Hoffmann and Some Medical Aspects of Witchcraft." *Clio Medica* 9 (1974): 299–309.

———. "Witchcraft and Medicine: Conflicts in the Early Eighteenth Century." In *Circa Tiliam: Studiae historiae medicinae Gerrit Arie Lindeboom septuagenaria oblata*. Leiden: Brill, 1974, 122–39.

Nemec, Jaroslav. *Witchcraft and Medicine, 1484–1793*. Washington D.C.: U.S. Department of Health, Education, and Welfare, 1974.

Piomelli, Daniele, and Antonio Pollio. "'In upupa o strige': A Study in Renaissance Psychotropic Plant Ointments." *History and Philosophy of the Life Sciences* 16 (1994): 241–73.

Schoeneman, Thomas J. "Criticisms of the Psychopathological Interpretation of the Witch-Hunts: A Review." *American Journal of Psychiatry* 139 (1982): 1028–32.

———. "The Role of Mental Illness in the European Witch Hunts of the Sixteenth and Seventeenth Centuries: An Assessment." *Journal of the History of Behavioral Sciences* 13 (1977): 337–51.

———. "The Witch Hunt as a Cultural Change Phenomenon." *Ethos* 3 (1975): 529–54.

Sidky, H. *Witchcraft, Lycanthropy, Drugs, and Disease: An Anthropological Study of the European Witch-Hunts*. New York: Peter Lang, 1997.

6. Women, Gender, and Witchcraft

Bailey, Michael D. "The Feminization of Magic and the Emerging Idea of the Female Witch in the Late Middle Ages." *Essays in Medieval Studies* 19 (2002): 120–34.

Barstow, Anne Llewellyn. *Witchcraze: A New History of the European Witch Hunts*. San Francisco: Pandora, 1994.

Blöcker, Monica. "Frauenzauber—Zauberfrauen." *Zeitschrift für schweizerische Kirchengeschichte* 76 (1982): 1–39.

Coudert, Allison P. "The Myth of the Improved Status of Protestant Woman: The Case of the Witchcraze." In *The Politics of Gender in Early Modern Europe*, ed. Jean R. Brink, Allison P. Coudert, and Maryanne C. Horowitz. Kirksville, Mo.: Sixteenth Century Journal Publishers, 1989, 61–94.

Dienst, Heide. "Zur Rolle von Frauen im magischen Vorstellungen und Praktiken—nach ausgewählten mittalterlichen Quellen." In *Frauen in Spätantike und Frühmittelalter: Lebensbedingungen—Lebensnormen—Lebensformen*, ed. Werner Affeldt. Sigmaringen, Ger.: Thorbecke, 1990, 173–94.

Dinzelbacher, Peter. *Heilige oder Hexen? Schicksale auffälliger Frauen im Mittelalter und Frühneuzeit.* Munich: Artemis, 1995.

Ehrenreich, Barbara, and Deirdre English. *Witches, Midwives and Nurses: A History of Women Healers.* New York: Feminist Press, 1973.

Garrett, Clarke. "Women and Witches: Patterns of Analysis." *Signs* 3 (1977): 461–70.

Harley, David. "Historians as Demonologists: The Myth of the Midwife-Witch." *Social History of Medicine* 3 (1990): 1–26.

Heinemann, Evelyn. *Witches: A Psychoanalytical Exploration of the Killing of Women.* Trans. Donald Kiraly. London: Free Association Books, 2000.

Hester, Marianne. *Lewd Women and Wicked Witches: A Study of the Dynamics of Male Domination.* London: Routledge, 1992.

Holmes, Clive. "Women: Witnesses and Witches." *Past and Present* 140 (1993): 45–78.

Horsley, Ritta Jo, and Richard A. Horsley. "On the Trail of the 'Witches': Wise Women, Midwives and the European Witch Hunts." In *Women in German Yearbook 3: Feminist Studies and German Culture*, ed. Mariane Burkhard and Edith Waldstein. Washington, D.C.: University of America Press, 1987, 1–28.

James-Raoul, Danièle. "La femme maléfique dans la literature Romanesque de la fin du Moyen Age." In *Le mal et le diable: Leurs figures à la fin du Moyen Age*, ed. Nathalie Nabert. Paris: Beauchesne, 1996, 11–33.

Kittell, Ellen E. "Toward a Perspective on Women, Sex, and Witches in the Later Middle Ages." In *Von Menschen und ihren Zeichen: Sozialhistorische Untersuchungen zum Spätmittelalter und zur Neuzeit*, ed. Ingrid Matschinegg et al. Bielefeld, Ger.: Verlag für Regionalgeschichte, 1990, 13–40.

Klaniczay, Gábor. "*Miraculum* und *maleficium*: Einige Überlegungen zu den wieblichen Heiligen des Mittelalters in Mitteleuropa." *Wissenschaftskolleg Jahrbuch* (1990/1991): 220–48.

Labouvie, Eva. "Männer im Hexenprozeß: Zur Sozialanthropologie eines 'männlichen' Verständnisses von Hexerei." *Geschichte und Gesellschaft* 16 (1990): 56–78.

McLachlan, Hugh. "Witchcraft and Antifeminism." *Scottish Journal of Sociology* 4 (1980): 141–66.

Monter, E. William. "The Pedestal and the Stake: Courtly Love and Witchcraft." In *Becoming Visible: Women in European History*, ed. Renate Bridenthal and Claudia Koonz. Boston: Houghton Mifflin, 1977, 119–36.

Opitz, Claudia, ed. *Der Hexenstreit: Frauen in der frühneuzeitlichen Hexenverfolgung*. Freiburg, Ger.: Herder, 1995.

Roper, Lyndal. *Oedipus and the Devil: Witchcraft, Sexuality and Religion in Early Modern Europe*. London: Routledge, 1994.

Weston, L. M. C. "Women's Medicine, Women's Magic: The Old English Metrical Childbirth Charms." *Modern Philology* 92 (1995): 279–93.

Wiesner, Mary E. *Women and Gender in Early Modern Europe*. Cambridge: Cambridge University Press, 1993.

Williams, Selma R., and Pamela Williams Adelman. *Riding the Nightmare: Women and Witchcraft from the Old World to Colonial Salem*. New York: Harper, 1978.

7. Magic and Occult Science in the Era of the Witch-Hunts

Cook, John W. "Magic, Witchcraft, and Science." *Philosophical Investigations* 6 (1983): 2–36.

Copenhaver, Brian P. "Scholastic Philosophy and Renaissance Magic in the *De vita* of Marsilio Ficino." *Renaissance Quarterly* 37 (1984): 632–80.

Couliano, Ioan P. *Eros and Magic in the Renaissance*. Chicago: University of Chicago Press, 1987.

Easlea, Brian. *Witch Hunting, Magic and the New Philosophy: An Introduction to the Debates of the Scientific Revolution 1450–1750*. Atlantic Highlands, N.J.: Humanities Press, 1980.

Gouk, Penelope. *Music, Science and Natural Magic in Seventeenth-Century England*. New Haven, Conn.: Yale University Press, 1999.

Idel, Mosche. "The Magical and Neoplatonic Interpretation of the Kabbala in the Renaissance." In *Jewish Thought in the Sixteenth Century*, ed. Bernard D. Cooperman. Cambridge, Mass.: Harvard University Press, 186–242.

Jobe, Thomas Harmon. "The Devil in Restoration Science: The Glanvill-Webster Witchcraft Debate." *Isis* 72 (1981): 343–56.

León-Jones, Karen Silvia de. *Giordano Bruno and the Kabbalah: Prophets, Magicians, and Rabbis*. New Haven, Conn.: Yale University Press, 1997.

Mebane, John S. *Renaissance Magic and the Return of the Golden Age: The Occult Tradition and Marlowe, Johnson, and Shakespeare*. Lincoln, Nebr.: University of Nebraska Press, 1989.

Merkel, Ingrid, and Allen G. Debus, eds. *Hermeticism and the Renaissance: Intellectual History and the Occult in Early Modern Europe.* Washington, D.C.: Folger Shakespeare Library, 1988.

Shumaker, Wayne. *The Occult Sciences in the Renaissance.* Berkeley, Calif.: University of California Press, 1972.

Tambiah, Stanley Jeyaraja. *Magic, Science, Religion, and the Scope of Rationality.* Cambridge: Cambridge University Press, 1990.

Walker, D. P. *Spiritual and Demonic Magic from Ficino to Campanella.* 1958. Reprint University Park, Pa.: Pennsylvania State University Press, 2000.

Woolley, Benjamin. *The Queen's Conjurer: The Science and Magic of Dr. John Dee, Advisor to Queen Elizabeth I.* New York: Holt, 2001.

Yates, Frances A. *The Art of Memory.* Chicago: University of Chicago Press, 1966.

———. *Giordano Bruno and the Hermetic Tradition.* Chicago: University of Chicago Press, 1964.

———. "The Hermetic Tradition in Renaissance Science." In *Art, Science, and History in the Renaissance,* ed. Charles S. Singleton. Baltimore, Md.: Johns Hopkins Unviersity Press, 1967, 255–74.

———. *The Occult Philosophy in the Elizabethan Age.* London: Routledge, 1979.

———. *The Rosicrucian Enlightenment.* London: Routledge, 1972.

Zambelli, Paolo. "Magic and Radical Reformation in Agrippa of Nettesheim." *Journal of the Warburg and Courtauld Institute* 39 (1976): 69–103.

———. *L'ambigua natura della magia: Filosofi, streghe, riti nel Rinascimento.* 2nd ed. Venice: Marsilio, 1996.

Zika, Charles. "Reuchelin's *De verbo mirifico* and the Magic Debate in the Late Fifteenth Century." *Journal of the Warburg and Courtauld Institute* 39 (1976): 104–38.

V. WITCHCRAFT IN MEDIEVAL AND EARLY-MODERN EUROPE: REGIONAL STUDIES

1. British Isles

Anderson, Alan, and Raymond Gordon. "Witchcraft and the Status of Women: The Case of England." *British Journal of Sociology* 29 (1978): 171–84.

Bostridge, Ian. *Witchcraft and Its Transformations c.1650–c.1750.* Oxford: Clarendon, 1997.

Byrne, Patrick. *Witchcraft in Ireland.* Cork: Mercier, 1975.

Clark, Stuart, and P. T. J. Morgan. "Religion and Magic in Elizabethan Wales: Robert Holland's Dialogue on Witchcraft." *Journal of Ecclesiastical History* 27 (1976): 31–46.

Cowan, Edward J. "The Darker Vision of the Scottish Renaissance: The Devil and Francis Stewart." In *The Renaissance and Reformation in Scotland*, ed. Ian. B. Cowan and Duncan Shaw. Edinburgh: Scottish Academic Press, 1983, 125–40.

Crawford, Jane. "Evidence for Witchcraft in Anglo-Saxon England." *Medium Aevum* 32 (1963): 99–116.

Deacon, Richard. *Matthew Hopkins: Witch-Finder General*. London: Muller, 1976.

Durston, Gregory. *Witchcraft and Witch Trials: A History of English Witchcraft and its Legal Perspectives, 1542 to 1736*. Chichester, Eng.: Barry Rose Law, 2000.

Gaskill, M. "The Devil in the Shape of a Man: Witchcraft, Conflict and Belief in Jacobean England." *Historical Research* 71 (1998): 142–71.

Geis, Gilbert, and Ivan Bunn. *A Trial of Witches: A Seventeenth-Century Witchcraft Prosecution*. London: Routledge, 1997.

Gibson, Marion. *Reading Witchcraft: Stories of Early English Witches*. London: Routledge, 1999.

Gregory, Annabel. "Witchcraft, Politics and 'Good Neighbourhood' in Early Seventeenth-Century Rye." *Past and Present* 133 (1991): 31–66.

Griffiths, Bill. *Aspects of Anglo-Saxon Magic*. Hockwold-cum-Wilton, Eng.: Anglo-Saxon Books, 1996.

Guskin, Phyllis J. "The Context of Witchcraft: The Case of Jane Wenham (1712)." *Eighteenth Century Studies* 15 (1981): 48–71.

Harley, David. "Mental Illness, Magical Medicine and the Devil in Northern England, 1650–1700." In *The Medical Revolution of the Seventeenth Century*, ed. R. K. French and A. Wear. Cambridge: Cambridge University Press, 1989, 114–44.

Holmes, Clive. "Popular Culture? Witches, Magistrates and Divines in Early Modern England." In *Understanding Popular Culture: Europe from the Middle Ages to the Nineteenth Century*, ed. Steven Kaplan. Berlin: Mouton, 1984, 85–111.

Holmes, Ronald. *Witchcraft in British History*. London: Muller, 1974.

Jolly, Karen Louise. "Anglo-Saxon Charms in the Context of a Christian World View." *Journal of Medieval History* 11 (1985): 279–93.

———. "Magic, Miracle, and Popular Practice in the Early Medieval West: Anglo-Saxon England." In *Religion, Science, and Magic in Concert and in Conflict*, ed. Jacob Neusner, Ernest S. Frerichs, and Paul Virgil McCracken Flesher. Oxford: Oxford University Press, 1989, 166–82.

———. *Popular Religion in Late Saxon England: Elf Charms in Context*. Chapel Hill, N.C.: University of North Carolina Press, 1996.

Kelly, H. A. "English Kings and the Fear of Sorcery." *Mediaeval Studies* 39 (1977): 206–38.

Lapoint, E. C. "Irish Immunity to Witch-Hunting, 1534–1711." *Éire-Ireland* 27 (1992): 76–92.

Larner, Christina. *Enemies of God: The Witch-Hunt in Scotland.* Baltimore, Md.: Johns Hopkins University Press, 1981.

———. "Witch Beliefs and Witch-Hunting in England and Scotland." *History Today* 31 (February, 1981): 32–36.

Levack, Brian. "The Great Scottish Witch-Hunt of 1661–1662." *Journal of British Studies* 20 (1980): 90–108.

———. "Possession, Witchcraft and the Law in Jacobean England." *Washington and Lee University Law Review* 52 (1995): 1613–40.

Macfarlane, Alan. *Witchcraft in Tudor and Stuart England: A Regional and Comparative Study.* London: Routledge, 1970.

———. "Witchcraft in Tudor and Stuart Essex." In *Crime in England 1550–1800,* ed. J. S. Cockburn. Princeton, N.J.: Princeton University Press, 1977, 72–89.

MacDonald, Michael, ed. *Witchcraft and Hysteria in Elizabethan England: Edward Jorden and the Mary Glover Case.* London: Routledge, 1991.

Maxwell-Stuart, P. G. "The Fear of the King is Death: James VI and the Witches of East Lothian." In *Fear in Early Modern Society,* ed. William C. Naphy and Penny Roberts. Manchester, Eng.: Manchester University Press, 1997, 209–25.

———. *Satan's Conspiracy: Magic and Witchcraft in Sixteenth-Century Scotland.* East Lothian, Scotland: Tuckwell, 2001.

Meaney, A. L. "Women, Witchcraft and Magic in Anglo-Saxon England." In *Superstition and Popular Medicine in Anglo-Saxon England,* ed. D. G. Scragg. Manchester, Eng.: Manchester University Press, 1989, 9–40.

Norman, Lawrence, and Gareth Roberts. *Witchcraft in Early Modern Scotland: James VI's Demonology and the North Berwick Witches.* Exeter, Eng.: University of Exeter Press, 2000.

Peel, Edgar, and Pat Southern. *The Trials of the Lancashire Witches: A Study of Seventeenth-Century Witchcraft.* 3rd ed. Nelson, Eng.: Hendon, 1985.

Rushton, Peter. "Women, Witchcraft, and Slander in Early Modern Europe: Cases from the Church Courts of Durham." *Northern History* 18 (1982): 116–32.

Sawyer, Ronald C. " 'Strangely handled in all her lyms': Witchcraft and Healing in Jacobean England." *Journal of Social History* 22 (1989): 461–85.

———. *The Bewitching of Anne Gunter: A Horrible and True Story of Deception, Witchcraft, Murder, and the King of England.* London: Routledge, 2001.

———. *Instruments of Darkness: Witchcraft in Early Modern England.* Philadelphia: University of Pennsylvania Press, 1996.

———. *Witchcraft in Early Modern England.* London: Longman, 2001.

———. *Witchcraft in Seventeenth-Century Yorkshire: Accusations and Counter-Measures*. York, Eng.: Bothwick Institute of Historical Research, 1992.

Sharpe, James. "Witchcraft and Women in Seventeenth-Century England: Some Northern Evidence." *Continuity and Change* 6 (1991): 179–99.

Stavreva, Kirilka. "Fighting Words: Witch-Speak in Late Elizabethan Docufiction." *Journal of Medieval and Early Modern Studies* 30 (2000): 309–38.

Swain, J. T. *Witchcraft in Seventeenth Century England*. Bristol, Eng.: Stuart Press, 1994.

Swale, J. K., and Hugh McLachlan. "Witchcraft and the Status of Women." *British Journal of Sociology* 30 (1979): 349–58.

Thomas, Keith. *Religion and the Decline of Magic*. New York: Scribners, 1971.

Tourney, Garfield. "The Physician and Witchcraft in Restoration England." *Medical History* 16 (1972): 143–55.

Unsworth, C. R. "Witchcraft Beliefs and Criminal Procedure in Early Modern England." In *Legal Record and Historical Reality*, ed. Thomas Glyn Watkin. London: Hambledon, 1989, 71–98.

Valletta, Frederick. *Witchcraft, Magic, and Superstition in England, 1640–70*. Aldershot, Eng.: Ashgate, 2000.

Willis, Deborah. *Malevolent Nurture: Witch-Hunting and Maternal Power in Early Modern England*. Ithaca, N.Y.: Cornell University Press, 1995.

2. Colonial America

Behar, R. "Sexual Witchcraft, Colonialism, and Women's Powers: Views from the Mexican Inquisition." In *Sexuality and Marriage in Colonial Latin America*, ed. Anunción Lavrin. Lincoln, Nebr.: University of Nebraska Press, 1989, 178–206.

Boyer, Paul, and Stephen Nissenbaum. *Salem Possessed: The Social Origins of Witchcraft*. Cambridge, Mass.: Harvard University Press, 1974.

Brown, David C. "The Case of Giles Cory." *Essex Institute Historical Collections* 121 (1985): 162–81.

Caporael, Linda R. "Ergotism: The Satan Loosed in Salem?" *Science* 192 (1976): 21–26.

Carlson, Laurie Winn. *A Fever in Salem: A New Interpretation of the New England Witch Trials*. Chicago: Ivan R. Dee, 1999.

Cervantes, Fernando. *The Devil in the New World: The Impact of Diabolism in New Spain*. New Haven, Conn.: Yale University Press, 1994.

———. "The Devils of Querétaro: Scepticism and Credulity in Late Seventeenth-Century Mexico." *Past and Present* 130 (1991): 51–69.

———. *Entertaining Satan: Witchcraft and the Culture of Early New England*. Oxford: Oxford University Press, 1982.

———. "John Godfrey and his Neighbors: Witchcraft and the Social Web in Colonial Massachusetts." *William and Mary Quarterly* 33 (1976): 242–65.

Demos, John. "Underlying Themes in the Witchcraft of Seventeenth-Century New England." *American Historical Review* 75 (1970): 1311–26.

———. "John Godfrey and His Neighbors: Witchcraft and the Social Web in Colonial Massachusetts." *William and Mary Quarterly* 33 (1976):245–65.

———. *Entertaining Satan: Witchcraft and the Culture of Early New English.*

Drake, Frederick C. "Witchcraft in the American Colonies, 1647–62." *American Quarterly* 20 (1968): 694–725.

Erikson, Kai T. "The Witches of Salem Village." In *On the Margin of the Visible: Sociology, the Esoteric, and the Occult*, ed. Edward A. Tiryakian. New York: Wiley, 1974, 209–14.

Fox, Sanford J. *Science and Justice: The Massachusetts Witchcraft Trials.* Baltimore, Md.: Johns Hopkins University Press, 1968.

Gildrie, Richard, P. "The Salem Witchcraft Trials as a Crisis of Popular Imagination." *Essex Institute Historical Collections* 128 (1992): 270–85.

———. "Visions of Evil: Popular Culture, Puritanism, and the Massachusetts Witchcraft Crisis of 1692." *Journal of American Culture* 8 (1985): 17–33.

Godbeer, Richard. *The Devil's Dominion: Magic and Religion in Early New England.* Cambridge: Cambridge University Press, 1992.

Gregg, Larry. *The Salem Witch Crisis.* New York: Praeger, 1992.

Hall, David D. "Witchcraft and the Limits of Interpretation." *New England Quarterly* 59 (1985): 253–81.

———. *Worlds of Wonder, Days of Judgement: Popular Religious Belief in Early New England.* New York: Knopf, 1989.

Hansen, Chadwick. "Andover Witchcraft and the Causes of the Salem Witchcraft Trials." In *The Occult in America: New Historical Perspectives*, ed. Howard Kerr and Charles L. Crow. Urbana, Ill.: University of Illinois Press, 1983, 38–57.

———. *Witchcraft at Salem.* New York: George Braziller, 1969.

Harley, David. "Explaining Salem: Calvinist Psychology and the Diagnosis of Possession." *American Historical Review* 101 (1996): 307–30.

Heyman, Christine L. "Specters of Subversion, Societies of Friends: Dissent and the Devil in Provincial Essex County, Massachusetts." In *Saints and Revolutionaries: Essays on Early American History*, ed. David Hall, John M. Murrin, and Thad W. Tate. New York: Norton, 1984, 38–74.

Hill, Frances. *A Delusion of Satan: The Full Story of the Salem Witch Trials.* New York: Doubleday, 1995.

Hoffer, Peter Charles. *The Devil's Disciples: Makers of the Salem Witchcraft Trials.* Baltimore, Md.: Johns Hopkins University Press, 1996.

———. *The Salem Witchcraft Trials: A Legal History.* Lawrence, Kans.: University Press of Kansas, 1997.

Kamensky, Jane. "Words, Witches and Women Trouble: Witchcraft, Disorderly Speech and Gender Boundaries in Puritan New England." *Essex Institute Historical Collections* 128 (1992): 286–306.

Karlsen, Carol F. *The Devil in the Shape of a Woman: Witchcraft in Colonial New England*. New York: Norton, 1987.

Kences, James E. "Some Unexplored Relationships of Essex County Witchcraft to the Indian Wars of 1675 and 1689." *Essex Institute Historical Collections* 120 (1984): 179–212.

Kibbey, Ann. "Mutations of the Supernatural: Witchcraft, Remarkable Providences, and the Power of Puritan Men." *American Quarterly* 34 (1982): 125–48.

Norton, Mary Beth. *In the Devil's Snare: The Salem Witchcraft Crisis of 1692.* New York: Knopf, 2002.

Owen, Dennis E. "Spectral Evidence: The Village Witchcraft Cosmology of Salem Village in 1692." In *Essays in the Sociology of Perceptions*, ed. Mary Douglas. London: Routledge, 1982, 275–301.

Pearl, Jonathan L. "Witchcraft in New France in the Seventeenth Century: The Social Aspects." *Historical Reflections* 4 (1977): 191–205.

Reis, Elizabeth. *Damned Women: Sinners and Witches in Puritan New England.* Ithaca, N.Y.: Cornell University Press, 1997.

———. "The Devil, the Body, and the Feminine Soul in Puritan New England." *Journal of American History* 82 (1995): 15–36.

Reis, Elizabeth, ed. *Spellbound: Women and Witchcraft in America.* Wilmington, Del.: Scholarly Resources, 1998.

Rosenthal, Bernard. *Salem Story: Reading the Witch Trials of 1692.* Cambridge: Cambridge University Press, 1993.

Simmons, Mark. *Witchcraft in the Southwest: Spanish and Indian Supernaturalism on the Rio Grande.* Lincoln, Nebr.: University of Nebraska Press, 1974.

Taylor, John M. *The Witchcraft Delusion: The Story of Witchcraft Persecutions in Seventeenth-Century New England, Including Original Trial Transcripts.* New York: Gramercy, 1995.

Weiseman, Richard. *Witchcraft, Magic, and Religion in Seventeenth Century Massachusetts.* Amherst, Mass.: University of Massachusetts Press, 1984.

Werking, Richard H. "'Reformation Is Our Only Preservation': Cotton Mather and Salem Witchcraft." *William and Mary Quarterly* 29 (1972): 281–90.

3. Eastern Europe

Kazhdan, Alexander. "Holy and Unholy Miracle Workers." In *Byzantine Magic*, ed. Henry Maguire. Washington, D.C.: Dumbarton Oaks, 1995, 73–82.

Kivelson, Valerie A. "Through the Prism of Witchcraft: Gender and Social Change in Seventeenth-Century Muscovy." In *Russia's Women: Accommodation, Resistance, Transformation*, ed. Barbara E. Evans, Barbara A. Engel, and

Christine D. Worobec. Berkeley, Calif.: University of California Press, 1991, 74–94.

Klaniczay, Gábor. *The Uses of Supernatural Power*. Ed. Karen Margolis. Trans. Susan Singerman. Princeton, N.J.: Princeton University Press, 1990.

Klaniczay, Gábor, and Éva Pócs, eds. *Witch-Beliefs and Witch-Hunting in Central and Eastern Europe*. Budapest: n.p., 1994. Special issue of *Acta Ethnographica Hungarica* 37 (1991–92).

Plakans, Andrejs. "Witches and Werewolves in Early Modern Livonia." In *Rättea: En Festskrift till Bengt Ankarloo*, ed. Lars M. Andersson et al. Lund, Norway: Nordic Academic Press, 2000, 255–71.

Pócs, Éva. *Between the Living and the Dead: A Perspective on Witches and Seers in the Early Modern Age*. Trans. Szilvia Rédey and Michael Webb. Budapest: Central European University Press, 1999.

———. *Fairies and Witches at the Boundary of South-Eastern and Central Europe*. Helsinki: Suomalainen Tiedenkatemia, 1989.

Ryan, W. F. *The Bathhouse at Midnight: A Historical Survey of Magic and Divination in Russia*. University Park, Pa.: Pennsylvania State University Press, 1999.

Tazbir, Janusz. "Hexenprozesse in Polen." *Archiv für Reformationsgeschichte* 71 (1980): 280–307.

Zguta, Russell. "The Ordeal by Water (Swimming of Witches) in the East Slavic World." *Slavic Review* 82 (1977): 220–30.

———. "Was There a Witch-Craze in Muscovite Russia?" *Southern Folklore Quarterly* 40 (1977): 119–27.

———. "Witchcraft and Medicine in Pre-Petrine Russia." *Russian Review* 37 (1978): 438–48.

———. "Witchcraft Trials in Seventeenth-Century Russia." *American Historical Review* 82 (1977): 1187–1207.

4. France and the Low Countries

Bordes, Françoise. *Sorciers et sorcières: Procès de sorcellerie en Gascogne et Pays Basque*. Toulouse: Edition Privat, 1999.

Briggs, Robin. *Communities of Belief: Culture and Social Tensions in Early Modern France*. Oxford: Clarendon, 1989.

———. "Witchcraft and Popular Mentality in Lorraine, 1580–1630." In *Occult and Scientific Mentalities in the Renaissance*, ed. Brian Vickers. Cambridge: Cambridge University Press, 1984, 337–49.

———. "Women as Victims? Witches, Judges and the Community." *French History* 5 (1991): 438–50.

Clark, Stuart. "The 'Gendering' of Witchcraft in French Demonology: Misogyny or Polarity?" *French History* 5 (1991): 426–37.

Delcambre, Etienne. *Le concept de sorcellerie dans le Duché de Lorraine au XVIe et au XVIIe siècle*. 3 vols. Nancy, 1948–51.

Diedler, Jean-Claude. *Démons et sorcières en Lorraine: Le bien et le mal dans les communautés rurales de 1550 à 1660*. Paris: Messene, 1996.

Dupont-Bouchat, Marie-Sylvie. "Sorcellerie et superstition: L'attitude de l'Eglise dans les Pays-Bas, XVIe–XVIIIe siècle." In *Magie, sorcellerie, parapsychologie*, ed. Hervé Hasquin. Brussels: Université de Bruxelles, 1984, 61–83.

Dupont-Bouchat, Marie-Sylvie, ed. *La sorcellerie dans les Pays-Bas sous l'Ancien Régime: Aspects juridiques, institutionnels et sociaux*. Courtrai, Belgium: UGA, 1987.

Dupont-Bouchat, Marie-Sylvie, Willem Frijhoff, and Robert Muchembled, eds. *Prophètes et sorciers dans le Pays-Bas XVIe–XVIIIe siècle*. Paris: Hachette, 1978.

Garrett, Clarke. "Witches and Cunning Folk in the Old Regime." In *The Wolf and the Lamb: Popular Culture in France from the Old Regime to the Twentieth Century*, ed. Jacques Beauroy, Marc Betrand, and Edward T. Gargan. Sarasota, Calif.: Anma Libri, 1976, 53–64.

Gauvard, Claude. "Paris, le Parlement et la sorcellerie au milieu du XVe siècle." In *Finances, pouvoirs et memoire: Mélanges offerts à Jean Favier*. Paris: Fayard, 1999, 85–111.

Gijswijt-Hofstra, Marijke. "The European Witchcraft Debate and the Dutch Variant." *Social History* 15 (1990): 181–94.

———. "Witchcraft in the Northern Netherlands." In *Current Issues in Women's History*, ed. Ariana Angerman et al. London: Routledge, 1974, 75–92.

Gijswijt-Hofstra, Marijke, and William Frijhoff, eds. *Witchcraft in the Netherlands: From the Fourteenth to the Twentieth Century*. Trans. Rachel M. J. van der Wilden-Fall. Rotterdam: Universitaire Pers Rotterdam, 1991.

Jacques-Chaquin, Nicole, and Maxime Préaud. *Les sorciers du carroi de Marlou: Un procès de sorcellerie en Berry (1582–1583)*. Grenoble, France: Millon, 1996.

Klaits, Joseph. "Witchcraft Trials and Absolute Monarchy in Alsace." In *Church, State, and Society under the Bourbon Kings of France*, ed. Richard M. Golden. Lawrence, Kans.: Coronado Press, 1982, 148–72.

Le Roy Ladurie, Emmanuel. *Jasmin's Witch*. Trans. Brian Pierce. New York: George Braziller, 1987.

———. *Montaillou: The Promised Land of Error*. Trans. Barbara Bray. New York: George Braziller, 1978.

Mandrou, Robert. *Magistrats et sorciers en France au XVIIe siècle: Une analyse de psychologie historique*. Paris: Seuil, 1968.

Monter, E. William. *Judging the French Reformation: Heresy Trials by Sixteenth Century Parlements*. Cambridge, Mass.: Harvard University Press, 1999.

——. "Toads and Eucharists: The Male Witches of Normandy, 1564–1660." *French Historical Studies* 20 (1997): 563–95.

Muchembled, Robert. *Les derniers bûchers: Un village de Flandre et ses sorcières sous Louis XIV*. Paris: Ramsay, 1981.

——. *Popular Culture and Elite Culture in France, 1400–1750*. Trans. Lydia Cochrane. Baton Rouge, La.: Louisiana State University Press, 1985.

——. *Sorcières, justice et société aux 16e et 17e siècles*. Paris: Imago, 1987.

——. "Witchcraft, Popular Culture, and Christianity in the Sixteenth Century, with an Emphasis upon Flanders and Artois." In *Ritual, Religion, and the Sacred,* Selections from the Annales—economies, sociétes, civilizations, vol. 7, ed. Robert Forster and Orest Ranum, trans. Elborg Forster and Particia M. Ranum. Baltimore, Md.: Johns Hopkins University Press, 1982, 213–36.

——. "The Witches of the Cambrésis: The Acculturation of the Rural World in the Sixteenth and Seventeenth Centuries." In *Religion and the People, 800–1700*, ed. James Obelkevich. Chapel Hill, N.C.: University of North Carolina Press, 1979, 221–76, 315–23.

Oates, Caroline. "The Trial of a Teenage Werewolf, Bordeaux, 1603." *Criminal Justice History* 9 (1988): 1–29.

Paravy, Pierrette. *De la Chrétienté romaine à la Réforme en Dauphiné: Evêques, fidèles et déviants (vers 1340–vers 1530)*. 2 vols. Rome: Ecole française de Rome, 1993.

——. "Faire Croire: Quelques hypothèse de recherche basées sur l'étude des procès de sorcellerie du Dauphiné au XVe siècle." In *Faire Croire: Modalités de la diffusion et la reception des messages religieux du XIIe au XVe siècle*. Rome: Ecole française de Rome, 1981, 119–30.

——. "Streghe e stregoni nella società del Delfinato nel XV secolo." In *Poteri carismatici e informali: Chiesa e società medioevali*, ed. Agostino Paravicini Bagliani and André Vauchez. Palermo, Italy: Sellerio, 1992, 78–92.

Rapley, Robert. *A Case of Witchcraft: The Trial of Urbain Grandier*. Montreal: McGill-Queen's University Press, 1998.

Rochelandet, Brigitte. *Sorcières, diables et bûchers en Franche-Comté aux XVIe et XVIIe siècles*. Besançon, France: Cêtre, 1997

Soman, Alfred. "Decriminalizing Witchcraft: Does the French Experience Furnish a European Model?" *Criminal Justice History* 10 (1989): 1–22.

——. "La décriminilisation de la sorcellerie en France." *Histoire, économie et société* 4 (1985): 179–203.

——. "The Parlement of Paris and the Great Witch Hunt (1565–1640)." *Sixteenth Century Journal* 9 (1978): 31–44.

——. *Sorcellerie et justice criminelle: Parlement de Paris (16e–18e siècles)*. London: Variorum, 1992.

——. "Trente procès de sorcellerie dans le Perche (1566–1624)." *L'orne littéraire* 8 (1986): 42–57.

———. "Witch Lynching at Juniville." *Natural History* 95 (1986): 6–15.

Villette, Pierre. *La sorcellerie et sa repression dans le nord de la France.* Paris: Pensée universelle, 1976.

Wilkins, Kay S. "Attitudes to Witchcraft and Demonic Possession in France during the Eighteenth Century." *Journal of European Studies* 3 (1973): 348–62.

5. German Lands

Ahrendt-Schulte, Ingrid. *Zauberinnen in der Stadt Horn (1554–1603): Magische Kultur und Hexenverfolgung in der Frühen Neuzeit.* Frankfurt: Campus, 1997.

Alfing, Sabine. *Hexenjagd und Zaubereiprozesse in Münster: Vom Umgang mit Sündenböcken in den Krisenzeiten des 16. und 17. Jahrhunderts.* Münster, Ger.: Waxmann, 1991.

Baumgarten, Achim B. *Hexenwahn und Hexenverfolgung im Naheraum: Ein Beitrag zur Sozial- und Kulturgeschichte.* Frankfurt: Peter Lang, 1987.

Behringer, Wolfgang. *Mit dem Feuer vom Leben zum Tod: Hexengesetzgebung in Bayern.* Munich: Hugendubel, 1988.

———. *Shaman of Oberstdorf: Chonrad Stoeckhlin and the Phantoms of the Night.* Trans. H. C. Erik Midelfort. Charlottesville, Va.: University of Virginia Press, 1998.

———. *Witchcraft Persecutions in Bavaria: Popular Magic, Religious Zealotry and Reason of State in Early Modern Europe.* Trans. J. C. Grayson and David Lederer. Cambridge: Cambridge University Press, 1998.

Benedikter, Hans. *Hexen und Zauberer in Tirol.* Bozen, Italy: Athesia, 2000.

Brauner, Sigrid. *Fearless Wives and Frightened Shrews: The Construction of the Witch in Early Modern Germany.* Ed. Robert H. Brown. Amherst, Mass.: University of Massachusetts Press, 1995.

Degn, Christian, Hartmut Lehmann, and Dagmar Unverhau, eds. *Hexenprozesse: Deutsche und skandinavische Beiträge.* Neumünster, Ger.: Wachholtz, 1983.

Dillinger, Johannes. *"Böse Leute": Hexenverfolgungen in Schwäbisch-Österreich und Kurtrier im Vergleich.* Trier, Ger.: Spee, 1999.

Dillinger, Johannes, Thomas Fritz, and Wolfgang Mährle. *Zum Feuer verdammt: Die Hexenverfolgungen in der Grafschaft Hohenberg, der Reichsstadt Reutlingen und der Fürstpropstei Ellwangen.* Stuttgart, Ger.: Steiner, 1998.

Gebhard, Horst Heinrich. *Hexenprozesse im Kürfurstentum Mainz des 17. Jarhhunderts.* Aschaffenburg, Ger.: Geschichts- und Kunstverein Aschaffenburg, 1989.

Gehm, Britta. *Die Hexenverfolgung im Hochstift Bamberg und das Eingreifen des Reichhofrates zu ihrer Beendigung.* Hildesheim, Ger.: Georg Olms, 2000.

Hsia, R. Po-chia. *The Myth of Ritual Murder: Jews and Magic in Reformation Germany.* New Haven, Conn.: Yale University Press, 1988.

Jerouschek, Günther. *Die Hexen und ihr Prozess: Die Hexenverfolgung in der Reichstadt Esslingen.* Esslingen, Ger.: Stadtarchiv, 1992.

Koppenhöfer, Johanna. *Die mitleidlose Gesellschaft: Studien zu Verdachtsgenese, Ausgrenzungsverhalten und Prozessproblematik im frühneuzeitlichen Hexenprozeß in der alten Grafschaft Nassau unter Johann VI. und der späteren Teilgrafschaft Nassau-Dillenburg (1559–1687).* Frankfurt: Peter Lang, 1995.

Kunstmann, Harmut H. *Zauberwahn und Hexenprozesse in der Reichsstadt Nürnberg.* Nuremberg, Ger.: Stadtarchiv, 1970.

Kunze, Michael. *Highroad to the Stake: A Tale of Witchcraft.* Trans. William E. Yuill. Chicago: University of Chicago Press, 1987.

Labouvie, Eva. *Verbotene Künste: Volksmagie und ländlicher Aberglaube in den Dorfgemeinde des Saarraumes (16.–19. Jahrhundert).* St. Ingbert, Ger.: Röhrig, 1992.

———. *Zauberei und Hexenwerk: Ländlicher Hexenglaube in der Frühen Neuzeit.* Frankfurt: Fischer, 1991.

Lambrech, Karen. *Hexenverfolgung und Zaubereiprozesse in den schlesischen Territorien.* Cologne: Böhlau, 1995.

Lehmann, Hartmut. "The Persecution of Witches as Restoration of Order: The Case of Germany, 1590s–1650s." *Central European History* 21 (1988): 107–21.

Lorenz, Sönke. *Aktenversendung und Hexenprozess: Dargestellt am Beispiel der Juristenfakultäten Rostock und Greifswald (1570/82–1630).* 2 vols. Frankfurt: Peter Lang, 1982–83.

Lorenz, Sönke, ed. *Hexen und Hexenverfolgung im deutschen Südwesten.* Ostfildern bei Stuttgart, Ger.: Cantz, 1994.

Lorenz, Sönke, and Dieter Bauer, eds. *Das Ende der Hexenverfolgung.* Stuttgart, Ger.: Steiner, 1995.

Midelfort, H. C. Erik. *Hexenverfolgung: Beiträge zur Forschung, unter besonderer Berücksichtigung des südwestdeutschen Raumes.* Würzburg, Ger.: Königshausen & Neumann, 1995.

———. "Heartland of the Witchcraze: Central and Northern Europe." *History Today* 31 (February, 1981): 27–31.

———. *A History of Madness in Sixteenth-Century Germany.* Stanford, Calif.: Stanford University Press, 1999.

———. *Witch Hunting in Southwestern Germany, 1562–1684: The Social and Intellectual Foundations.* Stanford, Calif.: Stanford University Press, 1972.

——. "Witchcraft and Religion in Sixteenth-Century Germany: The Formation and Consequences of an Orthodoxy." *Archiv für Reformationsgeschichte* 62 (1971): 266–78.

Niederstätter, Alois, and Wolfgang Scheffknecht, eds. *Hexen oder Hausfrau: Das Bild der Frau in der Geschichte Vorarlbergs.* Sigmaringendorf, Ger.: Glock & Lutz, 1991.

Pohl, Herbert. *Zauberglaube und Hexenangst im Kurfürstentum Mainz: Ein Beitrag zur Hexenfrage im 16. und beginnenden 17. Jarhrhundert.* 2nd ed. Stuttgart, Ger.: Franz Steiner, 1998.

Renczes, Andrea. *Wie löscht man eine Familie aus? Eine Analyse Bamberger Hexenprozesse.* Pfaffenweiler, Ger.: Centaurus, 1990.

Roper, Lyndal. "'Evil Imaginings and Fantasies': Child-Witches and the End of the Witch Craze." *Past and Present* 167 (2000): 107–39.

Rowlands, Alison. "Witchcraft and Old Women in Early Modern Germany." *Past and Present* 173 (2001): 50–89.

——. "Witchcraft and Popular Religion in Early Modern Rothenburg ob der Tauber." In *Popular Religion in Germany and Central Europe, 1400–1800,* ed. Bob Scribner and Trevor Johnson. New York: St. Martin's Press, 1996, 101–18, 245–49.

Rummel, Walter. *Bauern, Herren und Hexen: Studien zur Sozialgeschichte sponheimischer und kurtrierischer Hexenprozesse, 1574–1664.* Göttingen, Ger.: Vandenhoeck & Ruprecht, 1991.

Saatkamp, Marielies. *Bekandt daß sie ein Zaubersche were: Zur Geschichte der Hexenverfolgung im Westmünsterland.* Vreden, Ger.: Landeskundliches Institut Westmünsterland, 1994.

Sabean, David Warren. "The Sacred Bond of Unity: Community Through the Eyes of a Thirteen-Year-Old Witch (1683)." In David Warren Sabean, *The Power in the Blood: Popular Culture and Village Discourse in Early Modern Germany.* Cambridge: Cambridge University Press, 1984, 94–112.

Schmidt, Jügen Michael. *Glaube und Skepsis: Die Kurpfalz und die abendländische Hexenverfolgung 1446–1685.* Bielefeld, Ger.: Verlag für Regionalgeschichte, 2000.

Schormann, Gerhard. *Hexenprozesse in Deutschland.* 3rd ed. Göttingen, Ger.: Vandenhoek & Ruprecht, 1996.

——. *Hexenprozesse in Nordwestdeutschland.* Hildesheim, Ger.: Lax, 1977.

——. *Der Krieg gegen die Hexen: Das Ausrottungsprogramm des Kurfürsten von Köln.* Göttingen, Ger.: Vandenhoeck & Ruprecht, 1991.

Schulte, Rolf. *Hexenmeister: Die Verfolgung von Männern im Rahmen der Hexenverfolgung von 1530–1730 im alten Reich.* Frankfurt: Peter Lang, 2000.

Schwillus, Herald. *Kleriker im Hexenprozeß: Geistliche als Opfer der Hexenprozesse des 16. und 17. Jahrhunderts in Deutschland.* Würzburg, Ger.: Echter Verlag, 1992.

Scribner, Robert W. "Magic and the Formation of Protestant Popular Culture in Germany." In R. W. Scribner, *Religion and Culture in Germany (1400–1800),* ed. Lyndal Roper. Leiden: Brill, 2001, 323–45.

———. "Magie und Aberglaube: Zur volkstümlichen sakramentalischen Denkart in Deutschland am Ausgang des Mittelalters." In *Volksreligion im hohen und späten Mittelalter,* ed. Peter Dinzelbacher and Dieter R. Bauer. Paderborn, Ger.: Schöningh, 1990, 253–73.

———. "Witchcraft and Judgment in Reformation Germany." *History Today* 40 (April, 1990): 12–19.

Thieser, Bernd. *Die Oberpfalz im Zusammenhang des Hexenprozessgeschehens im süddeutschen Raum während des 16. und 17. Jahrhunderts.* Bayreuth, Ger.: Hagen, 1987.

Tschaikner, Manfred. *"Damit das Böse ausgerottet werde": Hexenverfolgungen im Vorarlberg im 16. und 17. Jahrhundert.* Bregenz, Austria: Vorarlberger Autoren Gesellschaft, 1992.

Walinski-Kiehl, Robert S. "The Devil's Children: Child Witch-trials in Early Modern Germany." *Continuity and Change* 11 (1996): 171–89.

———. "'Godly States': Confessional Conflict and Witch-hunting in Early Modern Germany." *Mentalities* 5 (1988): 13–24.

Walz, Rainer. *Hexenglaube und magische Kommunikation im Dorf der frühen Neuzeit: Die Verfolgungen in der Grafschaft Lippe.* Paderborn, Ger.: Schöningh, 1993.

Wilbertz, Gisela, Gerd Schwerhoff and Jürgen Scheffler, eds. *Hexenverfolgung und Regionalgeschichte: Die Grafschaft Lippe im Vergleich.* Bielefeld, Ger.: Verlag für Regionalgeschichte, 1994.

Zeck, Mario. *"Im Rauch gehn Himmel geschüggt": Hexenverfolgungen in der Reichsstadt Rottweill.* Stuttgart, Ger.: Ibidem Verlag, 2000.

6. Italy, Portugal, and Spain

Bertolotti, Maurizio. "The Ox's Bones and the Ox's Hide: A Popular Myth, Part Hagiography and Part Witchcraft." Trans. Eren Branch. In *Microhistory and the Lost Peoples of Europe,* ed. Edward Muir and Guido Ruggiero. Baltimore, Md.: Johns Hopkins University Press, 1991, 42–70.

Blécourt, Willem de. "Spuren einer Volkskultur oder Dämonisierung? Kritische Bemerkungen zu Ginzburgs 'Die Benandanti.'" *Kea: Zeitschrift für Kulturwissenschaften* 5 (1993): 17–29.

Bonomo, Giuseppe. *Caccia alle streghe: Le credenza nelle streghe dal sec. XIII al XIX con particolare riferimento all'Italia.* 3rd ed. Palermo, Italy: Palumbo, 1986.

Brucker, Gene A. "Sorcery in Early Renaissance Florence." *Studies in the Renaissance* 10 (1963): 7–24.

Cassar, Carmel. "Witchcraft Beliefs and Social Control in Seventeeth-Century Malta." *Journal of Mediterranean Studies* 3 (1993): 316–34.

——. *Witchcraft, Sorcery, and the Inquisition: A Study of Cultural Values in Early Modern Malta*. Msida, Malta: Mireva, 1996.

Centini, Massimo. *Streghe, roghi e diavoli: I processi di stregoneria in Piemonte*. Cuneo, Italy: L'arciere, 1995.

Corrêa De Melo, M. C. "Witchcraft in Portugal During the Eighteenth Century, Analysed Through the Accusations of the Tribunal do Santo Oficio de Evora." In *Transactions of the Eighth International Congress on the Enlightenment*, Studies on Voltaire and the Eighteenth Century, vol. 303. Oxford: Voltaire Foundation, 1992, 573–78.

Deutscher, Thomas. "The Role of the Episcopal Tribunal of Novara in the Suppression of Heresy and Witchcraft, 1563–1615." *Catholic Historical Review* 77 (1991): 403–21.

Fiume, Giovanna. "The Old Vinegar Lady, or the Judicial Modernization of the Crime of Witchcraft." Trans. Margaret A. Gallucci. In *History from Crime*, ed. Edward Muir and Guido Ruggiero. Baltimore, Md.: Johns Hopkins University Press, 1994, 65–87.

Gari Lacruz, Angel. "Variedad de competencias en el delito de brujería 1600–1650 en Aragón," in *La Inquisicíon Española: Nueva vision, nueva horizonte*. Ed. Joaquín Perez Villanueva. Marid: Siglo Veintiuno, 1980, 319–27.

Gemmo, Roberto. *Streghe e magia: Episodi di opposizione religiosa popolare sulle Alpi del Seicento*. Biella, Italy: ELF, 1994.

Gentilcore, David. "The Church, the Devil and the Healing Activities of Living Saints in the Kingdom of Naples after the Council of Trent." In *Medicine and the Reformation*, ed. Ole Peter Grell and Andrew Cunningham. London: Routledge, 1993, 134–55.

——. *From Bishop to Witch: The System of the Sacred in Early Modern Terra d'Otranto*. Manchester, Eng.: Manchester University Press, 1992.

——. *Healers and Healing in Early Modern Italy*. Manchester, Eng.: Manchester University Press, 1998.

Gil del Rio, Alfredo. *Inquisición y brujería*. Madrid: Casset, 1992.

Ginzburg, Carlo. *The Night Battles: Witchcraft and Agrarian Cults in the Sixteenth and Seventeenth Centuries*. Trans. John and Anne Tedeschi. Baltimore, Md.: Johns Hopkins University Press, 1983.

——. "Witchcraft and Popular Piety: Notes on a Modenese Trial of 1519." In Carlo Ginzburg, *Clues, Myths, and the Historical Method*, trans. John and Anne Tedeschi. Baltimore, Md.: Johns Hopkins University Press, 1989, 1–16.

Guggino, Elsa. *La magia in Sicilia*. Palermo, Italy: Sallerio, 1978.

Haliczer, Gustav. *Inquisition and Society in the Kingdom of Valencia, 1478–1834*. Berkeley, Calif.: University of California Press, 1990.

Henningsen, Gustav. "The Greatest Witch-Trial of All: Navarre, 1609–14." *History Today* 30 (November 1980): 36–39.

———. *The Witches' Advocate: Basque Witchcraft and the Spanish Inquisition.* Reno, Nev.: University of Nevada Press, 1980.

Loriga, Sabina. "A Secret to Kill the King: Magic and Protection in Piedmont in the Eighteenth Century." Trans. Margaret A. Gallussi and Corrada Biazzo Curry. In *History from Crime*, ed. Edward Muir and Guido Ruggiero. Baltimore, Md.: Johns Hopkins University Press, 1994, 88–109.

Martin, Ruth. *Witchcraft and the Inquisition in Venice, 1550–1650.* Oxford: Oxford University Press, 1989.

Monter, E. William. *Frontiers of Heresy: The Spanish Inquisition from the Basque Lands to Sicily.* Cambridge: Cambridge University Press, 1990.

Mormando, Franco. "Bernardino of Siena, Popular Preacher and Witch-Hunter: A 1426 Witch Trial in Rome." *Fifteenth Century Studies* 24 (1998): 84–118.

———. *The Preacher's Demons: Bernardino of Siena and the Social Underworld of Early Renaissance Italy.* Chicago: University of Chicago Press, 1999.

Nardon, Franco. *Benandanti e inquisitori nel Friuli del Seicento.* Trieste, Italy: Università di Trieste, 1999.

O'Niel, Mary. "Magical Healing, Love Magic and the Inquisition in Late Sixteenth-Century Modena." In *Inquisition and Society in Early Modern Europe*, ed. Stephen Haliczer. Totowa, N.J.: Barnes and Noble, 1987, 88–114.

———. "*Sacerdote ovvero strione*: Ecclesiastical and Superstitious Remedies in 16th-Century Italy." In *Understanding Popular Culture: Europe from the Middle Ages to the Nineteenth Century*, ed. Steven Kaplan. Berlin: Mouton, 1984, 53–83.

Paton, Bernadette. "'To the Fire, to the Fire! Let Us Burn a Little Incense to God': Bernardino, Preaching Friars, and *Maleficio* in Late Medieval Siena." In *No Gods Except Me: Orthodoxy and Religious Practice in Europe, 1200–1600*, ed. Charles Zika. Parkville, Australia: University of Melbourne History Department, 1991, 9–14.

Romeo, Giovanni. *Inquisitori, esorcisti e streghe nell'Italia della Controriforma.* Florence: Sansoni, 1990.

Ruggiero, Guido. *Binding Passions: Tales of Magic, Marriage and Power at the End of the Renaissance.* Oxford: Oxford University Press, 1993.

———. "The Strange Death of Margarita Marcellini: *Male,* Signs, and the Everyday World of Pre-Modern Medicine." *American Historical Review* 106 (2001): 1141–58.

Sánchez Ortega, M. H. "Sorcery and Eroticism in Love Magic." In *Cultural Encounters: The Impact of the Inquisition in Spain and the New World*, ed. Mary Elizabeth Perry and Anne J. Cruz. Berkeley, Calif.: University of California Press, 1991, 58–92.

——. "Women as a Source of 'Evil' in Counter-Reformation Spain." In *Culture and Control in Counter-Reformation Spain*, ed. Anne J. Cruz and Mary Elizabeth Perry. Minneapolis, Minn.: University of Minnesota Press, 1992, 196–215.

Scully, Sally. "Marriage or a Career? Witchcraft as an Alternative in Seventeeth-Century Venice." *Journal of Social History* 28 (1995): 857–76.

Tausiet, María. *Ponzona en los ojos: Brujería y superstición en Aragón en el siglo XVI*. Zaragoza, Spain: Institución Fernando el Católico, 2000.

Tedeschi, John. "The Roman Inquisition and Witchcraft: An Early 17th-Century 'Instruction' on Correct Trial Procedure." *Revue de l'histoire des religions* 200 (1983): 163–88.

Villarín, Juan. *La hechiceria en Madrid: Brujas, maleficios, encantamientos y sugestiones de la villa y corte*. Madrid: Avapiés, 1993.

Zabala, Mikel. *Brujería e inquisición en Bizkaia (siglos XVI y XVII)*. Bilbao, Spain: Ekain, 2000.

Zanelli, Giuliana. *Streghe e società: Nell'Emilia e Romagna del cinque-seicento*. Ravenna, Italy: Longo, 1992.

7. Scandinavia

Degn, Christian, Harmut Lehmann, and Dagmar Unverhau, eds. *Hexenprozesse: Deutsche und skandinavische Beiträge*. Neumünster, Ger.: Wachholtz, 1983.

Ellison, R. C. "The Kirkjubôl Affair: A Seventeenth-Century Icelandic Witchcraft Case Analysed." *The Seventeenth Century* 8 (1993): 217–43.

Henningsen, Gustav. "Witch Hunting in Denmark." *Folklore* 93 (1982): 131–37.

Jochens, Jenny. "*Hexerie eller Blind Allarm*: Recent Scandinavian Witchcraft Studies." *Scandinavian Studies* 65 (1993): 103–13.

——. "Magie et différences des sexes dans les mythes et la société germanico-nordique." *Cahiers de civilisation médiévale, Xe–XII siècles* 36 (1993): 375–89.

——. "Old Norse Magic and Gender." *Scandinavian Studies* 63 (1993): 305–17.

Johanesen, Jens Christian V. "Superstition and Witchcraft in Reformation Scadinavia." In *The Scandinavian Reformation: From Evangelical Movement to Institutionalisation of Reform*, ed. Ole Peter Grell. Cambridge: Cambridge University Press, 1995, 179–211.

Miller, W. I. "Dreams, Prophecy and Sorcery: Blaming the Secret Offender in Medieval Iceland." *Scandinavian Studies* 58 (1986): 101–23.

Mitchell, S. A. "Nordic Witchcraft in Transition." *Scandia* 63 (1997): 17–33.

Morris, Katherine. *Sorceress or Witch? The Image of Gender in Medieval Iceland and Northern Europe*. Lanham, Md.: University Press of America, 1991.

Neronen, M. "'Envious Are All the People, Witches Watch at Every Gate': Finnish Witches and Witch Trials in the 17th Century." *Scandinavian Journal of History* 18 (1993): 77–91.

Sörlin, Per. *Wicked Arts: Witchcraft and Magic Trials in Southern Sweden, 1635–1734.* Leiden: Brill, 1998.

Willumsen, L. H. "Witchcraft of the High North: The Finnmark Witchcraft Trial in the Seventeenth Century." *Scandinavian Journal of History* 22 (1997): 199–221.

8. Switzerland

Andenmatten, Bernard, and Kathrin Utz Tremp. "De l'hérésie à la sorcellerie: L'inquisiteur Ulric de Torrenté OP (vers 1420–1445) et l'affermissement de l'inquisition en Suisse romande." *Revue écclesiastique Suisse* 86 (1992): 69–119.

Binz, Louis. "Les débuts de la chasse aux sorcières dans le diocèse de Genève." *Bibliothèque d'Humanisme et de Renaissance* 59 (1997): 561–81.

Blauert, Andreas. *Frühe Hexenverfolgungen: Ketzer-, Zauberei- und Hexenprozesse des 15. Jahrhunderts.* Hamburg: Junius, 1989.

——. "Hexenverfolgung in einer Spätmittelalterlichen Gemeinde: Der Beispiel Kriens/Luzern um 1500." *Geschichte und Gesellschaft* 16 (1990): 8–25.

Blöcker, Monica. "Ein Zaubereiprozess im Jahre 1028." *Schweizerische Zeitschrift für Geschichte* 29 (1979): 533–55.

Borst, Arno. "The Origins of the Witch-craze in the Alps." In Arno Borst, *Medieval Worlds: Barbarians, Heretics, and Artists in the Middle Ages*, trans. Eric Hansen. Chicago: University of Chicago Press, 1992, 101–22.

Broye, Christian. *Sorcellerie et superstitions à Genève, XVIe–XVIIIe siècles.* Geneva: Concepte Moderne, 1990.

Burghartz, Susanna. "The Equation of Women and Witches: A Case Study of Witchcraft Trials in Lucerne and Lausanne in the Fifteenth and Sixteenth Centuries." In *The German Underworld: Deviants and Outcasts in German History*, ed. Richard J. Evans. London: Routledge, 1988: 57–74.

Choffat, Pierre-Han. *La sorcellerie comme exutoire: Tensions et conflicts locaux, Dommartin 1524–1528.* Lausanne, Switz.: Université de Lausanne, 1989.

Kamber, Peter. "La chasse aux sorciers et aux sorcières dan le Pays de Vaud: Aspects quantitatifs (1581–1620)." *Revue historique vaudoise* 90 (1982): 21–33.

Maier, Eva. *Trente ans avec le diable: Une nouvelle chasse aux sorciers sur la Riviera lémanique (1477–1484).* Lausanne, Switz.: Université de Lausanne, 1996.

Mazzali, Tiziana. *Il martirio delle streghe: Una nuova dramatica testimonianza dell'Inquisizione laica del Seicento.* Milan: Xenia, 1988.

Modestin, Georg. *Le diable chez l'évêque: Chasse aux sorciers dans le diocèse de Lausanne (vers 1460)*. Lausanne, Switz.: Université de Lausanne, 1999.

———. "Der Teufel in der Landschaft: Zur politik der Hexenverfolgungen im heutigen Kanton Freiburg von 1440 bis 1470." *Freiburger Geschichtsblätter* 76 (1999): 81–122.

———. *Witchcraft in France and Switzerland: The Borderlands During the Reformation*. Ithaca, N.Y.: Cornell University Press, 1976.

———. "Witchcraft in Geneva, 1537–1662." *Journal of Modern History* 43 (1971): 179–204.

———. "Wozu brauch man Hexen? Herrschaft und Verfolgung in Châtel-Saint-Denis (1444–1465)." *Freiburger Geschichtsblätter* 77 (2000): 107–29.

Monter, E. William. "Patterns of Witchcraft in the Jura." *Journal of Social History* 5 (1971): 1–29.

Ostorero, Martine. *"Folâtrer avec les demons": Sabbat et chasse aux sorciers à Vevey (1448)*. Lausanne, Switz.: Université de Lausanne, 1995.

Pfister, Laurence. *L'enfer sur terre: Sorcellerie à Dommartin (1498)*. Lausanne, Switz.: Université de Lausanne, 1997.

Strobino, Sandrine. *Françoise sauvée des flammes? Une Valaisanne accusée de sorcellerie au XVe siècle*. Lausanne, Switz.: Université de Lausanne, 1996.

Utz Tremp, Kathrin. "Ist Glaubenssache Frauensache? Zu den Anfängen der Hexenverfolgungen im Freiburg (um 1440)." *Freiburger Geschichtsblätter* 72 (1995): 9–50.

Zumsteg, Fabienne Taric. *Les sorciers à l'assaut du village Gollion (1615–1631)*. Lausanne, Switz.: Zèbre, 2000.

VI. THE DEVIL AND DEMONOLOGY, POSSESSION AND EXORCISM

Caciola, Nancy. "Mystics, Demoniacs, and the Physiology of Spirit Possession in Medieval Europe." *Comparative Studies in Society and History* 42 (2000): 268–306.

Certeau, Michel de. *The Possession at Loudun*. Trans. Michael B. Smith. Chicago: University of Chicago Press, 1996.

Clark, Stuart. "The Rational Witchfinders: Concensus, Demonological Naturalism and Popular Superstitions." In *Science, Culture, and Popular Belief in Renaissance Europe,* ed. Stephen Pumfrey, Paolo L. Rossi, and Maurice Slawinski. Manchester, Eng.: Manchester University Press, 1991, 225–38.

———. "The Scientific Status of Demonology." In *Occult and Scientific Mentalities in the Renaissance*, ed. Brian Vickers. Cambridge: Cambridge University Press, 1984, 351–74.

Dendle, Peter. *Satan Unbound: The Devil in Old English Narrative Literature*. Toronto: University of Toronto Press, 2001.

Elliott, Dyan. *Fallen Bodies: Pollution, Sexuality, and Demonology in the Middle Ages*. Philadelphia: University of Pennsylvania Press, 1999.

———. "Seeing Double: John Gerson, the Discernment of Spirits, and Joan of Arc." *American Historical Review* 107 (2002): 26–54.

Ferguson, Everett. *Demonology of the Early Christian World*. Lewiston, N.Y.: Mellen, 1984.

Finlay, Anthony. *Demons! The Devil, Possession and Exorcism*. London: Blanford, 1999.

Gérest, Claude. "Der Teufel in der theologischen Landschaft der Hexenjäger des 15. Jahrhunderts." *Concilium* 2 (1975): 173–83.

Goddu, André. "The Failure of Exorcism in the Middle Ages." *Soziale Ordnung im Selbstverständnis des Mittelalters* 12 (1980): 540–57.

Haag, Herbert. *Teufelsglaube*. Tübingen, Ger.: Katzmann, 1972.

Jelsma, Auke. "The Devil and Protestantism." In Auke Jelsma, *Frontiers of the Reformation: Dissidence and Orthodoxy in Sixteenth-Century Europe*. Aldershot, Eng.: Ashgate, 1998: 25–39.

Kelly, Henry Ansgar. *The Devil, Demonology and Witchcraft: The Development of Christian Beliefs in Evil Spirits*. Rev. ed. New York: Doubleday, 1974.

Kirsch, Irving. "Demonology and Science during the Scientific Revolution." *Journal of the History of Behavioral Sciences* 16 (1980): 359–68.

Kreiser, B. Robert. "The Devils of Toulon: Demonic Possession and Religious Politics in Eighteenth-Century Provence." In *Church, State, and Society under the Bourbon Kings of France*, ed. Richard M. Golden. Lawrence, Kans.: Coronado Press, 1982, 173–221.

Lecouteux, Claude. *Démons et genies du terroir au Moyen Age*. Paris: Imago, 1995.

Maggi, Armando. *Satan's Rhetoric: A Study of Renaissance Demonology*. Chicago: University of Chicago Press, 2001.

Midelfort, H. C. Erik. "Catholic and Lutheran Reactions to Demon Possession in the Late Seventeenth Century: Two Case Histories." *Daphis* 15 (1986): 623–48.

———. "The Devil and the German People: Reflections on the Popularity of Demon Possession in Sixteenth-Century Germany." In *Religion and Culture in the Renaissance and Reformation*, ed. Steven Ozment. Kirksville, Mo.: Sixteenth Century Journal Publishers, 1989, 99–119.

Muchembled, Robert. *Une histoire du diable, XII–XX siècle*. Paris: Seuil, 2000.

Neumann, Almut. *Verträge und Pakte mit dem Teufel: Antike und mittelalterliche Vorstellungen im "Malleus maleficarum."* St. Ingbert, Ger.: Röhrig Universitätsverlag, 1997.

Newman, Barbara. "Possessed by the Spirit: Devout Women, Demoniacs, and the Apostolic Life in the Thirteenth Century." *Speculum* 73 (1998): 733–70.

Nicholls, David. "The Devil in Renaissance France." *History Today* 30 (November, 1980): 25–30.

Nischan, Bodo. "The Exorcism Controversy and Baptism in the Late Reformation." *Sixteenth Century Journal* 18 (1987): 31–51.

Oldridge, Darren. *The Devil in Early Modern England.* Stroud, Eng.: Sutton, 2000.

Pagels, Elaine. *The Origin of Satan.* New York: Random House, 1995.

Pearl, Jonathan L. *The Crime of Crimes: Demonology and Politics in France 1560–1620.* Waterloo, Ont.: Wilfred Laurier University Press, 1999.

Petzoldt, Ruth, and Paul Neubauer, eds. *Demons: Mediators between this World and the Other: Essays on Demonic Beings from the Middle Ages to the Present.* Frankfurt: Peter Lang, 1998.

Russell, Jeffrey Burton. *The Devil: Perceptions of Evil from Antiquity to Primitive Christianity.* Ithaca, N.Y.: Cornell University Press, 1977.

———. *Lucifer: The Devil in the Middle Ages.* Ithaca, N.Y.: Cornell University Press, 1984.

———. *Mephistopheles: The Devil in the Modern World.* Ithaca, N.Y.: Cornell University Press, 1986.

———. *Satan: The Early Christian Tradition.* Ithaca, N.Y.: Cornell University Press, 1981.

Spanos, Nicholas P., and Jack Gottlieb. "Demonic Possession, Mesmerism, and Hysteria: A Social Psychological Perspective on Their Historical Interrelations." *Journal of Abnormal Psychology* 88 (1979): 527–46.

Stanford, Peter. *The Devil: A Biography.* London: Mandarin, 1996.

Veenstra, Jan R. "Stretching the Imagination: Demons Between Man's Body and Soul." In *Tradition and Innovation in an Era of Change,* ed. Rudolf Suntrup and Jan R. Veenstra. Bern, Switz.: Peter Lang, 2001, 203–25.

Walker, Anita M., and Edmund H. Dickerman. "'A Woman under the Influence': A Case of Alleged Possession in Sixteenth-Century France." *Sixteenth Century Journal* 22 (1991): 535–54.

Walker, D. P. "Demonic Possession used as Propoganda in the Later 16th Century." In *Scienze, credenze occulte, livelli di cultura: Convegno internazionale di studi (Firenze, 26–30 giugno, 1980).* Florence, Italy: Olschki, 1982, 237–48.

———. *Unclean Spirits: Possession and Exorcism in France and England in the Late Sixteenth and Early Seventeenth Centuries.* Philadelphia: University of Pennsylvania Press, 1981.

Walzel, Diana Lynn. "Sources of Medieval Demonology." *Rice University Studies* 60 (1974): 83–99.

VII. THEORISTS OF WITCHCRAFT, TREATISES AND LITERATURE ON WITCHCRAFT

Anglo, Sydney. "Melancholia and Witchcraft: The Debate between Wier, Bodin, and Scot." In *Folie et déraison à la Renaissance*. Brussels: Université de Bruxelles, 1976, 209–28.

Anglo, Sydney, ed. *The Damned Art: Essays in the Literature of Witchcraft*. London: Routledge, 1977.

Bailey, Michael D. *Battling Demons: Witchcraft, Heresy, and Reform in the Late Middle Ages*. University Park, Pa.: Pennsylvania State Universty Press, 2003.

Bonney, Françoise. "Autour de Jean Gerson: Opinions de théologiens sur les superstitions et la sorcellerie au début de XVe siècle." *Le Moyen Age* 77 (1971): 85–98.

Brauner, Sigrid. "Martin Luther on Witchcraft: A True Reformer?" In *The Politics of Gender in Early Modern Europe*, ed. Jean R. Brink, Allison P. Coudert, and Maryanne C. Horowitz. Kirksville, Mo.: Sixteenth Century Journal Publishers, 1989, 29–42.

Camerlynck, Elaine. "Féminité et sorcellerie chez les théoriciens de la démonologie à la fin du Moyen Age: Etude du *Malleus maleficarum*." *Renaissance and Reformation* n.s. 7 (1983): 13–25.

Caro Baroja, Julio. "Martín del Rio y sus *Disquisiciones mágicas*." In Julio Caro Baroja, *El señor inquisidor y ostras vidas por oficio*. Madrid: Alianza, 1968, 171–96.

Classen, Albrecht. "The End of the Middle Ages? Criticism of Sorcery and Witchcraft Through Johann Weyer in his *De Praestigiis Daemonum* of 1583." In *Zauberer und Hexen in der Kultur des Mittelalters*, ed. Danielle Buschinger and Wolfgang Spiewok. Greifswald, Ger.: Reineke, 1994, 27–43.

Darst, David H. "Witchcraft in Spain: The Testimony of Martín de Castañega's Treatise on Superstition and Witchcraft (1529)." *Proceedings of the American Philosophical Society* 123 (1979): 298–322.

Estes, Leland L. "Reginald Scot and His *Discoverie of Witchcraft*: Religion and Science in Opposition to the European Witch Craze." *Church History* 52 (1983): 444–56.

Fürbeth, Frank. *Johannes Hartlieb: Untersuchungen zu Leben und Werk*. Tübingen, Ger.: Niemeyer, 1992.

Haustein, Jörg. *Martin Luthers Stellung zur Zauber- und Hexenwesen.* Stuttgart, Ger.: Kohlhammer, 1990.

Henningsen, Gustav. "The Papers of Alonso de Salazar Frias: A Spanish Witchcraft Polemic, 1610–14." *Temenos* 5 (1969): 85–106.

Horowitz, Maryanne Cline. "Montaigne versus Bodin on Ancient Tales of Demonology." *Proceedings of the Annual Meeting of the Western Society for French History* 16 (1989): 103–10.

Houdard, Sophie. *Les sciences du diable: Quatre discours sur la sorcellerie (XVe–XVIIe siècle).* Paris: Editions du Cerf, 1992.

Jensen, Peter F. "Calvin and Witchcraft." *Reformed Theological Review* 34 (1975): 76–86.

Lange, Ursula. *Untersuchungen zu Bodins "Démonomanie."* Frankfurt: Klostermann, 1970.

Lehmann, Hartmut, and Otto Ulbricht, eds. *Vom Unfug des Hexen-Processes: Gegner der Hexenverfolgungen von Johann Weyer bis Friedrich Spee.* Wiesbaden, Ger.: Harrossowitz, 1992.

Leutenbacher, Siegfried. *Hexerei- und Zaubereidelikt in der Literatur von 1450 bis 1550: Mit Hinweis auf der Praxis im Herzogtum Bayern.* Berlin: Schweitzer, 1972.

Midelfort, H. C. Erik. "Johannes Weyer and the Transformation of the Insanity Defense." In *The German People and the Reformation*, ed. R. Po-chia Hsia. Ithaca, N.Y.: Cornell University Press, 1988, 234–61.

Monter, E. William. "Inflation and Witchcraft: The Case of Jean Bodin." In *Action and Conviction in Early Modern Europe: Essays in Memory of E. H. Harbison*, ed. Theodore K. Rabb and Jerrold E. Seigel. Princeton, N.J.: Princeton University Press, 1969, 371–89.

Paravy, Pierrette. "A propos de la gènese médiévale des chasses aux sorcières: Le traité de Claude Tholosan, juge dauphinois (vers. 1436)." In *Mélanges de l'Ecole Française de Rome: Moyen Age—Temps Modernes* 91 (1979): 333–79.

Pearl, Jonathan L. "Bodin's Advice to Judges in Witchcraft Cases." *Proceedings of the Annual Meeting of the Western Society for French History* 16 (1989): 95–102.

———. "Humanism and Satanism: Jean Bodin's Contributions to the Witchcraft Crisis." *Canadian Review of Sociology and Anthropology* 19 (1982): 541–48.

Petersohn, Jürgen. "Konziliaristen und Hexen: Ein unbekannter Brief des Inquisitors Heinrich Institoris an Papst Sixtus IV. aus dem Jahre 1484." *Deutsches Archiv für Erforschung des Mittelalters* 44 (1988): 120–60.

Rummel, Walter. "Friedrich von Spee und das Ende der kurtrierischen Hexenprozesse." *Jahrbuch für westdeutsche Landesgeschichte* 15 (1989): 105–16.

Segl, Peter. "Der Hexenhammer: Eine Quelle der Alltags- und Mentalitäts-geschichte." In *Mentalität und Gesellschaft im Mittelalter: Gedenkschrift für Ernst Werner*, ed. Sabine Tanz. Frankfurt: Peter Lang, 1993, 127–54.

———. "'Malifice . . . non . . . sunt . . . heretice nuncupande': Zu Heinrich Kramers Widerlegung der Ansichten *aliorum inquisitorum in viuersis reg-nis hispanie*." In *Papsttum, Kirche und Recht im Mittelalter: Festschrift für Horst Fuhrmann*, ed. Hubert Mordek. Tübingen, Ger.: Niemeyer, 1991, 369–82.

Segl, Peter, ed. *Der Hexenhammer: Entstehung und Umfeld des "Malleus Maleficarum" von 1487*. Cologne: Böhlau, 1988.

Stephens, Walter. "Tasso and the Witches." *Annali d'Italianistica* 12 (1994): 181–202.

———. "Witches who Steal Penises: Impotence and Illusion in *Malleus malefi-carum*." *Journal of Medieval and Early Modern Studies* 28 (1998): 495–529.

Taylor, Steven M. "Le procès de la sorcellerie chez Martin Le Franc: *Le Cham-pion des Dames*, Livre IV." In *Zauberer und Hexen in der Kultur des Mitte-lalters,* ed. Danielle Buschinger and Wolfgang Spiewok. Greifswald, Ger.: Reineke, 1994, 203–12.

Tschacher, Werner. *Der Formicarius des Johannes Nider von 1437/38: Studien zu den Anfängen der europäischen Hexenverfolgungen im Spätmittelalter.* Aachen, Ger.: Shaker, 2000.

Veenstra, Jan. *Magic and Divination at the Courts of Burgundy and France: Text and Context of Laurens Pignon's "Contre les devineurs" (1411).* Lei-den: Brill, 1998.

West, Robert H. *Reginald Scot and Renaissance Writings on Witchcraft.* Boston: Twayne, 1984.

Williams, Gerhild Scholz. *Defining Dominion: The Discourses of Magic and Witchcraft in Early Modern France and Germany.* Ann Arbor, Mich.: Uni-versity of Michigan Press, 1995.

Wilson, Eric. "Institoris at Innsbruck: Heinrich Institoris, the *Summis Desider-antes* and the Brixen Witch-Trial of 1485." In *Popular Religion in Germany and Central Europe, 1400–1800*, ed. Bob Scribner and Trevor Johnson. New York: St. Martin's Press, 1996, 87–100, 239–45.

Wunder, Heide. "Friedrich von Spee und die verfolgten Frauen." In *Die poli-tische Theologie Friedrich von Spees*, ed. Doris Brockmann and Peter Eicher. Munich: Fink, 1991, 119–32.

Zenz, Emil. "Cornelius Loos—ein Vorlaufer Friedrich von Spees im Kampf gegen den Hexenwahn." *Kurtrierisches Jahrbuch* 21 (1981): 146–53.

Ziegler, Wolfgang. *Möglichkeiten der Kritik am Hexen- und Zauberwesen im ausgehenden Mittelalter: Zeitgenössische Stimmen und ihre soziale Zuhörigkeit.* 2nd ed. Cologne: Böhlau, 1973.

VIII. WITCHCRAFT IN ART

Davidson, Jane P. "Great Black Goats and Evil Little Women: The Image of the Witch in Sixteenth-Century German Art." *Journal of the Rocky Mountain Medieval and Renaissance Society* 6 (1985): 141–57.

——. *The Witch in Northern European Art, 1470–1750.* Freren, Ger.: Luca, 1987.

Hoak, Dale. "Art, Culture, and Mentality in Renaissance Society: The Meaning of Hans Baldung Grien's *Bewitched Groom* (1544)." *Renaissance Quarterly* 38 (1985): 488–510.

——. "Witch-Hunting and Women in the Art of the Renaissance." *History Today* 31 (February, 1981): 22–26.

Hults, Linda C. "Baldung and the Witches of Freiburg: The Evidence of Images." *Journal of Interdisciplinary History* 18 (1987–88): 249–76.

——. "Baldung's Bewitched Groom Revisited: Artistic Temperament, Fantasy and the 'Dream of Reason.'" *Sixteenth Century Journal* 15 (1984): 259–79.

——. "Hans Baldung Grien's 'Weather Witches' in Frankfurt." *Pantheon: Internationale Zeitschrift für Kunst* 40 (1982): 124–30.

Link, Luther. *The Devil: The Archfiend in Art from the Sixth to the Sixteenth Century.* New York: Abrams, 1996.

Mesenzeva, Charmain. "Der Behexte Stallknecht des Hans Baldung Griens." *Zeitschrift für Kunstgeschichte* 44 (1981): 57–61.

Schade, Sigrid. *Schadenzauber und die Magie des Körpers: Hexenbilder der Frühen Neuzeit.* Worms, Ger.: Werner'sche Verlagsgesellschaft, 1983.

Sullivan, Margaret A. "The Witches of Dürer and Hans Baldung Grien." *Renaissance Quarterly* 53 (2000): 333–401.

Zika, Charles. "Dürer's Witch, Riding Women, and Moral Order." In *Dürer and his Culture,* ed. Dagmar Eichberger and Charles Zika. Cambridge: Cambridge University Press, 1998, 118–40, 225–28.

——. "Fears of Flying: Representations of Witchcraft and Sexuality in Early Sixteenth-Century Germany." *Australian Journal of Art* 8 (1989–90): 19–47.

——. "'Magie' — 'Zauberei' — 'Hexerei': Bildmedien und kultureller Wandel." In *Kulturelle Reformation: Sinnformationen im Umbruch, 1400–1600,* ed. Bernhard Jussen and Craig Koslofsky. Göttingen, Ger.: Vandenhoeck & Ruprecht, 1999, 317–82.

——. Representing Sorcery and Witchcraft: Images and Cultural Meaning in Europe, 1470–1590. In preparation.

——. "She-man: Visual Representations of Witchcraft and Sexuality in Sixteenth Century Europe." In *Venus and Mars: Engendering Love and War in*

Medieval and Early Modern Europe, ed. Andrew Lynch and Philippa Maddern. Perth, Australia: University of Western Australia Press, 1992, 147–90.

IX. WITCHCRAFT IN THE MODERN WORLD

1. Magic and Superstition after the Witch-Hunts

Argyrou, Vassos. "Under a Spell: The Strategic Use of Magic in Greek Cypriot Society." *American Ethnologist* 20 (1993): 256–71.

Conrad, John L. "Bulgarian Magic Charms: Ritual, Form, and Content." *Slavic and East European Journal* 31 (1987): 548–62.

——. "Magic Charms and Healing Rituals in Contemporary Yugoslavia." *Southeastern Europe* 10 (1983): 99–120.

Davies, Owen. "Cunning-Folk in England and Wales during the Eighteenth and Nineteenth Centuries." *Rural History* 8 (1997): 91–107.

——. "Cunning-Folk in the Medical Market–Place during the Nineteenth Century." *Medical History* 43 (1999): 55–73.

——. "Hag-Riding in Nineteenth-Century West Country England and Modern Newfoundland: An Examination of an Experience-Centred Witchcraft Tradition." *Folk Life* 35 (1996–97): 36–53.

——. "Healing Charms in Use in England and Wales 1700–1950." *Folklore* 107 (1996): 19–32.

——. "Methodism, the Clergy, and the Popular Belief in Witchcraft and Magic." *History* 82 (1997): 252–65.

——. "Newspapers and the Popular Belief in Witchcraft and Magic in the Modern Period." *Journal of British Studies* 37 (1998): 139–65.

——. "Urbanization and the Decline of Witchcraft: An Examination of London." *Journal of Social History* 30 (1997): 597–617.

——. *Witchcraft, Magic and Culture, 1736–1951.* Manchester, Eng.: Manchester University Press, 1999.

Denier, Marie-Claude. "Sorciers, présages et croyances magiques en Mayenne aux XVIIIe et XIXe siècles." *Annales de Bretagne et de Pays de l'Ouest (Anjou, Maine, Touraine)* 97 (1990): 115–32.

Devlin, Judith. *The Superstitious Mind: French Peasants and the Supernatural in the Nineteenth Century.* New Haven, Conn.: Yale University Press, 1987.

Favret-Saada, Jeanne. *Deadly Words: Witchcraft in the Bocage.* Trans. Catherin Cullen. Cambridge: Cambridge University Press, 1980.

——. "Unbewitching as Therapy." *American Ethnologist* 16 (1989): 40–56.

Gibbons, B. J. *Spirituality and the Occult: From the Renaissance to the Modern Age.* London: Routledge, 2001.

Greenwood, Susan. *Magic, Witchcraft and the Otherworld: An Anthropology.* Oxford: Berg, 2000.

Maple, Eric. *Superstition and the Superstitious.* London: W. H. Allen, 1971.

Owen, Alex. *The Darkened Room: Women, Power and Spiritualism in Late Nineteenth Century England.* Philadephia: University of Pennsylvania Press, 1990.

Schier, Barbara. "Hexenwahn und Hexenverfolgung: Rezeption und politische Zurichtung eines kulturwissenschaftlichen Themas im Dritten Reich." *Bayerische Jahrbuch für Volkskunde* (1990): 43–115.

Schiffmann, Aldona Christina. "The Witch and the Crime: The Persecution of Witches in Twentieh-Century Poland." *ARV: Scandinavian Yearbook of Folklore* 43 (1987): 147–65.

Schöck, Inge. *Hexenglaube in der Gegenwart: Empirische Untersuchungen in Südwestdeutschland.* Tübingen, Ger.: Vereinigung für Volkskunde, 1978.

Sebald, Hans. *Witch Children.* Amherst, N.Y.: Prometheus, 1995.

——. *Witchcraft: The Heritage of a Heresy.* New York: Elsevier, 1978.

Soman, Alfred. "Sorcellerie, justice criminelle, et société dans la France moderne." *Histoire, economie, et société* 12 (1993): 177–218.

Traimond, Bernard. *Le pouvoir de la maladie: Magie et politique dans les Landes de Gascogne, 1750–1826.* Bordeaux, France: Université de Bordeaux, 1988.

Worobec, Christine D. *Possessed: Women, Witches, and Demons in Imperial Russia.* DeKalb, Ill.: Northern Illinois University Press, 2001.

——. "Witchcraft Beliefs and Practices in Prerevolutionary Russian and Ukrainian Villages." *Russian Review* 54 (1995): 165–87.

2. Modern Wicca, Neo-Paganism, and Satanism

Adler, Margot. *Drawing Down the Moon: Witches, Druids, Goddess-Worshippers, and Other Pagans in America Today.* Rev. ed. Boston: Beacon, 1986.

Bovenschen, Silvia. "The Contemporary Witch, the Historical Witch, and the Witch Myth: The Witch, Subject of the Appropriation of Nature and the Object of the Domination of Nature." *New German Critique* 15 (1978): 83–119.

Crowley, Vivianne. *Wicca: The Old Religion in the New Millenium.* Rev. ed. London: Aquarian, 1996.

Culpepper, Emily Erwin. "Contemporary Goddess Theology: A Sympathetic Critique." In *Shaping New Vision: Gender and Values in American Culture,* ed. Clarissa W. Atkinson, Constance H. Buchanan, and Margaret R. Miles. Ann Arbor, Mich.: UMI Research Press, 1987, 51–71.

Eller, Cynthia. *Living in the Lap of the Goddess: The Feminist Spirituality Movement in America.* Boston: Beacon, 1995.

Gardner, Gerald B. *Witchcraft Today*. New York: Citadel, 1954.

Harmening, Dieter, ed. *Hexen Heute: Magische Traditionen und neue Zutaten*. Würzburg, Ger.: Königshausen & Neumann, 1991.

Hutton, Ronald. *The Triumph of the Moon: A History of Modern Pagan Witchcraft*. Oxford: Oxford University Press, 1999.

Kelly, Aidan. *A History of Modern Witchcraft, 1939–1964*. St. Paul, Minn.: Llewellyn, 1991.

King, Francis. *Ritual Magic in England: 1887 to the Present Day*. London: Spearman, 1970.

La Fontaine, J. S. *Speak of the Devil: Tales of Satanic Abuse in Contemporary England*. Cambridge: Cambridge University Press, 1998.

Leek, Sibyl. *The Complete Art of Witchcraft*. New York: Penguin, 1971.

Lewis, James R., ed. *Magical Religion and Modern Witchcraft*. Albany, N.Y.: State University of New York Press, 1996.

Luhrmann, T. M. *Persuasions of the Witch's Craft: Ritual Magic in Contemporary England*. Cambridge, Mass.: Harvard University Press, 1989.

Pearson, Jeanne, Richard Roberts, and Geoffrey Samuel, eds. *Nature Religions Today: Paganism in the Modern World*. Edinburgh: Edinburgh Unviersity Press, 1998.

Salomonsen, Jane. *Enchanted Feminism: Ritual, Gender and Divinity among the Reclaiming Witches of San Francisco*. London: Routledge, 2002.

Starhawk. *The Spiral Dance: A Rebirth of the Ancient Religion of the Great Goddess*. 20th anniversary ed. San Francisco: Harper, 1999.

Truzzi, Marcello. "The Occult Revival as Popular Culture: Some Random Observations of the Old and Nouveau Witch." *Sociological Quarterly* 13 (1972): 16–36.

Valiente, Doreen. *The Rebirth of Witchcraft*. Custer, Wash.: Phoenix Publishing, 1989.

X. NON-EUROPEAN WITCHCRAFT, ANTHROPOLOGICAL AND COMPARATIVE STUDIES

Bongmba, Elias Kifon. *African Witchcraft and Otherness: A Philosophical and Theological Critique of Intersubjective Relations*. Albany, N.Y.: State University Press of New York, 2001.

Crais, Clifton. *Magic, State Power and the Political Imagination in South Africa*. Cambridge: Cambridge University Press, 2002.

Crawford, J. R. *Witchcraft and Sorcery in Rhodesia*. Oxford: Oxford University Press, 1967.

Debrunner, Hans W. *Witchcraft in Ghana: A Study of the Belief in Destructive Witches and Its Effect on the Akan Tribes.* 2nd ed. Accra, Ghana: Presbyterian Book Depot, 1961.

Douglas, Mary. "Witch Beliefs in Central Africa." *Africa* 37 (1967): 72–80.

Douglas, Mary, ed. *Witchcraft Confessions and Accusations.* London: Tavistock, 1970.

Evans-Pritchard, E. E. *Witchcraft, Oracles and Magic among the Azande.* 2nd ed. Oxford: Clarendon, 1950.

Fisiy, C. F., and P. Geschiere. "Judges and Witches, or How Is the State to Deal with Witchcraft? Examples from Southeastern Cameroon." *Cahiers d'études africaines* 118 (1990): 135–56.

———. "Sorcery, Witchcraft, and Accumulation—Regional Variation in South West Cameroon." *Critique of Anthropology* 11 (1991): 251–78.

Fortune, Reo Franklin. *Sorcerers of Dobu: The Social Anthropology of the Dobu Islanders of the Western Pacific.* London: Routledge, 1963.

Geschiere, Peter. *The Modernity of Witchcraft: Politics and the Occult in Postcolonial Africa.* Trans. Peter Geschiere and Janet Rothman. Charlottesville, Va.: University of Virginia Press, 1997.

Hammond-Tooke, W. D. "The Cape Nguni Witch Familiar as a Mediatory Construct." *Man* n.s. 9 (1974): 128–36.

———. "Urbanization and the Interpretation of Misfortune: A Quantitative Analysis." *Africa* 40 (1970): 25–39.

Harris, Grace. "Possession 'Hysteria' in a Kenya Tribe." *American Anthropologist* 59 (1957): 1046–66.

Harwood, Alan. *Witchcraft, Sorcery and Social Categories among the Safwa.* Oxford: Oxford University Press, 1970.

Jackson, Michael D. "Structure and Event: Witchcraft Confession among the Kuranko." *Man* 10 (1975): 387–403.

Kennedy, John G. "Psychological and Social Explanations of Witchcraft." *Man* 2 (1967): 216–25.

Kluckhorn, Clyde. *Navaho Witchcraft.* 1944. Reprint, Boston: Beacon Press, 1967.

Kuhn, Philip A. *Soulstealers: The Chinese Sorcery Scare of 1768.* Cambridge, Mass.: Harvard University Press, 1990.

Lehmann, Arthur C., and James E. Myers, eds. *Magic, Witchcraft, and Religion: An Anthropological Study of the Supernatural.* Palo Alto, Calif.: Mayfield, 1985.

Lewis, I. M. *Ecstatic Religion: An Anthropological Study of Spirit Possession and Shamanism.* Harmondsworth, Eng.: Penguin, 1971.

———. "Spirit Possession and Deprivation Cults." *Man* 1 (1966): 307–29.

Mair, Lucy. *Witchcraft.* New York: McGraw-Hill, 1969.

Marwick, Max. G. "Another Modern Anti-Witchcraft Movement in East Central Africa." *Africa* 20 (1950): 100–12.

——. "The Continuance of Witchcraft Beliefs." In *Africa in Transition*, ed. Prudence Smith. London: Reinhardt, 1958, 106–14.

——. "The Social Context of Cewâ Witch Beliefs." *Africa* 22 (1952): 120–22.

——. *Sorcery in Its Social Setting: A Study of the Northern Rhodesian Cewâ.* Manchester, Eng.: Manchester University Press, 1965.

——. "The Study of Witchcraft." In *The Craft of Social Anthropology*, ed. A. L. Epstein. London: Tavistock, 1967, 231–44.

——. "Witchcraft as a Social Strain-Gauge." *Australian Journal of Science* 26 (1964): 263–68.

Marwick, Max G., ed. *Witchcraft and Sorcery: Selected Readings.* 2nd ed. New York: Penguin, 1982.

Middleton, John, and E. H. Winter, eds. *Witchcraft and Sorcery in East Africa.* New York: Praeger, 1963.

Nadel, S. F. "Witchcraft in Four African Societies." *American Anthropologist* 54 (1952): 18–29.

Niehus, Isak A. *Witchcraft, Power and Politics: Exploring the Occult in the South African Lowveld.* Cape Town, S.A.: Sterling, 2001.

Newall, Venetia, ed. *The Witch Figure: Folklore Essays by a Group of Scholars in England Honouring the 75th Birthday of Katharine M. Briggs.* London: Routledge, 1973.

Obeyesekere, Gananath. "Sorcery, Premeditated Murder, and the Canalization of Agression in Sri Lanka." *Ethnography* 14 (1975): 1–23.

Parrinder, Geoffrey. *Witchcraft: European and African.* New York: Barnes and Noble, 1963.

Reynolds, Barrie. *Magic, Divination, and Witchcraft among the Barotse of Northern Rhodesia.* Berkeley, Calif.: University of California Press, 1963.

Rose, B. W. "African and European Magic: A First Comparative Study of Beliefs and Practices." *African Studies* 23 (1964): 1–10.

Schapera, Isacc. "Sorcery and Witchcraft in Bechuanaland." *African Affairs* 51 (1952): 41–52.

Turner, Victor W. "Witchcraft and Sorcery: Taxonomy versus Dynamics." *Africa* 34 (1964): 314–24.

Walker, Deward E., ed. *Witchcraft and Sorcery of the American Native Peoples.* Moscow, Idaho: University of Idaho Press, 1989.

Watson, C. W., and Roy Ellen, eds. *Understanding Witchcraft and Sorcery in Southeast Asia.* Honolulu, Hawaii: University of Hawaii Press, 1993.

Willis, R. G. "Kamcape: An Anti-Sorcery Movement in South-West Tanzania." *Africa* 38 (1968): 1–15.

Wyllie, R. W. "Introspective Witchcraft among the Effutu of Southern Ghana." *Man* n.s. 8 (1973): 74–79.